BRINGING IN
BEAUTY

MALCOLM PULLEN

BALBOA.
PRESS
A DIVISION OF HAY HOUSE

Copyright © 2016 Malcolm Pullen.

All rights reserved. No part of this book may be used or reproduced by any means, graphic, electronic, or mechanical, including photocopying, recording, taping or by any information storage retrieval system without the written permission of the author except in the case of brief quotations embodied in critical articles and reviews.

Balboa Press books may be ordered through booksellers or by contacting:

Balboa Press
A Division of Hay House
1663 Liberty Drive
Bloomington, IN 47403
www.balboapress.com
1 (877) 407-4847

Because of the dynamic nature of the Internet, any web addresses or links contained in this book may have changed since publication and may no longer be valid. The views expressed in this work are solely those of the author and do not necessarily reflect the views of the publisher, and the publisher hereby disclaims any responsibility for them.

The author of this book does not dispense medical advice or prescribe the use of any technique as a form of treatment for physical, emotional, or medical problems without the advice of a physician, either directly or indirectly. The intent of the author is only to offer information of a general nature to help you in your quest for emotional and spiritual well-being. In the event you use any of the information in this book for yourself, which is your constitutional right, the author and the publisher assume no responsibility for your actions.

Any people depicted in stock imagery provided by Thinkstock are models, and such images are being used for illustrative purposes only.
Certain stock imagery © Thinkstock.

Print information available on the last page.

ISBN: 978-1-5043-6554-3 (sc)
ISBN: 978-1-5043-6556-7 (hc)
ISBN: 978-1-5043-6555-0 (e)

Library of Congress Control Number: 2016914362

Balboa Press rev. date: 09/02/2016

Contents

A Bit of Background 1
The Dance Begins 3
First Meeting 5
The Deal is Cast 7
A Bit of Groundwork 10
The First Feeding 12
Calls & Coordination 14
The Routine 16
The Naming 18
The Dance Continues 20
A Long, Cold February 23
The Drive Home – Times of Reflection 25
Cold & Wet Concerns 28
The Connection is Made 30
Some Things Don't Work 33
Offerings of Friends 36
A Week of Eternal Waiting 38
A Pause, Then More 41
Enjoy & Share 43
Hostile Elements 45
What Next? 48
First Treats 50
An Offering Accepted 52
Building Trust 54
Coming Closer 56
Towards Touch 58
A Leap in Closeness 60
Mind & Measuring 62

Yet Closer	64
Closer By a Bit	66
A Bit of Intimacy	69
There will be a Book	72
Always a Surprise	74
Connections with a Neighbor	77
Bravely Building Trust	80
Offers and Acceptance	82
Settling In	85
Bring out Fawn	88
Moving Towards Touch	92
Two in a Row	95
Allowing Protection	98
Doggy Intimacy	101
Towards a Pack	106
Bringing Beauty Closer	109
Cruelty Pushing Beauty Away	113
Getting Closer	116
Working on Trust	119
Lessons of Worry	122
Sweetness of Surrender	123
Becoming Family	126
A Step Backwards	129
Hiding, Then Returns	131
Her Approach	134
Work to do with Fawn	136
Three in a Row	140
Hiding from Young Hunters	144
Startled into Flight	145
Roller Coaster of Feelings	150
Others Want Her	155
A Bold New Move	161
From the Car	167
Brief and Meaningful	173
Empty Absence	177
Trusting Again	179

Toy Time	182
She Offers Herself	186
Enjoying Attention	190
Handling My Dog	194
Showing Me Her Space	198
Taking my Hand	202
Intimacy and Play	205
So Much Grooming Needed	210
Our Field	212
A Ritual of Connection	215
A Bit Surreal	218
Towards Being on Leash	221
Effort Rewarded	224
Where Is The Balance	228
More Relaxed and Organic	232
Just Being Us	236
From One Step to the Next	238
Settling More into Us	241
Sudden Terror	245
A Bit of Car Exposure	250
Setting Boundaries	252
A Boundary Accepted	254
Rainy Days and Boundaries	257
A Step Barely Noticed	259
A Quick Visit	265
Getting Fawn to Accept Beauty	268
Introducing Ute	273
Maybe My Sister	276
Family	279
Trust and the Car	284
Declaring 'Us' to Others	290
Time for Focus	294
Little Progress	298
A Step in the Right Direction	301
Crossing Over	304
Day of Chase	307

Help from the Neighbors	309
With Me Inside	312
Beauty and the Cat	315
More Socializing	317
Unleashing Fear	321
What Pains Her	323
Inner Weavings	327
Transition to Leash	330
Sorrow and Separation	334
Speaking with the Police	336
Announcing 'Us'	339
Quick Visit	343
Jumping In	344
Thanks and Goodbyes	348
Subtle Changes	351
Quiet Day Getting Ready	352
Time to Plan	353
More Willingness to Trust	356
Easy Day	358
The Future Arrives	362
Four Years Later	369
About the Author	371

A Bit of Background

Ute has been a friend for many years. Our shared interest in dogs holds the friendship together. Well, that is a guy description, quite true but lacking the intricate details and interplay involved. You see I am a guy, an older guy, raised in the 50s and 60s in a logging community, living on the grounds of a mental hospital. Now at 63 I have been given a challenge, given a task to step beyond my masculine patterns, to share more than simple statements. Please realize the guy part of me is protesting, "Too much energy for what payback?" "What? No, we keep that part within so it won't interfere with what we must do?" "And just how will this serve others?" "Hey, that exposes too much." "Look, we made it work. Why talk about what has already happened?" It will, indeed, be a challenge. Even now the guy part of me is eager to begin describing, letting you know what the pieces are and how they fit together. My mind is arguing that letting you know what my writings will include is important. From within I receive guidance, what my rational mind translates as "Be open, be organic, let the energies bring it forth."

I expect many of you are now ready to stop reading. "Nut case!" "Airy Fairy" "Total loss of reality." and other judgments. Some will be uncomfortable. Some will hide behind a "Why bother?" It is your choice. If the play between the rational and the mysteries of life amuse you I invite you to join me. My plan is to interweave the rational, the descriptive, feelings (the body's experiences), and phrases pointing to quiet knowings from within. For those of you who enjoy a challenge keep the title in your awareness. Notice the many subtle inferences connecting to the title. If you wish, share with me at <u>BringingInBeauty@</u>

gmail.com. I can just hear some of you, "You can't share your email in a book!" Well, it is my book and I just did.

Ute and I's relationship goes deeper than "an interest in dogs". It goes deeper than that and is more complex than that. I was the person who validated, agreed with, her assessment that a withdrawn dog, long in the pound, could be drawn out, drawn into a dog-person relationship. Shiva was Ute's first dog, a creature found tied out in a field with signs of being used as a bait dog. He yearned to connect with "his" person yet held back afraid of what that might bring. Yes, there are similarities between Shiva and I. Perhaps you can find traces of the same fears within you. I won't speak for Ute, that would be folly. (grin)

There have been other "rescues" Ute and I shared in various way. The fate of some dog or cat needing rescue is common discussion between us. Even more common are discussions of what is happening in rescued animal's lives. Ah, perhaps this will help you get a feeling for Ute and I's connections. Ute was involved in my finding, taking on, adopting, all four of my current animals, two dogs and two cats. Now the guy part of me is clearly stating, "That is enough information!" There is more to tell! I am grateful for and occasionally annoyed by the diet, behavior, and logistical help Ute is providing me, helping me provide a richer life for the animals that share my home. The guy part of me is afraid I will expose myself by sharing what I provide for Ute. I was directly involved in her bringing home two of her three dogs. I also support her in providing for them. I am their "backup" people, caring for them when Ute is busy.

Oh, this page is almost ended, I better get on with it on the next page.

THE DANCE BEGINS

On a December day before Christmas Ute tells me that a mutual friend, one who already has three dogs, has spotted a stray dog and hopes somehow she (the friend) can find the resources to have the dog rescued. As I listen my mind put together reasons I should not be involved. My heart sympathizes with our friend and the dog but remains quietly tucked behind my mind's rational presentations. Deep within, deep in my lower belly I feel stirrings, a familiar alert, an unformed call to action, a whisper of *"The choice is already made."*

A complex, intricate, shifting, ever changing dance begins. The people and music shift and change, some stepping in, some stepping out, partners changing, some dancing by themselves. The music is often slow and soft only to shift into strident tones and quick step beats.

Chery, the mutual friend, has found a rescue organization that will help. The rescue has found a sponsor to help cover costs while the dog is being fostered. Each day I hear from Ute, sometimes from Chery, what is happening. Everything is lining up, they just need someone to foster the dog. With a knowing that I am "getting involved" I ask about the dog, what kind, how big, how close has Chery been to the dog, and other questions. I have the feeling of being pulled out onto the dance floor. The stirrings in my lower belly shift from an alert to a *"pay attention to your choices"*. My mind continues to provide reasons I should insistently remain in watch mode. My ego is surprisingly quiet.

As the reader you may be wondering why my mind would be in insist mode. What I haven't shared is that I have fostered several dogs for a local rescue. Of greater concern to my mind is that both Ute and Chery know I have fostered dogs. My mind is also acutely aware that both Ute and Chery hope I will step onto the dance floor by agreeing to foster the stray. I admit that Chery's description of the dog suffering through a cold, wet winter pulls at me.

Through the days I inch my way closer to the dance floor. Then one day the stirrings in my belly trigger my mind to ask, "What is needed for this to work? What step should we take?" My mind happily begins to examine, measure, contrast, and structure a plan. The people from rescues have tried several times to "capture" the stray. They have seen him but have not been close to him. Chery has made several trips and has left food with similar results. As Ute describes the events to me one evening on the phone from my belly I receive a sense, *"It is time to visit the stray, to step onto the dance floor."* I hear myself saying to Ute, "**I will go out and visit him.**" as my mind is busy placing the information into the framework it has created for the "stray dog problem". Processing Ute's pleasurable response keeps my mind and ego busy for almost a minute. Busy with planning my mind does not start raising objections until half an hour later as it plans the trip. My ego is uncertain as it reviews possible exposures vs rewards.

The next day with a description of the dog and where it has been seen I drive. Deep within there is a sense of contentment. My body sensations and emotions tell me I am calm and worried, afraid of what I am creating and yet pleased with the possibilities. My mind repeats, "There is no real commitment yet, no need for more plans right now. Its cool. Just gathering information we will process later." Paying attention in the way I have been taught I sense a warmth in my lower belly, gentle energies circling, some flowing up to my heart to ease my worries. I know this is more than a simple visit, the currents of change are being stirred, new possibilities being shaped. With all of this my mind keeps busy being annoyed by the poor timing of the traffic lights. Quietly under it all I am worried, knowing I might be called upon to bear my essence to the stray, to experience it's sorrow.

First Meeting

I turn off the main road, see the hedge along the bar parking lot and choose to turn in and park my car close to the hedge. My ego and mind worry about parking at a business I am not going to visit. I get out of the car and head to the right, planning to circle around the hedge and then turn left to slip between the hedge and the battery shop. As I make the second turn my body comes alive and time shifts into a slow, fluid state. My mind and ego quiet. One step, two steps, three steps, as I make the fourth step I slow, glancing along the hedge. A very slow fifth, then sixth step, then seventh, I notice him, the red of his fur, his head's movement, his energy. He is laying down looking in my direction. Time slows again, my awareness slips into a place where physical, energetic, and deeper knowings play together.

In the long moments before my next step I know I will continue forward, my steps taking me in his direction but not directly towards him. A step, he watches, another step, he watches. The distance closes to 15 feet and he sits up, his uncertainty flowing to me. A moment and yet an eternity pass as I sense myself kneeling and then experience my body kneeling. As my knees meet the wet ground and the cold moisture of the grass soaking through my pants registers, my full attention shifts to the stray. I look in its direction, not at it. The dog seems puzzled. As I sense it's wondering I lower a hip to the ground, greeted by the cold, wetness of the ground. The dog relaxes a bit, pauses, looks away from me, looks back, and lays back down.

As the stray's elbows meet the ground I feel myself relax and take a breath. As the breath moves out of my body a warmth spreads in my lower belly and flows to my heart. The stray lays there looking in my direction while I only glance at it out of the corners of my eyes. I notice the cold wetness of the December ground. Each breath marks a little progress. Its head goes down, resting on its paws. I shift my body so I am facing it less directly. Time moves very slowly, a breath at a time, small movements marking times passage. Perhaps 20 seconds later I notice I am smiling, pleased that the stray has chosen to remain close. The dance of our energies begins, connecting, checking, noticing, disconnecting, withdrawing then floating back. I am holding my awareness gently, quietly within, allowing it to float out and drawing it back in when I sense his uncertainty growing.

Five, maybe six minutes later he raises his head, looks at me. As he gets up I sense *"Too much, get away"* from him. The stray stands, then turns away, and slowly walks along the hedge, away from me. I watch and somehow know the best I can do is to remain quiet, to remain seated, accepting the stray's decision to leave. Several times as he walks away he looks over his shoulder, checking to see if I am following, if he needs to move faster. As the distance increases I experience pleasure at having been so close and sorrow that he is leaving. My mind inserts, "Well, that was a bust." and my ego worries that others from the rescue will find my efforts lacking. It all blends together.

As the stray moves out of sight, 100 feet away, I get up and walk out into the field, away from the hedge. Within two minutes I know it is time to leave. It is not my mind but a deeper sense that I can best translate as *"Your done for now. Drive away but don't let go."* I do just that. As I walk to the car and then drive home a myriad of thoughts and feeling move within me. My mind busily crafts what I will share with Ute when I talk with her. In true masculine fashion my mind's plan carefully expresses facts and only the vaguest hints of emotions. My ego frets that I will be judged as not having done enough. My emotions are a blend of satisfaction, sorrow, regret, and worry. Deep within there is calm and stirrings that extends into the future.

The Deal is Cast

I talk with Ute that evening. I describe what happened including very little about my feelings. She offers occasional encouragement as she listens. I also tell her what I am considering offering the rescue to help, what I will do and what I will require of them. Ute offers, "**I understand why you want that but I don't think they will go for it.**" Once my tale is finished Ute tells me I have to talk with Chery and the conversation moves on to how she and her dogs are doing.

I call Chery and share with her my visit. I am surprised when I hear an excited, "**You got that close to him? He stayed close to you laying down for that long? He has never let me close to him.**" My ego does a little happy dance knowing that our efforts have brought positive responses.

I image you are wondering what my plan includes. I tell Chery that in addition to fostering the stray I am willing to feed the stray for a few weeks and to see if I can get the stray to come to me. Her expression of relief stops when I tell her there is a condition that needs to be agreed upon. I tell her, "**I can't have people spooking him. People in the rescue have to agree that they will not try to catch him unless I okay it. I don't want any progress I make walked on. I will be the one going out every day.**" With reservation in her voice Chery agrees to talk with the others and let me know what is decided.

During my conversation with Chery I experience an almost constant pushing back and forth of my inner awareness, mind, ego, and my masculine instincts to make Chery happy. After hanging up the phone I take some time to sit quietly, to remember, to feel, to sense, what has just happened. Part of me hopes that Chery will call back with a "doesn't work for us." My mind is busy figuring out what the daily feedings will look like. From within a quiet inner space comes a knowing that my plan is already in effect.

When Chery calls back she says that the people from the rescue, Bobby and Fran, have agreed to my plan. She also let me know Bobby and Fran are planning on visiting the site that evening. She has given them my phone number so they can call me if they have a chance to catch the stray. As I hang up the phone I feel a familiar slightly sick feeling, my fears are not happy, I have just stepped into a several week process that is vague and that offers possibilities of conflict. "Take a breath, feel my feet, relax my belly, another breath, open space in my body, ah, better."

That evening Bobby calls. The stray is in an enclosure. He is sure that he can sneak in undetected and catch the stray. I ask few questions about the setup. Feeling Bobby's confidence and hearing how well he has it planned I say okay. As I hang up the phone I quiet, letting myself sense whether the stray might be in my home that evening. I sense a faint *"maybe"*. That is enough for my mind to begin figuring, "back bedroom, may be some damage, only a maybe on tonight, don't waste effort planning yet." With that I settle into a nervous waiting, busying myself with reading.

The call comes about an hour and a half later. While Fran stayed at the enclosure entrance Bobby snuck in using training the military had provided during the Vietnam era. Bobby was undetected by the stray until the last moment when he made his move. The stray bolted keeping Bobby from getting a strong hold. The stray surprises both Fran and Bobby by heading to the locked chain link double gates. He charges it with full force, forcing the gates apart, forcing his way out. Bobby is calling while he and Fran wait to see if the stray returns. They have tied the bottom of the chain link gates and hope to have a second chance yet that night. They will call if they have any luck. The stray does not return.

Not long after Chery calls. We talk about the results and what is next. Chery has been feeding the stray when she could and offers to give me the box containing the supplies. I am pleased by her offer and happily arrange to pick up the box. As I sit quietly before going to bed

I allow myself to notice the many, many energies and ideas busy trying to prepare me for what lays ahead. Things are stirring, things my mind and ego seem unable to know. Calm, worry, excitement all quietly dance within me.

A Bit of Groundwork

End of December

*A*fter picking up the box with feeding supplies I drive out to feed the stray. As I drive my attention moves to everyone referring to the stray with the masculine pronoun, he. The stray has been cautious, quiet, observing intently yet carefully, and withdrew when uncomfortable. As I quiet myself and sense the energies of different dogs I know and have known I wonder if the stray isn't female. Beyond the reserved energies is an inner strength, an inner knowing. On our encounter the stray had not challenged me in any way. Rather than test me the stray seemed to carefully sense my intent by creating a gentle connection. My mind and ego will only accept that the stray might be female. My fears of being wrong caution me not to share my suspicions yet. Deep within I know she and I are destine to learn together.

Several days earlier Chery had placed a water bowl inside the enclosure where the stray sometimes sleeps. In addition to the gates there is a break in the chain link. My mind quickly let me know that I will be using the break in the fence to enter and replenish water in the water bowl. My mind, fears, and ego also decide that the best place to put the food bowl I have with me is next to the water bowl. As I walk to the break in the fence my fears and my desire to honor other people's property stop me. I stand at the unofficial entrance, others have used it but… In the moments of indecision a delivery truck arrives and parks close to the gates. As the driver gets out he looks at me with questioning attention. I feel myself relax, an easy solution is presenting itself. I greet the driver and quickly tell him I am working with a rescue and plan to begin feeding the stray. "**Good luck with that**" is coupled with a relaxing of his shoulders. My telling the driver I want to let the owner know what I plan is rewarded with a smile and "**He'll be fine with it. He just wants to know what is going on**." With that the driver heads into the spa shop.

As I stand watching the driver walk away my protocol sensitive father's words play in my head, "First things first." Okay, the owner or manager would be busy for a while. It seems a good time for me to walk the field, to see if the stray is anywhere around. When the delivery truck leaves I will talk with whoever is in the shop.

As I walk the large field I whistle an occasional single whistle, one note beginning low and raising in pitch and volume until I run out of breath. As I walk the field I see people in the apartment building across the field watching me. My mind, ego, and fears raise protests, I am in unfamiliar territory with no invitation, without permission. My masculine need to provide the service I have committed to overrides the protests of exposure which my mind prods me with at least once a minute. When I notice the delivery truck leaving, I gratefully head to the business.

As I enter the business I am pleased to notice no customers. The man there returns my greeting and looks at me expectantly. When I tell him I am with a rescue group and would like his okay to put a food bowl next to the water bowl in his enclosure and to feed the stray every day he responds with, "**That will be fine. Whatever you can do to help him will be good. I manage the shop and just need to know what you are doing**." "Great! I will keep you informed." I then spend a couple minutes letting him know that I plan to feed the stray each day hoping to win the stray's trust. The manager's posture and tone when he says, "**He runs away every time I go out the back door into the enclosure.**" gives me the sense that he will watch my attempts with amusement and no expectation of success. I find myself responding easily with, "**I will feed the stray for at least four or five weeks. As long as I see progress I will keep feeding him.**"

The First Feeding

As I round the corner to the back of the business I scan the field for the stray and whistle, a single, long note starting low and raising in pitch. The whistle will become my signal to the stray that I am in the area, a distinctive sound that a dog can be easily hear blocks away.

The area behind the business includes the enclosure, pavement circling the building, and an old Quonset hut. A grass field of perhaps six acres extends beyond the pavement. Across the field, about 180 feet away, is a chain link fence that separates the field from several two story apartment buildings. The field extends to the left, behind the business next door. A tall hedge separate the field from a parking lot further left. On the right the field extends about two blocks, circling behind old apartments that look as though they had once been an inexpensive single story motel. Their appearance remind me of trips my family took in the mid 50s.

I have parked at the far left corner of the pavement, next to the field. I go to the passenger side of my car, open the rear door, and begin preparing the stray's food, half a can of wet food and a couple of scoops of dry food. With the food mixed I walk the 60 feet back of the enclosure, as I walk my mind and ego worriedly chatter about "encroaching on other people's property". At the enclosure my masculine sense of honor remind me 'You have a commitment to fulfill.' and I step up through the break in the chain link fence. Worried and determined I circle to the right of the pool and deck, placing the food bowl just under the deck about half way back towards the business. As I step back from the deck and look out to scan the field I whistle and then hear myself saying, **"Your food is here, girl."** As I step out of the enclosure I smile with the pleasure of having allowed my inner awareness and masculine honor to shape my choices.

As I walk back to my car my mind and intuition play an all too familiar "yeah, but" game, my intuition giving my mind a sense of it's knowing and my mind countering with it's thoughts. Being limited to words here I have translated my intuition's knowing into words that carry a sense of the understanding. "Yes, *girl*." "Yeah, but Chery and the manager referred to him as he." *"Yes and, my sense in that she is female."* "Yeah but you can't know that, you have only seen him once." *"Yes and 'him' does not match my sense of her."* "Yeah but he has too much fur to see whether he is male or female." *"Yes and sight will only verify my knowing."* "Yeah but others are referring to him as he and we don't want to be wrong." *"Yes and that is group think, a projection."* "Yeah but we will look silly if we are wrong." *"Yes and we don't have to say anything yet."* "Oh, quiet and safe is good."

Thankfully the act of getting into the car and starting it interrupt the 'discussion'. As I turn the car on to leave within I sense stirrings, questions of what I have started. Happy to have the opening my mind chimes in with, "What makes you think this will go anywhere? In a few weeks we will stop this silliness and waste of resources." *"Yes and we have made a commitment. So help us make the best of it."* "The best of it would be to stop now and conserve resources." *"Yes and we are going to do it for at least four weeks."* "Okay, I will plan how to use the fewest resources and keep the looking silly to a minimum." *"Great! I know we are doing what we should, looking silly or not."*

I imagine that about now some of you are wondering how I have avoided becoming a resident in a mental hospital. Others are wondering, "Hey! You do it too?" Others are simply uncomfortable. A few have all three going on in a hodgepodge of thoughts and feelings. As a side note I did grow up on the grounds of a mental hospital. (grin)

Calls & Coordination

That evening I talk with Ute reporting that there was little to report other than the manager at the shop being good with my feeding the stray within the enclosure. My comment of not seeing the stray and not being sure when I would see him brings a "**You will just have to keep feeding him.**" from her. I countered with, "**I will feed him for four to six weeks and see. If I see progress I will consider continuing.**" I won't bore you (or expose myself) with the additional back and forth.

During the conversation with Ute I consider saying something about the stray's gender. My mind is quick to insert, **"You said we would wait. We need more evidence."** " *Okay, we will wait to see what else shows up.*" **"Good, we do need to maintain credibility."** "*Strange, credibility vs integrity*" Part of Ute and I's discussion involve my reiterating that my commitment is to bring the stray in and foster him until the rescue finds him a home. During the conversation I experience stirrings within my lower belly, intuition letting me know I am denying something I already know.

After talking with Ute I call Chery and update her. She expresses concern about the cold, rainy December weather the stray is living with. I offer that I hope things will progress quickly. We talk about my role as the one who would bring the stray in and then foster him until the rescue finds a home for him. The stirrings in my lower belly become stronger.

Next comes a call to Bobby from the rescue to let him know the feeding has begun. He shares how he usually just grabs dogs and that somehow they understand that he is giving them no choice. I say I plan a slower approach to winning trust, one that will probably take several weeks but that feels right to me. His response is that he hopes it will work leaves me hoping his trust will prove merited. Bobby tells me that he has already found a sponsor who will pay for food while I am feeding the stray and fostering him. The inner stirrings shift and become a sense of "*foster and more.*" I am careful to not open and explore the *"and more"*.

After the calls my ego and mind team up to make sure I know my ego is feeling very exposed. People are trusting me in ways my ego cannot. My mind points out that there is no logical reason to think my method will work. To make things worse it points out "the plan" is incredibly vague. "Feed the dog and see what happens. We need more details." Being alone in my home with few distractions I become quiet, open my awareness, ask "What haven't I seen? Is there something I should be aware of? Is the path I am on where I should be?" What comes to me is a sense of peace flowing from deep within. Slowly my ego's worry quiets and my mind accepts that it is time to "plan and guide" other parts of my life. There is a quiet knowing that I am being given a chance to open beyond limitations I have been accepting as necessary.

It is worth noting that at the time I begin feeding the stray I plan to be without dogs. I have a list of several countries I plan to visit, being gone a month at a time. Those plans and living alone make having a dog or dogs problematic. The simplest situation will be to remain "dog free" until my travels are completed.

The Routine

*A*nd so it begins. For the most part I drive the eleven miles to the Rockwood area in the early afternoon. I try to keep feeding time between 1 PM and 2 PM hoping the stray will begin showing up for feedings.

In the first two months seeing the stray seems to be a matter of whether the stray happens to be in the area or not. Either she is there when I arrive or she is not. From watching her I know that she has several other areas that she frequents. There are times when I have the sense she has been spooked by someone and left the area of the field for two or three days.

At first I call Bobby with regular reports. After a couple weeks the reports begin to be spaced out more and more. There simply is not much to report. At first the stray leaves the immediate area of the enclosure when I show up. She will move to the far left corner of the field, to a mound of dirt 150 feet away and disappear over the mound.

The second week of feeding against my ego's wishes I nervously tell Ute that I feel the stray is female. Ute points out that everyone else seems to think the stray is male. An "**I know. But my sense is that it is a she, not a he.**" brings a question of why I think that. My ego is not happy, "See she thinks we are wrong." My mind with exasperation kicks in, "Now I will have to give reasons I haven't formulated yet." I offer to Ute, "**I am not sure. The way she moves. The way she connects with me.**" "**What else?**" "**I can't really say. Saying he does not feel right, feels dishonest. Saying she is easy; feels right**." Thankfully Ute pauses allowing herself to sense what I offer. "**Okay, have you told Chery.**" "**Not yet, when it is time I** will." "**Chery will want to know**." "**And she will. I will tell her when it feels right**."

A couple of days later with more confidence I tell Chery. Chery excitedly asks if I have actually seen, had I been that close? My ego tells me Chery is disappointed when I say, "**No, I haven't been closer than the 15 feet when I first saw her. She just feels like a she.**" With Chery's "**Oh, okay.**" my ego offers, "See. She questions our sensing." and my mind offers, "Now we have lost credibility." From deep within comes, "*We spoke truth. We experience her.*"

A few days later I head into the shop attached to the enclosure. I have a sense that it is time to update the store manager on what is going on. I tell the store manager what I am noticing, that little has changed but that I am hopeful. After his quiet thanks for keeping him updated I feel a push from inside and hear myself saying, "**My sense is the stray is female. I haven't seen one way or the other. I just feels like it is a she.**" "**Oh, everyone has been saying he. And you expect it is she?**" "**Yeah, movement, the way she responds. Just feels like the stray is female.**" "**It will be interesting if we ever find out for sure.**" "**Yes, it will.**" As I leave the store and walk back to my car my ego and mind keep offering comments questioning my choice. After a couple of "*We will see*"s from within they quiet.

The Naming

*T*he first two weeks of feeding the stray span New Years. The weather is often rainy and cold. As I drive out to the site I often hear an inner voice asking, "Why are we doing this?". My mind and ego repeat that we have made a commitment with my mind often adding, "It is just for four to six weeks." From deeper within comes an unstated knowing of, "*or until*" with a sense of "*until what is planned occurs*".

In those first few weeks I have a sense that my presence is unwelcome. People from the apartment complex across the field seem suspicious and uncertain. They will hear me whistling and see me wandering through the field. Even more suspicious is my driving up behind the business and parking my car where I have a full view of the apartments. More than once I notice curtains pulled back and then quickly closed. More than once my mind and ego urge me to simply driving away.

Almost every evening I talk with Ute. If I have anything of significance I will also call Chery. Major events merit a call to Bobby from the rescue. By the end of the third week the phone calls to report progress dwindle to very few. On a few days the stray is laying across the field about 120 feet away. At first she will simply get up and walk out of sight. Some days I will see the stray, some days I will not.

About the end of the third week there is a new behavior. When I arrive and the stray sees me she gets up and begins walking away. She goes go up the small incline 140 feet away glancing back just before disappearing.

Somewhere during the third week when I drive between the two shops and the field comes into view I see the stray's red color out in the green field. The color contrast is striking, bringing a smile to me. She appears to be walking towards the enclosure. As my foot moves to the brake pedal she stops, raises her head, and seems to send her energy to scan 'the intruder'. I am pleased that she does not immediately turn and run and at the same time disappoint that a moment after I stop the car she turns and heads towards the raise off to the left. She is heading towards her exit.

By the time I park and get out of the car her slow pace has taken her half way to the raise. As I get out I whistle and watch as she turns to look at me and then increases her speed. Her movements and her energy tell me she is determined to leave, to escape to freedom. As she walks further and further from me I hear myself saying, "**Hey Beauty. You are certainly a beauty. Will you be my Beauty?**" Her glance back at me fills my body with warmth. As I stand there watching her leave my mind and ego seem to be tucked away, and seem to have not heard what I had just given voice. Finally my mind chimes in, "She is beautiful." blocking out the noticing of deeper possibilities of meaning in what I have said.

In the next couple weeks when I catch a glance of the stray leaving I find myself repeating what I had first said. Unnoticed by my mind and ego inner whispers are being given voice. "**You certainly are a beauty.**" My mind and ego are kept unaware that beauty is becoming part of my life, part of my growth. A long haired, reddish, chow chow mix, Beauty is beginning to allow her inner presence to show and to tease my inner knowing forth. At the time I do not understand. With Beauty's help I understand now. I cannot tell you when my mind and ego recognized that the stray had been given a name. It would be several months later that my mind would notice how Beauty coming into my life signaled my opening to beauty, opening to enriching my life.

The Dance Continues

As the third week in January approaches, week four of my quest, I wonder whether I will go past week six. As I drive out I ask myself, "What might I do to help Beauty trust me?" As I ponder that question another appears, "What might I do to increase my trust in Beauty, my trust in the Universe's intent?" My mind and ego respond immediately, "Oh, crap. Now we are in for it. The cat is out of the bag. There is more than us involved here." The stirrings in my lower belly verify the presence of other energies. Fortunately from within come stirrings, a sense of *"all is as it should be"*. I relax and return to wondering what I might do next.

When I arrive I am surprised to see Beauty just beyond the pavement, within 30 feet of the enclosure. Excitement jumps into my chest, a warmth expands to fill my body. As soon as she sees my car she begins walking slowly towards the rise. Her movement away brings sorrow and desire to connect blending with my excitement. She is 30 feet away when I cautiously get out of the car. I close the car door gently and turn towards her. As I notice her moving slowly away I find myself smiling and repeating outloud, **"Hey Beauty."** When the distance has reached 80 feet I whistle to her. She turns her head long enough to glance at me as she continues. At 100 feet I whistle again. Again she looks back. As she reaches the top of the rise 140 feet away I whistle yet again. To my surprise she turns her head, slows her walk, turns her body part way towards me and stops. Her pause lasts only a few seconds. In those few seconds I sense her energy touching me, then penetrating me. I am filled with a sense of worry and hope, a need for connection. At the moment she turns I sense, "*Too much, must get away.*" and she disappears beyond the rise.

My body is buzzing with energy. I barely notice as I retrieve her bowl, mix her food, and return the bowl to it's place inside the enclosure. I can already feel myself calling Ute and Chery with the news. For the first time Beauty has responded in a way that is more than just leaving.

When I report to Ute she asks, "**So you will keep feeding her?**" With discomfort stirring I reply, "**Possibly. I have seen some progress. Let's see what happens over the coming week to 10 days**." Whether it is present or not my ego detects displeasure as Ute responds with, "**Yeah, okay. You need to call Chery.**" I am not surprised when Chery asks the same question.

The following day as I drive to the sight my mind offers, "We have seen progress. We may need to go longer than six weeks." My ego immediately protests, "If you hadn't called people last night we could quit in a couple weeks and be safe."

Much to my disappointment Beauty is not at the field when I arrive. With a sullen mood I retrieve her bowl, fill it, and place it back in the enclosure. I am not ready to leave so I walk the field whistling my lone note in hopes of Beauty showing up. Twenty minutes later I get into my car and drive off. The drive home is populated with uncertainty and unending questions about what is happening. As I turn into my driveway a sense of "*everything is okay*" settles in. My mind and ego happily tuck the 'problem' away.

The next day I scan field as I arrive. No Beauty. Against all odds I whistle as I place her food and then walk the field, a sense of sorrow blending with quiet indignation.

The third day she is there again, laying about 30 feet from the slight rise. As I get out of the car she gets up and heads up the rise. As she gets to the top of the rise I whistle and to my delight she turns and looks at me, watches me for perhaps a minute before walking out of sight. Another positive change. She has responded to my whistle by turning to look at me. I enjoy a quiet confidence blended with a sense that she and I are opening to further connections. For the next few days if she is at the site she will start to leave and then pause to look at me when I whistle to her. Each day she stays a bit longer atop the rise before leaving.

Then, one day, she is there, on the pavement close to the entry of the enclosure. Time slows, still awareness opens within me, I can sense every blade of grass, every detail. As I park the car and get out she watches, waiting until I move towards the enclosure to begin her retreat. She is in no hurry and I sense that she is more curious about me than afraid. She walks slowly watching me, letting me sense her energy, until she is 50 feet away. Once again I whistle when she is about 80 feet away. This time she turns her head, pauses for a few seconds, and then walks on. At the bottom of the rise she glances back at me without my having whistled. I smile and without thinking allow a gentle warmth to flow towards her. I whistle as she reaches the top. She stops, turns fully towards me and watches, a minute and then two. Then to my surprise and delight she sits down. In the moment her butt settles on the ground I know I will be continuing beyond six weeks. In the moments that follow pleasure and contentment raise in me and I hear myself gently shouting, **"Good girl, Beauty. Thank you."** I am tempted to walk towards her, I am stopped by a deep knowing that it is not time.

To my delight Beauty stays sitting on the rise watching me as I retrieve her bowl, fill it with food at the car, and return it to the enclosure. I move with gentle intent, slow, easy, relaxed. As I am returning to the car I notice her stand. My immediately slowed pace reflects my disappointment and gives me time to open more fully to Beauty. I am holding my breath, she is still facing me. As I reach the car she turns and pauses. As I open the door she walks out of sight. I swing my body into the car, smiling and feeling the pull of wanting more.

There was a reason for driving out each day. The small, incremental progress deepens my knowing.

A Long, Cold February

The day the stray stops when I whistle I respond to the urge to share by going into the store to share the news with the shop manager. He notices my enthusiasm and as I describe what has occurred I sense him being polite and skeptical. I can almost hear him thinking, "Boy not much has happened. This guy is really paying attention. No real change though."

It is the end of the first week in February, the stray has responded to my whistle, remaining to watch me several times. When I show up she is not in sight. I prepare and place her food. I am here, it isn't raining, and I wonder whether the stray is around, waiting out of sight, watching me. With a gentle nudge from within I begin a walk out into the field and around the edges whistling our single note intermittently, hoping to see her. Suddenly she there laying by the blackberry bushes and gets up as soon as she notices me. I stop, pause a few seconds, and then turn back towards the car. My mind and ego seem far away. She watches me walk away, seeming puzzled by my retreat. As soon as I am 40 feet or so away she begins walking towards the rise. I get back to my car when she is half way to the rise. When I whistle she looks over at me, pauses, and then continues. As she reaches the base of the rise I whistle again. She stops, turns, and watches me for perhaps 30 seconds. Turning back to the rise she begins the short climb. As she reaches the top I whistle once again and holler **"Hey Beauty!"** To my surprise she stops and turns back to look at me. Time moves ever so slowly as 5, 10, 15, 20 seconds pass. In the stillness I sense her wondering, wanting more. She shifts her weight and to my surprise sits down facing me.

I am awe struck. Even though I approached her she has chosen to stop and watch me. Even better she has decided to sit down and continue watching me. As the urge to jump up in celebration wells within me an equal urge to not scare Beauty keeps me quiet. She sits, I watch and fidget. In the silence we seem to be discussing what is and negotiating trust. Slowly, gently we are opening to each other, accepting possibilities, wondering if we might share more. After about five minutes Beauty gets up and turns to leave. A whistle causes her to stop and turn her head back to look at me. In the few seconds she looks at me I hear myself thinking "Thank You". As she turns and leaves I sense from her *"Thank you so much."*

It is another night for calling people to report progress. Ute is pleased that I am reporting and seems most pleased that with progress I will continue to feed Beauty. I call Chery and let her know what I have experienced. She too is pleased and wonders whether it will only be three or four weeks before Beauty is home with me. I tell Chery that it would be nice but that I think it will be at least two months. A quick call to Bobby brings a thanks for the update followed by chatting about what is going on with the rescue dog he is caring for.

Within a week and a half it becomes routine that when I find Beauty in the field and approach her she will head to the rise and sit on the rise watching me while I mix and place her food. Each time she moves a bit more slowly away from me and stops more often when I whistle to her. Then one day I whistle when she is about 40 feet from the rise, she stops, turns, seems to consider what to do and then sits down facing me. Warmth and pleasure flow through me as from there she watches me fix her food and place it in the enclosure. To my surprise when I turn back to the field she is laying down. I freeze and am flooded with delight and puzzlement, should I wait so she stays where she is or should I return to the car, perhaps causing her to get up and leave. As *"let's see what she does"* floats to my mind I head to the car. She sit up, watching me. I step out of the enclosure and she shifts her weight but remains seated. She watches as I slowly walk the 40 feet to my car, walking in her direction. As I get to the car and walk to the side of the car nearest her she gets up and heads to the rise. I feel familiar disappointment swell within me. I whistle and she continues her quick walk towards the rise. Finally she stops at the top of the rise, looks back at me for a few seconds and then disappears.

The Drive Home – Times of Reflection

*A*s I watch her disappear I feel pride, pleasure, disappointment, hope, and sorrow all tumbling within me, each coming forward only to be replaced by another. I notice myself open the car door, get in, start the engine. And there I sit for three or four minutes simply feeling the sensations of each emotion as it comes forward. Soon I hear my mind insist, "Okay, let's go!" and respond by reaching over, putting the car in gear, and heading out of the parking area.

Once I am a few blocks away from the field I let myself settle into an easy flow of understanding coming forward with my mind inserting occasional cautions. "*Wow... That was real progress.*" "But not much. How long will it take?" "*She trusted me enough to stay closer and even lay down.*" "And how many more weeks will we spend using $30 in gas?" "*She did more and then didn't stop at the rise.*" "It is cold and wet and will be every day." "*I wonder if she will be here tomorrow. I hope so.*" "Yeah, hope... and probable disappointment." "*Ah, progress, I feel good.*" "Feels good? What about results?"

That becomes my pattern. Wondering about what I will find, about possibilities, as I drive to the site. Letting the experiences generate quiet awareness, emotions, and thoughts as I drive home.

By the middle of February Beauty no longer leaves when I show up. Whether she is on the rise or laying closer in, she simply remains where she is laying, watching me prepare and place her food.

Towards the end of February one day I arrive to find Beauty is nowhere to be seen. The following day I do not see her. As I walk the field whistling our single note, checking to see if she is laying down somewhere a person from the apartments nods to me for the first time. I wave and feel a bit of tension leave my body. For the first time I feel a bit of acceptance that I am here. Perhaps as the weather warms so will the neighbors' acceptance.

We settle into a familiar pattern. Beauty will choose to trust a bit, to stay a bit closer, and then will disappear the next day or two.

Also at the end of February one day when I arrive I notice Beauty is in the enclosure. She spots my car and carefully watches as I drive to my usual parking spot, perhaps 40 feet from the enclosure. Time slows and my movements begin to come from someplace beyond my thoughts. My mind and ego observe as I park, turn off the engine. Beauty has gotten up but has not moved towards the entry. I roll down my window and whistle the single rising note. Her body relaxes a bit. I sit still, suspended in time a few seconds before reaching for the door handle. I unwind my body out of the car and watch as Beauty stays where she is. I have a sense of her being puzzled, more driven by curiosity than fear. Very slowly, rhythmically I begin walking towards the enclosure. She watches carefully and soon understands I am head to where she is. She begins a hurried walk towards the enclosure's entrance. I freeze and hold my breath! She freezes watching me. Within 10 seconds her body shifts, relaxes a bit, and she walks to the entry, jumps out and begins a relaxed walk out into the field. I whistle, she turns to look at me as I begin walking again. She is in the middle of the field when I step up into the enclosure. I turn and whistle to her. To my delight she stops, turning back to face me, sitting down as I walk to retrieve her bowl. As I bend and reach out for her bowl I feel as though Beauty is right there, experiencing my arm's movement, my fingers opening and then closing, the cool feel of her bowl, my hand moving back to my body as my legs engage and I stand up. Cool! She gets up and watches as I walk with measured pace back to the entry. I am noticing each muscle cooperate with other muscles as I walk, a strange new sensation. When I step down out of the enclosure, she turns and begins walking away. As soon as I turn away from her heading to the car I whistle. She stops, watching me, waits for about six of my steps and then turns towards me and sits. I am grinning like a second grader and filled with elation, tempted to skip back to my car. Beauty delights me by staying there, in the middle of the field, perhaps 60 feet away.

Preparing Beauty's food in her bowl somehow is more meaningful. I have a sense of Beauty accepting, even appreciating, that I am taking actions for her. Each small movement reflects and strengthens the connections each of us is beginning to allow. As I pick up her bowl I glance out to her and in her glance at me I can almost hear her whisper, "*You give my food.*" and I have a sense of Beauty smelling the food, bending her head down, taking a bite into her mouth, being pleased with the now familiar tastes and textures. Time is crawling, small movements with each detail I perceive. It seems to take a minute or more to stand up and turn towards the enclosure. A few steps towards the enclosure I have a sense of "*too much*", then Beauty breaks contact, stands and begins walking towards the rise. Her gate is relaxed and determined. As I step up into the enclosure Beauty reaches the top of the rise and turns to look at me. I raise the her bowl and shout, **"This is your food Beauty!"** By the time my next foot lands on the ground Beauty is out of sight. As I walk the last few feet to place her bowl I cannot sense her. Bending to place her bowl is used by my mind and ego to ask if I am not bending over too far for her. I have no answer, my only feeling a faint whisper from within my belly of "*as it should be*".

The drive home is mechanical. I barely notice the traffic and guiding my car. Something is working deep within me, something I am not allowed to understand yet.

Cold & Wet Concerns

Most days the weather is wet and cold, typical Portland February and March weather. There are occasional days with broken clouds or even sunshine. Often when I talk with Ute and almost every time I talk with Chery Beauty's well being in the cold, wet weather is part of the discussion. I sense their attempts to increase my pace, there is no push from within to go faster. By the end of February I hear that the two are considering borrowing a trap so that Beauty can be brought in sooner.

During the discussions leading up to them borrowing and placing a trap I am in turmoil. Yes, Beauty is exposed. On the other hand she has a long coat and did okay through December and January. With the daily feeding she has added a bit of weight, still she is under weight. The masculine within me feels dishonored.

When Ute tells me they have lined up a trap and will be picking it up within the week my angst becomes palpable. My plan is to build Beauty's trust. Trying to trap her is in direct conflict with my intent. And I know Chery and Ute's plan is valid. The day I hear that Chery has arranged for the trap I can wait no longer. I must find a solution that will allow me to honor my intent, my unspoken agreement with Beauty.

I call Chery and talk with her about the trap. I tell her that I cannot be involved with the trap, I can't help them place the trap, I can't put food in the trap. Chery's consternation and confusion is evident in her tone. My mind and ego want to provide an acceptable reason but are unable to generate anything. After hanging up I sit with my inner conflict of wanting to make Ute and Chery happy and my need to honor my path. Which should be first? Have I missed a possibility? Finally I choose honoring my path with Beauty as my focus. I won't participate,

I will coordinate with Chery so I don't interfere with her efforts to trap Beauty.

Chery and I chat about how we can make it work. I let Chery know that I will continue to show up each day and propose that unless they say otherwise I will place Beauty's food in the usual place. Chery reasonably asks about how we will handle not feeding Beauty to entice her to go for the food in the trap. I hear myself saying to her, "**Let me know and I will not place food if you don't want me to. I do need to continue visiting each day.**" The deal is cast.

An evening a couple of days before Chery and her husband, Tony, are going to pick up the trap and place it in the enclosure she calls me. My thoughts of, "Tomorrow I will not place food." triggers another round of doubts. As soon as I hang up my mind and ego begin to search for a solution, "*How can we make it all reasonable and safe?*" Fortunately 15 minutes later when I choose to feel my feet on the floor and take a long slow breath I sense a quiet, "*It is as it should be. Let it go.*" With a second breath my body relaxes, with a third breath my mind releases it's tension and shifts to planning details for coordinating efforts.

With the trap in place I see less of Beauty. She is smart. First she collapses the back of the trap to get the food. Next she triggers the trap but is not caught. Stray cats are caught and as agreed are released by the fellow in the shop. By the end of a week it is evident that the trap is unlikely to work with Beauty. I find myself left with an interesting blend of pride, disappointment, and relief. Pride with Beauty's awareness, disappointment that she is not yet coming to my house, relief that the focus is returning to daily feeding, Beauty and I are returning to my methods, the methods she has accepted.

With the shift I agree I will gradually move the feeding bowl closer to the trap and then into it. When I do begin placing her food in the trap within a few days Beauty will go just far enough into the trap to catch the falling door with her butt, eat, and back out. The trap does not work. A sense of impudent pride in her wisdom forms within me.

The Connection is Made

The first week in March, towards the end of initial attempts to trap Beauty, it seems that Beauty is beginning to connect me with the daily feeding. Several days when I show up I find Beauty out on the edge of the field or even in the middle of the field paying attention to the enclosure. She will watch me retrieve her bowl, return to the car, fix her food, and place her bowl. Her tentative trust warms me as energies of deep contentment and pleasure flow from within.

One day in mid March she is sitting in the middle of the field when I arrive. As I leave the enclosure after placing her food I feel a pull to walk slowly towards her. I surrender and rather than head away from her towards the car I walk slowly across the pavement to the edge of the field, almost directly towards her. A couple of steps into the field time shifts and my world collapses to the pavement, the field, Beauty, and my movement. Beauty sits, facing me. One step on the grass, she stays. A second step on the grass, she shifts. A third step towards her, she looks toward the rise. A fourth step and she begins to get up facing towards the rise. Time slows further as my fifth step becomes going down onto my knees and quietly saying, "**Hey Beauty**." She turns back to me and my world becomes she, I, and the 30 feet between us. I hear myself saying, "**Its okay girl. I won't chase you.**" and notice myself shift so that I no longer face directly at her. She freezes, shifts her weight slightly towards me, and her ears come slightly up and forward. I can almost hear her asking, "*What?*" as she slowly sits down. Within a moment I notice warmth filling my body and myself smiling as I note her body is facing more towards the rise than me while her face is mostly towards me.

I cannot tell you whether it was 10 seconds or 10 minutes that we sat there within 30 feet of each other. I can tell you that at some point Beauty looked towards the rise and then back and forth between me and the rise. Soon the pull of the rise wins and Beauty gets up, she looks away and begins walking quickly towards the rise. Several times she glances back slowing her retreat with each glance. As Beauty begins her brief climb up the rise I feel sorrow beginning to impinge upon my awe and pleasure. As she reaches the top of the rise she glances back and pauses. With a whistle she pauses perhaps 5 seconds then disappears. The shift in time seem to leave with her. I am alone, kneeling on the ground, very aware of how wet and cold my knees are, wondering why, experiencing quiet stirrings of awareness within my lower belly.

Children shouting as they happily come out of their apartment 120 feet away bring the world back to me. I remain kneeling a few moments and get up, unwinding my now stiff legs, discomfort reminding me I am 62. I am quiet, a contentment flowing gently and messages stirring within. Mechanically I get into the car, back up, turn and head towards home. The quiet contentment remains and is slowly replaced by stirrings in my belly. Beauty pushed her comfort. She will not be around tomorrow. She has connected me with her daily food. She has allowed me to approach her. Somehow I need to draw her to me, get her to allow me to touch her. I allow the openness of the question *"How?"* and notice the stirrings in my energies. *"Stay open. The stirrings will bring awareness of the next action."*

I call Ute and Chery that evening. I am disappointed that news of Beauty and I's progress seems over ridden by their intent to have trapping Beauty work, to bring Beauty in quickly. My angst softens when I remember and say, **"Beauty cannot be hurried."**

The next day as I drive out I consider placing her food bowl outside the enclosure, sitting close by, and taking the food with me if she does not approach. Perhaps after a day or two without food she will come closer. As expected she is not there. She has trusted me more. Within there is only a deep, solid knowing that now is not the time for changes. I place her food and find myself hoping she will show up the next day.

On the drive home I am stirred to review the flow and timing of events. I have the sense of some inner knowing placing each event before

Malcolm Pullen

my mind and ego. As each event is brought forward inner knowings trace out it's significance within the flow of events. In knowings beyond words my ego and mind are shown progress is being made, progress is accelerating somehow guided by knowings that are vague whispers to my mind and ego. My mind and ego are a bit surprised and disturbed as they recognize I had stepped onto the grass, moving towards Beauty without their involvement in the choosing. They have a vague sense of there being beauty within allowing inner awareness to guide our choices.

Some Things Don't Work

The next day I do not see her when I first arrive. I park the car and get out, heading towards the enclosure to get her bowl. As I take in a breath to whistle Beauty walks around the Quonset hut that forms the east side of the enclosure. Both of us are startled and stop dead in our tracks. Noticing my tension I shift my weight back onto my heels, breath in, and relax my shoulders as I breath out. I am rewarded by seeing Beauty relax a bit and shift her movement towards the field. I watch, almost holding my breath. Another breathe, relax, open, allow, notice. To my surprise she goes about 35 feet out into the field, turns to face the enclosure, and sits down. I can almost hear her, *"Okay. Food. Waiting."* In the same moment I have the sense of chewing food in my own mouth. I look at her in surprise and sense her being pleased, *"Oh, you noticed. Maybe."* I sense an easing of the barriers between she and I. We seem to share a bit more space together. As I turn and walk to the enclosure I am very aware of my body moving within the physical world. I have purpose for living beyond myself.

Somehow Beauty is with me as I retrieve her bowl, return to the car, and mix her food. In a moment I notice I am smiling in response to realizing she is laying down, watching me, trusting me a bit more. Her food in hand I walk towards her rather than heading to the enclosure. She immediately sits up. Within four of my steps she is standing, facing away from me. "Not working." floats into my mind and I stop. As she begins to move away from me I whistle, she keeps walking away from me. She stops and turns with my second whistle. Without thinking I raise her bowl, **"Here girl."** She watches as I bend, place the bowl on the ground, and take several steps backwards. The openness I sensed between us earlier is now gone. I drop to my knees. Beauty pauses a few seconds and as she turns to walk away I sense from her, *"Not right, different, not safe, need distance."*

I watch her walking away. Before I notice what I am doing I retrieve her bowl, turn to the enclosure, walk that direction, and hear myself saying, "**Hey Beauty. It is okay.**" As I step up into the enclosure I notice she is sitting on the rise. As I place her bowl I know deep within that placing her bowl anywhere but the usual place will not work. I am puzzled. Beauty watches as I walk to back to the enclosure entry and as soon as I step out of the enclosure she gets up, turns, and disappears. By the time I reach the car she has also disappeared energetically as if she has shifted into another reality. As I turn to the driveway I have a brief sense of her then she is gone again. As my mind considers reaching out to her from within I sense, *"Let her be."* and I do.

It is three miserable days before I see her again. Several times a sense of *"No Beauty in my life."* floats from deep within. That third day I do not see her at the field. After placing her food I drive out of the lot, carefully looking to see if she is laying on the grass across the parking lot of the Mexican Restaurant. With a jolt I notice her too late to turn in and so nervously drive around the block to get back to the lot. As I drive into the lot I roll down my window and whistle. Beauty's ears come up. Half way across the lot I park and get out of the car. Beauty is now standing. I pause and with a breath contain my excitement while allowing my pleasure to flow to Beauty. With my next whistle she begins walking towards the field and enclosure. I smile as warmth flows through me and I walk slowly in her direction. She turns her head to look towards me and immediately increases her pace as she sees I am walking in her direction. As she disappears out of site I think, "Go ahead girl. The food is there for you." As I walk back to my car I notice that I am calm, both satisfied and disappointed. My mind and ego seem curious and accepting.

The drive home is occupied by tumbling thoughts and questions. What can I do? I have to keep putting her bowl in the enclosure. How will I get her to let me close to her? *She will have to chose to trust me.* How? What can I do? *No changes, only additions.* What do I add? It needs to change soon. What new interactions? Talk with Ute and Chery. The rest of the drive I alternate between worrying I will fail and my mind offering possibilities. Within my belly energies are stirring, a signal something is being arranged within the unknown. I am too focused in pondering, in thoughts to engage the subtle stirrings I notice.

Offerings of Friends

I call both Ute and Chery in the evening. I need to sense their support, to know there are others helping to hold the spaces in which Beauty and I work.

I can feel Ute's concerns as we talk, concerns for Beauty, concerns for me, a gentle fear that I will give up. I sense her connecting with my worry that I am missing something, with my questioning what to try next. As we chat she offers several possibilities. Eventually I accept the unfinished thought that I will have to place the food, stay around for an hour or so, and then take the food if Beauty does not show up to eat it. As we say goodbye I can feel Ute's support and confidence in contrast to my uncertainty.

I call Chery and report the current status and share what Ute and I have come up with for the next step. As Chery reminds me of how much progress has been made I feel myself relax. Her positive initial comments make it easier to listen to her voice her concerns of Beauty's well being during the miserable weather. Fortunately I am able to hear her concerns without judging myself for not doing better. As I hang up I sense how each of them provide different forms of support.

The next day is one of those gray days where my awareness of the cold varies with the comings and goings of the rain. My mind is focused on the plan of taking the food if Beauty does not come. Deep within I am unsettled from the sense that there is something I am not noticing, something has shifted. With gentle jolt I sense that my plan is somehow destructive.

As I pull in behind the store and park I do not sense Beauty's energy.

My whistle as I get out of the car seems to float out never touching Beauty. I do not sense Beauty other than as a distant hiding.

I go through the ritual of retrieving Beauty's bowl, filling it with food, and replacing it. As I return to the car I know Beauty will remain hiding. I sit in the car reading the book I have brought with little interest. Something is tugging at me, something is stirring in my lower belly insisting I allow quiet rather than read. After half an hour of pretending to read what I am sensing becomes a feeling of *"You can't do that."* Within moments and with a deep breath in the feeling shifts into thoughts, "You can't take Beauty's food away. You can't violate her trust that way. Manipulation collapses the spaces you and she connect within." Suddenly my body relaxes. I put the book down and allow my energies to seek out Beauty. This time I sense her responding and can almost hear her whisper to me, *"It's okay now. I will stay here. I will move to get food later."* I sit there, relieved, embarrassed to have allowed my mind to dominate my choices, grateful to know I finally opened to my inner knowing, grateful to sense that Beauty and I are moving together again.

A dozen slow, deep, relaxed breaths and I am ready to drive away. As my mind begins to look for next steps my inner awareness quiets it with a, *"Be still for now. Simply notice what you learned about our purpose. Trust and love is to be at the center of what we are doing."*

A Week of Eternal Waiting

In reflection of what I am experiencing my mind quips, "How long is a week? How slowly can time creep as we wait for movement?" For five days I sense a separation between Beauty and I. It feels as though she is holding me at a distance, waiting to see if I will be trustworthy.

The next day there is no sign of Beauty other than the food has been eaten. A part of me senses that some other animal has eaten her food. The field seems empty and there is no welcoming energy as I arrive. A thought, " it cannot be over". There is a null space, an emptiness. I am a robot going through the routines burned into my circuitry through repetition. I place Beauty's food and then walk the field not really expecting to see her. At the car I open the door and collapse into the driver's seat. My arm reaches up, inserts the key, starts the car. Back, turn, forward, stop at the street, turn towards home. I am most of the way home before time and space return. Life returns as I sense Fawn waiting for me, as I anticipate her welcoming me home.

Oh, I should tell you a bit about Fawn. Fawn was at the county pound, withdrawn and untrusting. When people visited she would cower at the back of her pen. Her time was almost up. Deemed unadoptable the staff had put out word to rescues who sometimes fostered dogs like her. When I first visited Fawn at Ute's request I took her for a walk. She would not look at me. My only hope was her seeming to whisper to me, "*I like doing this with you.*" half way through our walk. A rescue I had worked with agreed to find her a new home if I would foster her. When I visited the second time the rescue had talked with the county and things were suddenly very formal. The staff member who had been accepted by Fawn went with Fawn and me to a play area.

Bringing In Beauty

When we were in the play area the fellow removed Fawn's leash and frowned when Fawn quickly walked away from us. Without me noticing my mind and ego slipped into the background. I noticed myself kneeling, facing mostly towards Fawn. As she looked at me with curiosity I began a series of play bows and bouncing myself back and forth. Suddenly her ears came up followed by her tail and she charged at me growling. Without thought I turn sideways to her and turning my head away from her exposing my neck to her. I sensed the staff member's shock at what was happening. Three feet from my exposed neck Fawn veered away and I lunged after her. We played that way for several minutes. As I stood up from our play and reality returned I noticed the staff member's skin tone had blanched and sensed him recovering from the shock of how Fawn and I's play began. With the help of a kind staff member Fawn came home with me a couple hours later.

Within two weeks of Fawn being at my home I knew it was her home too. Fawn is a cattle dog, reddish in color. We share many easy, trusting connections.

The next day going to visit Beauty's area is the same, mechanical, empty, meaningless movements that simply hold what may be in place, no movement, just waiting while energies play beyond my awareness. The actions, the worries, the aching desires are all background noises in the stillness, in the waiting. I sense no trace of Beauty's energy in the field. The food has been eaten. Am I feeding the raccoon? How far away is Beauty? Get in the car and drive away. A sorrow and slight worry mix with mechanical movements.

A third, fourth, fifth, and sixth day, as I go through the process. There is something building, something I am not permitted to understand. Beauty is busy with something. Twice I see her as I drive past the Mexican restaurant when leaving. Both times she leaves as soon as she sees the car.

Dare I say, "and on the seventh day." As I make the 11 mile drive to the field the emptiness is gone. Once again I notice landmarks and enjoy a sensation of quiet anticipation. As I drive into the field I notice Beauty sitting at the top of the rise. Something is different. As I get out of the car and call to her she stands up, her ears are up and she seems to be leaning towards me. As I call out, "**Are you hungry?**" I am dumbfounded by her slowly beginning to walk down the rise towards me. Everything is surreal as she takes step after step. I feel reality jolt back into existence when she stops and sits down about 100 feet from me. The impact of the event, her first steps towards me, flood into my awareness as I notice my butt leaning back onto the car fender. I prattle words of greetings and praise. Sensing Beauty's *"Well, are you going to feed me or not?"* pulls me back into reality. Numb with surprise and elation I stand up and head for the enclosure. I keep glancing back to check on Beauty and get a sense of *"Yeah, you do it for me."* Beauty stays seated while I retrieve her bowl and then return to mix her food at the trunk of the car. As I stand back up from placing her food in the enclosure I notice she has moved another 30 feet closer and is standing watching me. I call to her, "**Are you my Beauty?**" A sense of *"Maybe."* returns as she sits down. My walk to the enclosure entry is tentative. My turn towards Beauty and my car is even more tentative. For a brief moment I consider walking directly towards Beauty and notice my body has already decided to begin walking to my car. Beauty sits there, ears partially pulled back, very alert, and yet somehow confident in her posture. At the car I open the door and turn towards Beauty with a "**Hey, Beauty. You are a Beauty!**" As I slump into the car Beauty gets up and watches me start the car, back up, and turn to the street. As I leave I glance in the rearview mirror and notice Beauty is walking towards the enclosure. Warmth and gratitude fill me. As I turn onto the street I notice I am both elated and numb. During the drive home I sense a deep satisfaction and know it will take several hours for the importance of the events to expose themselves.

A Pause, Then More

The next day when I arrive at the field Beauty is not in view. A sense of sorrow and acceptance floats within me as I go through the ritual of putting her food in place. As I walk the field after placing her food I sense her energies present in the field. When I relax and let an inner quiet reach out I sense her responding to me. I can almost hear a whisper of, "*Not today. Quiet, space for now.*"

That evening as I chat with Ute we speak of the pattern. Whenever Beauty and I make a shift in behavior she is gone for a day or two. I appreciate Ute listening, allowing me to voice my concerns and my hopes. Somehow it helps release my sorrows and engage my hope.

Driving out the next day I am filled with pleasure and anticipation. Sitting at the left turn signal waiting to turn into the parking area by the field I sense Beauty waiting for me. As I drive into the parking area I am surprised and hear my self whispering **"Wow"**. Beauty is there, sitting up waiting but not on the rise 140 feet way. My amazement grows as my eyes measure the distance, she is only 80 feet or so from where I park my car. As I get out of my car she stands, her ears up and for the first time her tail is up, not fully up, rather just above her back. Being part ChowChow Beauty's tail when fully up curls up and over to her back much like a husky. I hear myself saying, **"Hi Beauty. I like that you are here**." In turn I sense her energy, her tentatively accepting the energy I offer in connection. As I turn to retrieve her food bowl I hear myself saying, **"You are certainly looking good today.**" Was that a slight wag of her tail? With a second glance back at her I see she is sitting down watching my movements. Back at the car I talk to her as I prepare her food. She seems to know it is her food. As I head for the enclosure I raise her bowl and exclaim, "**For you!**". She shifts her ears more forward and seems to say, *"Yes, good you."*

As I step up into the enclosure I notice there is more bounce in my step. Bending to place her bowl is somehow more meaningful and I notice I am smiling as I straighten up. When I step down out of the enclosure Beauty stands up, alert and ears forward. I walk across the pavement and slow as I reach the grass of the field, *"Tread carefully."* floats in my mind. Beauty is waiting, one step, two steps, she shifts her body. I speak, "**Hey Beauty**." and take two slow steps. Before I recognize what I am doing I bend down onto my knees. As the cold water from the ground soaks through my pants I see Beauty's ears come forward and feel my mouth drop open as she begins walking towards me. "**Oh, girl, my Beauty**." floats up and out of me as she approaches. Then 50 feet away she slows, a few more steps and she stands there a mere 40 feet away, facing directly at me, head up, ears forward. My outer calm is challenged by my inner exuberance. I hear myself say in a quiet voice, "**You are a Beauty. Will you get closer? Another day?**" Instinctual I shift and sit on a hip, facing only partially towards Beauty. As the cold water bathes my hip my mind questions my wisdom in choosing to sit. By the time the question is formed I have my answer as I see Beauty sit down. In the quiet warmth of our progress my mind interjects, "So what do we do now? Yeah, it is good but now what? I feel silly."

For perhaps five minute I sit there with Beauty. Within I am calm, delighted, a deep peace. My mind is busy trying to get me to do something, anything. Finally Beauty gets up, turns away, turns her head back to me and then begins slowly walking away. I sit and wait. When 20 more feet away Beauty turns back to me and seems to whisper, *"You go now. I get food."* As I stand up Beauty sits down and watches me walk to the car. As the car door closes with my pull, Beauty stands up. I start the car, backup, and turn to the street. As my car begins to roll forward I notice Beauty has begun walking to the enclosure.

Enjoy & Share

As I look right and then left to turn out of the parking area I sense myself reconnecting with the physical world. I am calm and elated, a warm glow filling me, making the drive home easy. I find myself puzzled as I notice a lack of outward celebration and the presence of a deep sense that things are as they should be, that I have done well, that I and Beauty have done well.

The first two miles of the drive over busy streets I notice how the jangle of driving contrasts with the quiet within. I notice a mild resentment as my outer reality impinges on my fully engaging the deep satisfaction within me. I find myself grateful as the car descends the gentle slope and the road arches through a gradual curve transitioning from busy streets to an area with more trees and grassy fields with a few warehouses mixed in. Connecting with my surroundings relaxes and opens me and I find Beauty is there with me in the peace. She is acknowledging our growing connections with warmth and pleasure as my driving increases the physical distance between us. Her certainty, her acceptance helps me stay open and connected as my mind begins asking for attention.

I pull into the driveway at home and know that I will call both Ute and Chery that evening. Part of me wants to call right away while another part is happy to have the quiet time to honor and revel in the expanding connections Beauty and I's developing trust is allowing. As Fawn barks in greeting I wonder how she will respond to Beauty, how Beauty will respond to her. In those moments I sense the possibility of Beauty living with me and notice vague imaginings of fixing food for her on the kitchen counter floating in my awareness.

Malcolm Pullen

When I chat with Ute that evening she seems distracted with things at work. I quickly share the superficial facts of my time with Beauty and find I don't seem to be able to open the space to share what is asking to flow from within me. Ute shares some of what is going on at work and talks about her concerns. It is a time for me to hold space and listen. I suspect that in a few days she and I will talk, as she explores how she will respond to her work concerns. As I hangup feeling a bit cheated, a bit denied contrasts with the satisfaction of having helped by holding space and listening.

A couple hours later I call Chery and share what happened with Beauty. I am rewarded as I sense Chery connecting with the possibilities that have opened up. Chery's congratulations and appreciation of my efforts allow me to sense more of what has transpired. When I mention that with the progress I will continue feeding Beauty the conversation naturally turns to Beauty's well being in the stormy early spring weather. Chery asks how much longer and I offer a guess of 4 to 6 weeks, maybe eight. Chery voices her concern with the delay and mentions that she thought that it was time to try to trap Beauty. With a strong internal, "*I can't.*" I simply tell Chery I will have to sit with how we might be able to have that work. I feel that familiar tug between my planned approach and changing my approach to provide the service a friend wants. On the one hand I am making progress with Beauty following actions that resonate with my values and inner awareness. Now Chery's desire for having Beauty's situation resolved, for taking more direct action brings forward my values of providing for people who matter to me. Dueling values! I manage to step past my momentary urge to blame Chery for my quandaries and sense myself allowing time for my inner awareness to work out a solution that honors both value sets. I grin as I remember earlier years when dueling values generated frustration and then anger and often blame. Life is easier now that slowly earned patience and trust allow me to accept and sit with the discomfort as my inner awareness finds a path honoring multiple value sets.

But I digress.

Hostile Elements

Over the next week a couple of days I am disappointed by Beauty not being at the field. On the days that she is there I place her food and then go to the edge of the field and kneel down. Each day she gets up and walks towards me, sometimes remaining 70 to 80 feet away, sometimes coming closer but never closer than the 40 feet. Each day she seems more relaxed, each day her ears and tail spend more time up.

In conversations with Ute I have been mentioning I am not sure how to make the transition to touching Beauty. The subject of using treats comes up several times as something to try when the time is right. One morning, soon after, I notice myself sensing it is time to begin using treats. Ute and I talk about what to use. I have just purchased three pounds of hotdogs and decided to try those first. I pick up a package of hotdogs, well actually kosher franks, as I go out the door heading to feed Beauty and visit with her.

As I park my car and scan the field my disappointment grows, she is no where in sight. As I get out of the car I whistle and let my energy flow out into the field. I do not sense her and let my energies to flow out further, still no response. My actions become mechanical. Walk to the enclosure, get the bowl, walk to the car, fix Beauty's food at the trunk. As I pick up the bowl I sense a gentle, fear laced connection, "*Maybe tonight*", followed by sorrow and then nothing. I freeze and become quiet. Within a few moments I have a sense of Beauty offering, "*dangerous*" and have a sense of teenage boys chasing her. Anger and concern wash through me as my mind and ego begin to search for a way I can protect Beauty. "*She is safe. They are not your concern. Be with her.*" floats into my awareness and I sense calm space opening within me, space filled with sorrow for her fear. As I stand up from placing her food my body movement and surroundings become my focus. There is little I can do other than sense the connections we have begun.

It seems time to mention that in my younger years I never allowed myself to consciously, purposefully sense the presence or absence of the energies of a person or animal. In my 40s and 50s I began allowing myself to notice that often in my life I had allowed an 'inner knowing' to guide me. In my younger years I was careful to always have a nice, neat rational explanation for how I made any choice. Now in my 60s and with Beauty for motivation I have begun allowing myself to notice the energies of my 'inner wisdom' and the energies of other beings, especially Beauty's energies. Thirteen years of study with a mystic have opened my awareness and opened the choice of allowing myself to expand my perceptions to include subtle energies. My decision to 'bring in Beauty' brought an awareness that the possibilities would exist only if I expanded my 'awareness' to include the flow and interplay of Beauty's and my energies. With each day I am being challenged to step beyond my comfort with 'figuring it out' into the realms of subtle knowings.

The next day brings relief. Beauty is not in sight as I park and get out. As I whistle I do not sense her in the field. There is only a faint awareness of our connection. I retrieve her bowl from the enclosure and return to the car to mix her food. As I am mixing in the kibble I feel a gentle pull and look up. She has just come into view about 200 feet away walking slowly towards me, ears back, head down, tail tucked down. I notice myself smile and send out a warm, "Well hi, girl" and listen to myself whistle to her. My smile deepens as her head comes up and her ears shift slightly forward. When she is about 100 feet away I hear myself saying, "**Hi Beauty. I am glad you are here.**" In response her ears come further forward and her tail slips out of it's tucked position. When 50 feet away she stops, seems to consider what to do and then sits as I say, "**I have your food now.**"

I pick up her bowl, close the trunk, and head for the enclosure. As I walk I sense her sorrow, her fear of pursuit mixed with desires to trust. My mind and ego begin generating vengeful energies intended for projection towards her unseen tormentors. A quiet warmth within shifts my attention back to Beauty, to the connections she and I both desire. From within a quiet knowing, "*With vengeance they win. Be with Beauty.*" Opening to my sorrow for Beauty's pain opens quiet spaces within where Beauty and I share hopeful connections. As I place her bowl in the enclosure a sense of gratitude and purpose cut the edges off my worries for Beauty's well being.

That evening I talk with Ute about my sense of the need to bring Beauty closer to me, the need to build her trust in me. Ute's "**And your trust in her.**" provides a gentle jolt. I know Ute's words will play in my awareness for several days, effecting my choices for many days.

WHAT NEXT?

*O*ver the next week Beauty often is waiting in the field when I arrive and watches from afar seeming to test if I will allow her space. Each day I am warmed by the sight of her ears coming up and forward when she sees me. Each day she stands as I return to the car after placing her food. When I speak to her her ears first shift back, her tail comes up, a pause, and her ears shift forward again. I can almost hear her whisper, *"Yes, those are my signals."*

One of the days she arrives at the field as I bring her food bowl back to the car to fix her food. When I first see her I tense with anticipation and notice that her movement into the field slows and her tail lowers. Oops... I relax my shoulders, take a breath, and breath out saying, "**Hi Beauty. I am glad you're here.**" I am rewarded with her tail coming back up and her continuing to the center of the field. As I prepare her food she sits watching. As I measure her distance from me I notice her position in the field. I smile in recognition that my path back to the enclosure will take me closer to her. I sense stirrings of awareness within and notice a *"Yes"* coming from Beauty as my mind registers that she has decided to place herself so that she in involved with my feeding her. All my mind can manage is a "Wow" as a I sense the bonding Beauty is offering and asking for.

Having the food prepared I lift the bowl high and hear myself saying, "**For you, Beauty**." and internally hear, *"For us."* Beauty stands, ears up and forward, tail almost fully up and gently wagging. I sense a *"Good for us. Yummy."* from her as her energy joins me in the walk to the enclosure. As I stand from placing her bowl I notice she has taken a few steps towards the enclosure. By the time I have taken the few steps to the enclosure entry I am nervously noticing her position means walking closer towards her. She seems amused by my concern. When I consider walking towards her a "*No*" floats up from within so I turn and continue on to the car.

At the car I turn, **"Hey Beauty. Are you going to get your food?"** She simply stands there watching me until I open the door and get in. I start the car, back, and turn. When I glance in the rear view mirror I notice Beauty has gotten up and is walking towards the enclosure. As her behavior being another first registers I smile. Beauty is allowing me to see her move towards the enclosure, moving to accept my offerings.

As I drive home I know it is time to begin offering treats. My mind and ego assess the situations lining up all the considerations. Deeper within my masculine awareness tests the linking of thousands of possibilities against my values, resource costs compared with possibility of success. Beauty is coming close enough that I can toss the treats in her direction. I can't throw them at her, I will have to aim for a spot ten to twelve feet in front of her. The hotdog pieces will be light so I can't expect a toss of more than about 25 feet, 30 feet at the most. The toss does need to be gentle, non threatening. The grass is tall enough that having the hot dog piece land within 10 feet is important so she can find it. Using an underhand toss will be less violent and create an arch Beauty can watch. Kneeling will be better but will make the underhand toss only 15 feet. That won't land the pieces close enough. We will have to be away from the areas with longer grass. Doing it after placing the bowl will be best, that is when she seems most ready to be closer to me. I need to take the package of hotdogs with me when I place her food. Other things will come to mind. With a plan sketched out I relax and enjoy the drive home.

First Treats

The next day Beauty is waiting for me out in the field when I arrive. I notice I am automatically assessing whether her position will work for tossing treats. She is lying too far away. As I retrieve her bowl and move to the car I notice her get up and move closer. I grin as she walks to where she can see what I am doing at the trunk of the car and then sits with her ears forward and her tail up. Another first. I hear myself talking to her. "**Yes, girl, this is for you. Some wet food. And now I am mixing it with kibble. That does it. Your food is ready.**" When I glance up it seems as though Beauty is amused and slightly puzzled by my talking.

As I pick up her bowl I think of the hotdogs. Before I know I have made a choice I pick up the hotdogs, tuck them in my pocket, and walk towards the enclosure. With her food in place I exit the enclosure and move to the spot in the field, just off the pavement where she had first come towards me when I knelt. From 60 feet away she watches as I take the package of hotdogs out of my pocket and take one out of the package. For reasons that puzzle my mind I take a bite of the hotdog being careful to notice the texture and flavor in my mouth as I look in her direction. Her ears come up and forward as she stands there. I hold my hand high and hear myself saying, "**Hey Beauty. Do you want some of this?**" She watches me, after a minute or so it is clear she will not walk closer. My ego is disgruntled, my mind is unhappy that we need to close the gap between us and Beauty, a tricky, uncertain task. Within I notice a gentle playfulness.

From within floats, *"We can only try and see."* as I begin to slowly walk in Beauty's direction. Three steps and Beauty is standing, tail down.

Another two steps and her ears come down. With the next step she starts to turn away from me. Instinctively I stop, turn a quarter turn away from her, drop to my knees, and hear myself saying, "**It's okay, girl. I won't come any closer**." As my mind chases after what to do I notice her look back at me and pause. Without thinking I raise my hand with a piece of hotdog, notice the taste still in my mouth, and say, "**Do you want some?**" Her ears come back up and she turns slightly more towards me. Somehow I know this is the best I will get. Reality changes, opening to a rich and detailed world of just Beauty and I.

I break off a large piece and draw my hand back over my shoulder getting ready to toss it. I freeze as her ears go back and she takes a step backwards. Oops. Now what. An under handed toss won't make it to her and an over handed toss will scare her away. I feel trapped until from deep within comes a sense of, "*Underhanded, to her, for her, taste in your mouth*". My hand floats down and back, "**Hey Beauty, this is for you.**", my hand arches forward and releases the piece of hot dog in a long arch.

As the piece of hot dog takes flight time shifts, the world consists of only Beauty, me, and the piece of hotdog arching towards her. I watch as Beauty watches the object arching in her direction, curious and uncertain. We seem to blend as I sense both of us focus on the arch of the hotdog within the air. It seems to float, independent of earthly time. Beauty watches it, I watch Beauty, deep changes are afoot. The hotdog drops to the field. As it disappears in the grass I sense how the future has disappeared behind the choices Beauty and I are about to make. Beauty looks at me seeming uncertain. Instinctively I step back, pause, and consider another step. I relax as Beauty steps toward the hotdog and then stops to check on me. As I wait the wet, cold drizzle of rain moves into my awareness. I sense how my accepting the cold wetness reflects my acceptance of the discomfort brought with waiting in the moment, allowing discomfort in the space of possibilities. The cold contrasts with the warmth that fills me as Beauty relaxes and saunters over to find her chunk of hotdog.

An Offering Accepted

She searches for a few moments, each moment seems to be eternal. She sniffs the hotdog and raises her head to look at me. I have a distinct sense of *"Is that all?"* Her head goes down, she sniffs, her head comes up with no hotdog in her mouth. On the surface I feel a sudden panic arise, "It's not working." Within is a quiet calm. It seems automatic, I am tearing off another piece of hotdog and tossing it in her direction. It seems to travel a bit faster than the first hot dog piece, it's dropping to the ground seems to carry more weight. Beauty takes a few steps and lowers her head to sniff. She seems unconvinced, raises her head to look at me. Again a hotdog piece arches towards her. Again she takes a few steps, sniffs, and raises her head to look at me. Her stance shifts a bit and I sense a *"Well, okay."* as she bends down and picks up a hot dog piece, chomps twice, and swallows it. I sense relief and yet feel a bit of a failure. She goes to the second piece of hotdog and unenthusiastically picks it up and swallows it. At the third hot dog piece she sniffs, looks at me, sniffs, looks at me, and sits down. There she sits as I dismember a second hot dog and arch each piece in her direction. She sniffs the first piece and simply watches as the second, third, and fourth pieces arch to resting places close to her. There she sits, watching me, ears forward, seemingly unimpressed.

 I kneel looking at her as a sense of embarrassed failure mixes with an urge to do better and pleasure with the progress that has just been made. My ego offers, "That didn't work so good." My mind puzzles, "Now what?" and from within, *"We have made progress and will find something better."* My mind unhappily offers, "Jeez, now we have to try Ute's idea of roasted chicken." and my masculine ego winces a bit.

I return to normal time as my body almost shouts, "cold, wet knees, not pleasant, not good". I get up and watch Beauty stand in response. She and I begin to turn away at the same time. With my first step away she sits back down and watches as I return to the car. She seems to be protecting what is now hers, in her watching she lets me know she has accepted my marginal offering and values that I gave to her. What I have offered seems trivial. Her accepting is mixed with complex messages. *"I won't be easy. I will choose what is worthy of my acceptance. I like that you offered. You give me space to choose a new life. I will accept in my own time. I will measure and perhaps choose each step you offer."*

On the drive home my mind and ego are busily trying to make sense of what happened so they can plan something better. Inside there is a quiet warmth, a gentle celebration that Beauty choose to trust me throwing something in her direction, that Beauty choose to cautiously accept what I offered. When I decide to talk with Ute my mind and ego quiet. We have a plan to find a plan and somehow that is enough! Awareness of Beauty's fear of those pursuing her bring a sense of urgency. The process is now more serious, heavier. Without words I sense that my commitment to Beauty has deepened. In offering her treats somehow she has become mine. I know I will never own her. She will not allow that. I have accepted responsibility for protecting her, providing for her, in that way only she will be mine.

As I get out of the car and open the gate into the backyard I notice for the first time a sense of Beauty being in the backyard. It is a wispy possibility unattached to any timeline.

My ego and mind are on edge as I talk with Ute. My masculine ego seems tender. My values of providing and finding a solution outweigh my value of self mastery. As we talk I carefully keep my emotions tucked out of the way. Sharing emotions is a luxury affordable only when my world lines up in expression of the values of great importance to me. Earning Beauty's trust and acceptance looms before me.

BUILDING TRUST

The next day I am disappointed and not surprised to find that Beauty is not at the field. As I go through the ritual of preparing and placing her food I have a sense of her connecting with me from out beyond the field. The sense is encouraging and puzzling at the same time. My mind and ego seem unusually quiet, happy with the routine. The flow of my movements seems to bring with them a flow of connections to safety.

After my divorce, as suggested in the 'Divorce Adjustment' class I took I began asking myself, "What is important to me? Why am I here?" Whenever I was doing something that took little direct attention I would open space within by asking theses questions. The easiest words I find to hopefully connect you with my process is, "Having a calm time I reach within, then withdraw my fingers of worry from touching the surface of deeper spaces within me. It is as if I take my fingers off chimes of awareness deep within. Repeating the question creates a gust of energy. I am quiet so I may sense chimes within tinkling with resonance that reaches my subtle energies. Each repetition of the question opens more space, more chimes are exposed to the gusts of energy, and the resonance becomes a bit stronger. With each repetition the resonance comes further into the physical world. Finally, a day later, four months later, repeating the question brings a few words that resonate so strongly I am stunned by the physicality. It is as if I have finally freed a huge bell that extends from the Void into the physical and my question has swung the clapper strongly enough to contact the bell. My entire being resonates with new awareness."

Not long after taking the Divorce Adjustment course I was driving

Bringing In Beauty

back to work on the freeway. Traffic was light. I was in a section where there was no space beside the freeway to pull off and stop. I had been repeating the question "What am I here for?" for perhaps three minutes. Suddenly time and space became only a surface and I sense, feel, and hear, "Creating Beauty". The clapper has struck the inner surface of the bell and I am resonating with energies that shatter boundaries of awareness. Tears of joy, of sorrow, of belonging, of touching home well up in me. The feel of the steering wheel causes me to place a bit of attention on the outer world forcing me to retain openings between the flood of awareness within and the physical world. Thirty seconds of driving is an eternity. I want to pull to the side but I cannot. While in several realities I must drive. As I drive the ten additional minutes back to work I retain a careful awareness of the physical as threads of awareness weave paths of connection from the Void into my body and into my mind. At work I sit in the parking lot for another ten minutes before ushering the strangeness of my body into the building.

"Creating Beauty" floats into my mind as I begin the routine of feeding Beauty this day. My inner awareness begins to tease my body awareness and my mind with connections. Creating beauty and Beauty is her name. Creating trust and acceptance so Beauty can relax into being who she is. Does beauty have my trust? Will beauty and Beauty trust me more? I must never try to bend beauty or Beauty to my will, she will not be owned. Each day, each offering, each acceptance allows Beauty to relax into being with me. Each action guided by the whispered wisdom of love within me opens new threads allowing beauty's expression in the physical. Each action shaped from fear severs threads of awareness. With time, with my choices, with her acceptance, Beauty is coming closer, allowing more threads of energy to connect us, giving up the mournful safety of separation, opening to the strange safety connection bring. When will Beauty allow me to touch her? When will Beauty walk with me? When will Beauty come home to be with me?

As I pull into the driveway at home I sense the Navajo blessing, "Walk in Beauty". The clapper has struck the edge of the bell again and I resonate with energy threads opening my awareness to new understanding woven within those threads. Is understanding simply the fabric formed by the threads of connection we foster?

Coming Closer

The next day Beauty is again absent from the field. Her food has been eaten and I have no sense of her having been the one who ate it. After placing her food I decide to talk with the fellow who manages the store. When I go to the front of the shop I notice he is with customers. Within a moment I sense myself walking the field whistling for Beauty and then returning. I do just that.

While I am walking near the apartments I notice a mother in the traditional Arab robe step out to check on her two children. The kids look at me and seem to be asking her something about me. I am warmed when from 20 feet away she nods to me and asks, "**You look for dog?**" Her children face me and relax into leaning against her as I respond. Over the days I had been feeding Beauty some people in the apartments seem to accept my presence. The kids who are outside when I walk the field no longer go inside as soon as they see me. I sense myself smiling as I gratefully respond, "**Yes. She is not here today.**" and hear, "**She is your dog?**". "**No, I hope she will be my dog.**" A question from one of her children takes her attention and she carefully ushers them inside. As I continue walking I notice I am more relaxed. It is the first time an adult from the apartments has acknowledged me. It is the first time I have shared my hopes about Beauty and I with a stranger.

When I swing back to the front of the shop I see that the customers have left. As I enter the shop the fellow looks up and smiles. We greet each other and for the first time I sense him accepting me as a person rather than a curiosity. "**Hey, you know the driver who sometimes delivers here? He bought a hamburger for the dog. She let him get close and ate pieces as he broke them** off." In the moment before I answered I noticed my ego and mind trying to figure out the best response. While they were still considering the possibilities and feeling a bit cheated by someone else being seen as having the honor of being the first I hear myself saying, **"Great! She has decided to trust and accept food. That helps a lot. She let me throw a hotdog to her a couple of days ago. She was about 25 feet away so the driver did even better."** As the fellow shared more details I have the sense his curiosity is peaked by my unexpected response, **"She has made a choice to trust. That is important. Tell the driver thank you for me."** His brow furrows as he responds, **"Yeah, I will."** My ego and mind are uncomfortable as I sense shopkeeper considering the possibility that it isn't just about me, that I considered myself, Beauty, the shopkeeper, all a team.

As I walk back to the car I sense Beauty. She does not cloak her energy as she senses me, she does not extend her energy to me. She seems to simply accept my connection. As I allow my gentle sorrow in not seeing her a *"Too much, close to man for food, scary different."* floats to me from her. As I get into the car I release, "You did well. Thank you." to her, carried within the warmth I feel in connection with her.

As I drive towards home I still sense Beauty. The combination of wanting time to enjoy what I am sensing and the pull of the park and walking trails along the slough cause me to pull off into the park's parking lot. As I get out of the car I know that being in the quiet of nature will help me be available for changes that are weaving themselves within me, changes that include both myself and Beauty. Thankfully my mind and ego are quiet allowing me to notice threads of connections rearranging themselves. Within moments I am walking in nature, walking with nature. I smile as "Walk in Beauty" floats into my mind. Deep within I sense Beauty smiling, offering *"Yes, like this we meet."*

TOWARDS TOUCH

$\mathcal{T}$he next day as driving toward the field I find myself turning right to head to Costco. As I complete the turn my mind offers, "cheap, big, roasted chicken" and I sense my immediate intent lining up with my longer term intent. I smile as I sense cutting off a piece of chicken then tossing it in Beauty's direction. "No knife! Buy one or what?" I relax as I sense myself using my fingers to tear off a piece and then using the paper towels in the car to wipe the chicken juices and fat off my hands.

About a mile away from the field I sense Beauty waiting and notice my mind's skeptical "Yeah, we will see." As I turn onto the pavement that flows back to the edge of the field I notice I am alert and relaxed, more curious than worried. Before I begin the turn to park I notice her laying in the field about 60 feet from the pavement, closer than before. As I park she sits up, ears back. As I open the door and step out she stands, ears back, tail tucked. A whistle and as I enjoy her tail ascending and her ears coming up I notice my mood rising. As I close the door and face her I hear, **"Hi girl. I have a treat for you today."** I smile as her ears come forward, her mouth opens, and her back lowers slightly into a relaxed posture. Within I sense a, *"give food now"* from her and enjoy the warmth that flows into and through my body as I head to get her bowl.

Once I am back at the car trunk Beauty moves closer, perhaps 30 feet away, positioned so she can see what I am doing. As I reach to pick up her bowl I sense a gentle urge, a sense of using an underhanded toss to release a piece of chicken towards her, her whispers within me. Picking up the container with the roasted chicken seems easier than picking up the bowl so that is what I do. My mind is happily giving me reasons why tossing a piece of chicken before placing Beauty's food is a good thing to do. Have you ever tried to rip a piece of chicken off by hand when it is still quite hot? I start with the breast and quickly withdraw my hands as my fingers protest in pain. Now what? One chicken leg seemed to poke forward so I reach for it. Still hot but workable. The thigh and leg come off easily. I grin as I notice my mind switching to the more comfortable thigh and drumstick creating an illusion of the carcass before me not being connected with a living creature. The heat when I touch the thigh causes me to switch to the drumstick. It is just cool enough for my fingers to accept the slight pain of tearing off a piece. I look up to notice Beauty sitting up watching me. A step back away from the car so she can see my whole body, letting myself sense her attention as I enjoy the smell of the chicken. Her ears come fully forward and I sense her uncertain curiosity. "**Here you go.**" and the piece of chicken begins it's arch towards her. She stands and watches as I watch her, sense her. She begins her movement towards where the piece of chicken will land before it touches the ground. I smile with pleasure at the signal of trust. She sniffs the chicken and looks up at me.

With an inward, "Oh well" I pick up her bowl, close the trunk and head to place her food. As she bends to sniff the piece of chicken once more I have the sense of her trying to decide '*follow or sniff food here?*' As I walked the 50 feet to the enclosure I glance back to see what she is doing. As I stand up from placing her bowl I notice her bend her head, pick up the piece of chicken, chew it a few times, swallow, and then walk to a spot in the field perhaps 25 feet from what is becoming our spot to meet, just off the pavement perhaps five feet into the field. As I leave the enclosure she sits and watches me return to the car, get the chicken out of the trunk and saunter back towards her. She stands watching me approach 'our spot' With her standing, ears back I slow my movement and allow myself to sense the smell of the chicken and tossing pieces to her. I relax again as her ears come forward and she sits again. As I kneel and feel the now familiar cold wetness soak in around my knees I grin and feel my body fill with warmth as I notice Beauty only 25 feet away, sitting, watching with a relaxed and attentive trust.

A Leap in Closeness

My senses are alive with pleasure and anticipation. This is the closest Beauty has been since my first meeting her. Her attention is directly on me. With wonder and enjoyment I sense the space we share opening, shifting, becoming what I had hoped for often. Time slips away, the world becomes a circle with a bit of pavement, wet grass and earth she and I sit upon, Beauty, me, and the chicken I am offering her. Within I sense her whisper of *"I can trust now."* For a long few moments I sit with her. Her uncertainty, desire for connection, new trust, and warm pleasure blend with mine. When it becomes too much I sense her attention shift to the package of chicken. I sense her *"Well?"* and her eagerness to experience the smell and taste of the chicken in her nose and then mouth. Within I sense a quiet, *"Well, okay girl."*

As I reach for the chicken and open the container I notice my hands seem to be energy as much as physical. As I first touch the chicken and it's smell fills my nose my fingers detect the cooler more acceptable temperature. A glance at Beauty re-enforces my sense of her connecting with each movement I make. The chicken leg and thigh seem to offer themselves and my hand slips over to grasp the drumstick. I am a bit surprised by how easily the drumstick and thigh break off. A touch tells me the thigh is still to hot to tear apart with my fingers. A sense of Beauty smelling the chicken brings my eyes up to her. She is standing, her tail wagging slightly, her ears up and forward, a slight tension of anticipation. When I look back down my hands have done their work separating some of the drumstick's flesh, a chunk with enough weight to toss 20 of the 25 feet separating us. My hand moves back with an intent to get the chicken as close to Beauty as possible. As my hand swings down and forward somehow from within my intent shifts to tossing the piece perhaps 10 feet away. As my mind begins to comprehend the new intent the piece arches a mere 9 to 10 feet from me and plops on the cold wet ground. *"Warm chicken on cold ground."* flits through my awareness. As the piece of chicken leaves my hand Beauty takes a step forward and now after two or three steps she stands looking at me. I have a sense of *"too close"* from her. To relieve the building tension I tear off another piece of chicken, gently say, "**Hey girl.**", and underhand toss the chicken just beyond the first one. Beauty relaxes and watches the arch. I find myself smiling as she steps forward before the piece of chicken reaches the peak of it's arch. She pauses for the moment it takes for the piece to drop to the ground. I am not breathing and find myself smiling as Beauty steps forward. Her four steps forward seem to take an eternity, the moments stretching out to express their significance. Her head down she smells the chicken and then raises her head to look at me. As her head goes back down and she begins to sniff once again it seems as if she is considering whether to surrender to a new future. I wait as a gentle struggle stirs within, my ego wanting to take action, my inner awareness urging stillness and space ..for Beauty's choice. I sense a quiet whisper of, *"Honor her."*

As my attention returns to her I observe her picking up the piece of chicken tentatively, tenderly. She seems to be teasing me as she moves it around in her mouth. As she swallows I sense a warmth open within my body, somehow she is closer to me, somehow her future and mine have blended. Absorbed in sensing the shifts in timelines I barely notice her few steps forward to the second piece of chicken and her few sniffs of it. The sense of her taking the piece in her mouth brings me back. She has turned away from me and after four or five steps has turned back to face me. I am puzzled when she puts the piece of chicken down and begins sniffing it once again. Uncertain I tear off and toss two more pieces of chicken, each one close to her.

Time shifts and suddenly I am simply a man standing up, backing away from a dog who still does not trust me. I am puzzled by the contrast of starkness now with the magic of a few moments ago.

Mind & Measuring

As I walk the few steps back to the pavement and then turn to see what Beauty is doing the world somehow makes no sense. Beauty moving from one piece of chicken to the next to sniff plays out before me. My sense of a knowable future is nowhere to be found. With the fog of possible timelines denying me a sense of any possible futures, life has now become very stark, very physical, a world with only the flow of physical events. After sniffing each piece Beauty finally picks up one and eats it. I see her, I do not sense her. She seems in a separate world. I sense very little and feel even less. I find myself shrugging, turning, and walking back to my car. I glance back at Beauty before getting in. She has moved perhaps 20 feet from the chicken and is sitting, watching me. I sense a quiet, *"Not with you here."* followed by emptiness. Getting into the car and the drive home are mechanical. The physical world is the same. Somehow I am not the same in the physical world. Part way home my mind makes the association. I have been in this space before when the mystic I was studying with opened my perception and allowed me to sense what is beyond the physical world. I relax accepting that for a few hours, for a few days, I will be suspended in the physical world as my awareness shapes threads, weaving patterns my mind will not notice and will never understand.

As I turn into the driveway I am surprised by sensing Beauty. She is with me wondering what her new home will be like. I notice a smile on my face as I get out of the car. Now and the future have reconnected a bit. It will be another day or two before life becomes blended together again.

It is a strange feeling. There is a sense that somehow Beauty is linked

Bringing In Beauty

into my physical awareness. She notices the gate, notices how opening the gate opens into a large backyard. She seems to be measuring the space, checking to see if her energies will blend with the energies already there. My mind offers, "Crazy!" and my ego winces with the judgment. A small bit of reality has returned. As I raise my foot to the first step up to the back porch Beauty leaves me. My mind is quiet, my ego seems to be napping. From within, *"Quiet now, reality when it is time."*

I spend a quiet afternoon doing simple tasks. In the evening I consider calling Ute and Chery. I look towards the phone and find no impulse, no energy to take the few steps needed. The tea I am stirring absorbs my need for physical movement. Now is not the time to share. My mind and ego seem to be tucked aside while parts of me with no names, no labels arrange new understanding, understanding I must experience in ways my mind cannot provide.

Yet Closer

The next day as I drive out to feed Beauty, long before I arrive at the field, before my mind notices, my energies begins scanning the field for her. *"Is she there? Is she waiting? No, empty field. Where?"* My mind and ego insert their judgment, "Boy, it is good no-one can hear us! We would be headed for the funny farm for sure!" Playful energy flows within me as my mind and ego proudly and happily repeat, "Funny Farm For Sure!" Deep within myself I sense Beauty, lying down, energy carefully contained, away from the field. A vague, "N*eed separation, quiet, no changes right now."* from her floats up within me and I sense my body relaxing. I draw my energies back within myself, honoring her bubble. The drive becomes mechanical.

As I drive back to my usual parking place I scan the field noticing how my habit of searching runs even though I do not expect to see her. By the time I park the physical world and my 'inner process' blend once again. No Beauty. My mind offers, "Well, at least the weather is cool so the chicken will be fine in the trunk for a day or two. We shouldn't waste our resources."

It is mechanical from then on. Park the car. Get out and retrieve her bowl. Return to the car and mix her food at the trunk. Close the trunk. Walk to the enclosure and place her bowl. As I walk back to the entrance to the enclosure a wave of sorrow flows through me, my insides seem as empty as the enclosure. As I take the large step down out of the enclosure I sense Beauty's energy within me. A sense of *"I am grateful for the food and you."* arises within me. I smile and notice my walk back to the car is easier, more fluid. *"Thank you girl."* floats within me, to her.

As I turn into the driveway at home I am surprised to sense Beauty connecting with me. She seems curious and a bit playful. As I open the back gate I have a sense of her running happily out into the backyard. My mind and ego begin to protest the craziness and thankfully give up as I smile and sense, *"Yes Beauty, this is yours too."* Warmth flowing within whispers, *"Yes, it will be."* The warmth seems to intensify slightly with Beauty's agreement.

That evening I talk with Ute. As we speak I notice my 'report' is factual and dry. We talk about what foods might work better than chicken. Hotdogs, bacon, various kinds of dog treats. Discussions of Beauty being exposed to the weather and people who seem to want to harm her. The shop keeper's amused support of my activities and surprise with my continuing efforts. We talk of me taking Fawn, the dog I fostered and decided to keep, out to visit Beauty. Will they get along or not? We talk about how her dogs are doing and other things. Through our talk the blending of energies Beauty and I are sharing remains unmentioned, held within, unready to be exposed.

Later I call Chery and give her an update. Chery shares her concern for Beauty's safety, shares the urgency she feels in having Beauty in a safer environment. I feel regret within that I can't be more aggressive as Chery desires. It is a feeling I have had many, many times in my life. Being urged by a woman in my life to move faster while knowing I must honor the timeline I know within is working. As I hang up I notice Chery turning her focus to Beauty, scanning to see if she is safe.

Closer By a Bit

The next day as I pull onto the pavement and drive between the two shops to the edge of the field I am drawn to park closer to the entry of the enclosure. My mind and ego scan the space, "We need to park so delivery trucks can get in and out. Maybe we shouldn't change." "*No, trust, allow, step beyond fear.*" As I turn towards the enclosure I feel and see Beauty sitting in the field watching. She seems puzzled yet accepting of the change. As I brake to a stop my eyes scan to measure if I have obtained the optimal spot, room for trucks and well positioned for interacting with Beauty. My mind offers, "This will work." as I get out of the car. Before I have fully stood up I hear myself whistling for Beauty and glance over to see that with the newness she has taken a couple of steps away from me. With the whistle she turns back towards me, pauses, and then sits. As her butt touches the ground I have a sense of her saying a heavy, "*Okay.*"

"**Hey girl**." brings her ears forward. I find myself smiling as I notice a warmth within and notice her mouth opening. My body and energy tell me she is smiling and relaxing into connection. My mind and ego jibe me with, "She is a dog. Since when do dogs smile?" I grin and notice my mind and ego seem to have less authority. My grin broadens when I sense the energy of, "*Well good.*" from Beauty. My grin broadens further as I notice how my current experience reminds me of younger years and talking with a few of the patients at the mental hospital my father ran. As I turn towards the enclosure I sense a, "*Yes, you do food.*" from Beauty and notice my mouth feels as though it is watering in anticipation of food.

As I pick up Beauty's bowl and turn back to the gap in the enclosure's fence I notice that Beauty has gotten up and moved closer to the car. Concern arises as I notice I will have to walk closer to her than she has allowed before. As I step down, out of the enclosure I have the sense of her noticing her bowl in my hand as a signal of 'us' existing now. She notices my uncertainty of walking closer to her and seems to be both tense and to whisper, "*Oh, silly.*" With my next step I notice a smile forming and I relax into accepting the risk of walking close to her. My mind and ego are unhappy as an awareness floats into me, "*I am more afraid than she.*" My body relaxes and as I walk closer to her I hear myself saying, "**Yes, this is your bowl.**" She turns slightly, ready to move away, and then turns back as soon as my path takes me past her towards the car. I barely notice preparing her food, my attention is full with noticing my own fears of success with Beauty and how my mind and ego do not want me to notice. With the food ready I look up and notice Beauty sitting there seeming amused and intent on supporting my providing her food. One hand for her bowl, one hand for the chicken, close the trunk, and put the chicken on the top of the car before walking towards the enclosure. Beauty stands and does not turn away as I walk close to her on my way to the enclosure. As I go through the ritual of placing her food it seems her attention is on the chicken atop the car. A glance shows me she is looking at the chicken rather than at me. As I turn back to the car I sense Beauty waiting for me to pick up the chicken and move to our spot.

I relax and open into simply being with Beauty. Movement is easier, it is as if Beauty and I have finally agreed upon today's dance steps. I pick up the chicken and turn towards Beauty who is now slowly walking to a spot just beyond "my spot". She stops, turns mostly towards me, and watches me as I walk towards her, towards my spot. Her ears and tail are up and her mouth is closed with ears only partially forward. I slow my pace, each step is measured, three, four, Beauty watches, five, six, and Beauty turns towards me as my feet come together and I kneel towards the ground. She is perhaps 30 feet away as my knees meet the ground and as the chicken package meets the ground her ears come forward, her tail wags a bit, her mouth opens and to my surprise and delight she saunters a few steps towards me. Time shifts as I become aware of the dichotomy, my body is frozen, an unearthly stillness, while within my energies dance in warm delight.

Beauty chooses to wait and watch as I open the chicken package and tear off a piece of chicken, she stands only 20 feet from me, relaxed and ready to come forward. I hold up a piece of chicken, her tail wags more quickly, and I sense a *'Well?'*. I wave my hand and hear myself saying, "**Are you going to come get it?**" She sits as I sense a simple *'No'*. I am surprised to notice the clean simplicity of her response and grin as a *"Perhaps, someday, we will be that relaxed and honest."* floats into my awareness.

A Bit of Intimacy

*B*eauty shifts her weight just a bit and her mouth makes a smacking sound as it opens and closes. I sense her desire to taste what she is smelling, floating on a desire to explore, to test, to open a bit more to 'us'. She seems to sense each small movement of my fingers as I remove the lid, reach in, and tear off a bit of chicken. Before my mind and ego notice I am reaching forward to place the piece of chicken on the ground in front of me. As my body leans so my hand extends further I sense Beauty's curiosity. A glance up, seeing her ears are a bit more forward, her head raised perhaps ½ an inch verifies what I sensed. I grin as I notice her curiosity with only a hint of concern. As my butt settles back on my heels Beauty stands and shifts back and forth on her feet a few times. "**Well, girl?**" brings a bit more uncertainty and she sits back down. I reach back to the chicken and tear off several pieces. An urge floats up from within and I find myself focusing my attention to a spot another foot beyond the piece I already placed. I come up on my knees, leaning forward, place my empty hand on the ground. Beauty tenses a bit and shifts her weight back. I keep my focus on 'the spot' as I turn my other hand palm up showing the chicken, lean forward another six inches, and tilt my hand so the piece of chicken tumbles to the ground maybe a foot beyond the first piece. Beauty turns her head a bit, looking away from me and I sense her considering leaving. Inside I am calm and a bit playful, a gentle warmth flowing in my lower belly and chest. My mind and ego seem curious and watchful. As I shift my weight back to sitting in the red of her fur I see the black of a collar. Something deep inside me relaxes, I know my mind will process what I have seen later. Beauty turns her head back towards me.

As I settle back Beauty's attention seems to move with me, maintaining the connections. Beauty is now standing, unsure whether to venture closer or not. I grin and show her the pieces still in my hand. I almost laugh as I notice her relax into her sitting position once again curious about what I am doing. As my arm swings forward in an underhanded arch I notice my arm moves with a playful, inviting energy with just a tinge of challenge to Beauty. In response, as the piece of chicken floats through the air she stands, her ears forward, tail wagging, and mouth open. The third piece is a foot closer to her. I wait, she waits and a long ten seconds later I arch the fourth piece of chicken yet closer to her. As I settle back on my haunches I almost hear myself saying, *"Okay, now it is your turn."*

Beauty and I are suspended in time, time frozen waiting for her decision. When she looks away towards her escape route my heart sinks and from within I sense a, *"Oh girl, it is for you."* As Beauty looks back she looks into my eyes and I sense her surrendering to what she and I desire. In that moment her weight shifts forward and she takes a step. It is amazing how detailed observations are when time is floating. The second or two it takes for her body to shift forward, her foot to float up gracefully and then swing forward bringing her body along until her foot finally begins to descend and I watch her toes spread out against the ground as her foot settles, contains more than an hour of unconscious observing. It seems strange to be noticing myself noticing.

My body is quiet, my mind occupied with observing, my lower belly stirring with delight and hope. A second step, a third, a fourth, as the Beauty chooses to come closer and closer. She stops at the piece closest to her, sniffs it and then looks at me. In a mere second she and I have a whole conversation without saying a word. *"Yeah, I know, luring me closer and closer." "Yes, I want you close." "That is surrender, not brave choice." "Oh? manipulative, not direct." "You expect too little of me. More challenge is better." "Okay, now what?" "I choose it all. Clean, bold, simple."* Beauty's head comes up a bit, time no longer exists, our world consists of her opening her energy to me and walking forward a few steps to smell and then pickup the piece of chicken closest to me. I am in awe. My mind and ego unable to fathom what has just happened, are reluctant to consider I had just been given a lesson. As Beauty chews the chicken I sense the taste,

Bringing In Beauty

the texture, flesh surrendering to her gently applied powerful jaws. I sense her muscles beginning her swallow and feel myself challenged to swallow the lesson she has provided me.

Time returns towards normal as I sense from her a, *"Oh, that was a bit scary... and fun."* as Beauty turns to pick up the next piece of chicken away from me, her body turns partly away from me. Three sniffs, a bit of consideration, and a decision to pick up the piece and move to the piece furthest away from me. I watch, the observer, nothing else to do. Beauty turns back to me, glances up at me, then lowers her head and opens her mouth to drop the one piece next to the other. She seems both proud and a bit uncertain. She glances at the piece one step closer to me, looks down at her two. My mind and ego offer, "She should eat those two." along with a bit of peeved energy. I sense a *'pay attention'* floating from within and my mind and ego reluctantly drop back to observer mode after a 'What is she doing?' Beauty looks at me, pauses, and then sits. She seems both proud and worried.

There will be a Book

*I*t takes me 20 or 30 seconds to relax and accept the knowing floating from within, her letting me know what she intends. "*Enough new, kind of scary, these are mine, eat when alone.*" I notice myself smiling and saying, "**Your a good girl. We did good. Look at you, only 10 feet from me, sitting down. That is so wonderful.**" As I relax a bit more, settling on my haunches I notice warmth flowing in my belly, expanding, filling my chest, floating out to her. As her warm energies return I sense the space we share, the ground we sit upon, she and I, the grass, a bubble of perhaps 20 feet. Our space, the world gently excluded by the warm connections we share. As I relax into just being with Beauty my mind is surprised to notice Beauty lays down and I sense a simple '*yes*' from her.

Soon I notice my mind is working on phrasing to use when I tell Ute that Beauty lay only 10 feet from me. In the same moment Beauty sits up, cloaking her energy, the cold and wet of the world speaks to my body. I stand and pick up the package of chicken, pleased that Beauty stays sitting, protecting 'her treats'. Without really noticing I return to the car, get in, and drive home. From within I sense Beauty imagining herself stretching her neck to take a piece of chicken from my hand. Warmth and gentle pleasure fill me.

At home I feel a struggle. Do I call and share? Do I wait, allowing understanding to flow into my awareness? Within an instant I understand that calling, bringing what I have experienced into words will greatly diminish the understanding available to me. Better to leave my experiences beyond the limiting frameworks my mind will impose so that I may speak of them. Perhaps tomorrow I will call.

Bringing In Beauty

As I sit at home, a glass of stout near by, Fawn laying near, I sense sharing my experiences in a book. It has the feel of something that was decided long ago. The only influence my mind and ego will have is over when the book will be done. I am a bit surprised that most of the questions my mind and ego offer have to do with the logistics of writing and releasing a book. The usual worries float into my awareness. I grin noticing the gentleness of their offerings. For many years such concerns were screamed and in later years yelled. I am delighted to notice that this time my mind and ego are putting most of their effort into the 'How' rather than the 'Why we should not'.

Suddenly my mind and ego have a project! So many wonderful questions, so much delightful planning, so many juicy details, ideas to push around, shape, play with, measure, color. A puzzle with wonderful new complexities. New learning required within a nice tight, limited project.

Immediately my mind offers "So much detail. How do we remember?" A possibility floats from within in the form of my sensing myself journaling my experiences. My mind's response is, 'Oh yes, key words and timeline. Sometimes more detail. That will not be too much work.' I feel a grunt of despair as my ego realizes, 'Crap. The timeline up until now will take so much work. That won't be much fun. I hope we can delay and lose more detail. Keep the scope small!'

Once started my ego takes off offering one objection after another. With a smile I notice that my ego and mind seem less cooperative with each other. My ego is unable to take full focus onto 'the problems ahead'. I am surprised by the energy stirred when my ego worries "What if it sells well? What if it stirs questions? What about all the people who will be angry? Attention is not safe." Before I really notice it I sense a flow from within to my ego, '*It is happening. All valid concerns. Thank you. Guidance will be provided.*" I can't help smiling as I notice my ego relaxing into a quieter state.

With a smile I reach for my laptop and begin what turns out to be three peaceful and often pleasant hours of remembering and writing. At the end of the three hours I feel satisfied and relaxed. Time for some food. Later I will write a bit about today.

Always a Surprise

The next day as I drive out I expect to find the field empty. Yesterday was a bit more intimate and Beauty's pattern is to not be around after greater intimacy. Sorrow and emptiness fill my belly then chest. The task I am doing seems to offer only the satisfaction of my doing what I committed to do. As I am driving up the hill, about two miles from 'the place' the Wendy's sign and building remind me I have not eaten lunch. As I consider pulling off to get a burger my passing the driveway makes the choice for me. When I think, "On the way home." my body relaxes a bit while protesting the delay. I notice the drive is suddenly less mechanical. I sense the field and subtle stirrings in my belly. Something is up. Just as quickly I drop back into 'just driving' mode.

As I turn into the left turn lane my senses seem to open up, I am curious and relaxed, a perfect state to notice details. The wait for the left turn signal seems to take more time than usual and to my annoyance there are more cars than usual ahead of me. The presence of many rich physical details seems to stretch time into a slow, linear process. Finally I am turning into the parking lot, driving past the shop, scanning the field. No Beauty, just what seems a vast, empty expanse of cold, wet grass. As I begin the turn to park I feel disappointment. *'What? Really?'* And finally my mind catches up registering that Beauty is laying down inside the enclosure under the deck perhaps 8 feet from her food bowl. Suddenly I am alive with awareness, each second contains a thousand considerations. As I sense my foot on the brake bringing the car to a stop I notice Beauty's energy and body. I sense a *"It's okay"* from her as her head comes up and she watches me carefully. Her connections with me and her level of attention are almost palpable. She seems far more curious than fearful.

With the car turned off I sit uncertain what to do. I do not want to spook her. What is best? As Beauty begins to sit up I have a sense that my delay in showing myself is uncomfortable for her and my hand floats to the door handle. As the door opens and I unwind my body out of the car, with my back to Beauty I sense her relaxing and laying back down. When I turn towards her my eyes provide verification. She is lying there, head up, looking at me. As my mind and ego try to understand, try to find the best actions I notice myself turning away from the opening to the enclosure. Instead of going to the opening I walk along the fence, moving closer to Beauty with the fence as a shield for her. I hear myself saying, "**Hey Beauty. What are you doing? This is new.**" I turn my body partially towards her and turn my head a bit more so I am looking at her. She is lying there relaxed, head up, and seems a bit amused by my caution. In a moment, before my mind fully understands her head comes up a bit more, her ears come fully forward, she tilts her head and I sense a gentle, *"Maybe you can be my people."* As my mind notices a warmth flowing into me from deep within, as I relax and open my energies to her, the bargain is struck, signed, and anchored in time. As I breath out and smile, the bond, the deep agreement to 'be together', is completed. My delight within is quickly covered with my mind and ego taking more energy as my focus shifts to 'feeding my dog'.

Looking back I notice how the complexities of what Beauty and I had agreed to was hidden, buried deep within. A seed had been selected, placed in fertile soil and then covered, buried deeply, left in darkness so that roots that would sustain it could grow eventually allowing a newness to emerge into the physical world.

As 'reality' returns Beauty stands up and meanders to the opening of the enclosure. I turn and parallel her movements waiting 20 feet from the opening as she jumps down onto the pavement and continues out to the field. When she is half way across the pavement I turn, walk to the opening and step up into the enclosure. A glance back shows she is just reaching the edge of the field.

After picking up the bowl and turning back to the car via the opening I notice Beauty is wandering in the field seemingly unaware of me. Trunk opened, food mixed, a bit of canned food, a bit of dry kibble. I pick up Beauty's bowl, reach up to close the trunk and notice Beauty is sitting perhaps 50 feet away watching me. As I turn my back to her, turn towards the opening, I have a sense that she is watching me 'be her people', feeding her as I should. Without my really noticing a grin on my face reflects my pleasure. As I bend to place her bowl just under the deck it is all somehow different. I am no longer fulfilling an agreed upon project, I am feeding my dog.

As I step down, out of the enclosure I sense no draw to offer Beauty treats. The backdoor of the shop opens and in a moment I am heading over to talk with the shopkeeper. He smiles as he sees me approach and asks how things are progressing. I let him know that Beauty is almost taking treats from my hand and speculate that before the end of the week she will take a treat from my hand. The shopkeeper's, **"That will be good progress**." seems to cover regret mixed with pleasure. Fortunately my mind and ego let the awareness slip away and go into explaining to him the steps that I have planned. As we are talking we notice that Beauty has wandered to a spot where she can see both of us. She seems to approve of us talking about her.

Goodbyes release me to return to the car. Beauty is watching me. My ego and mind wondering about doing treats do not get enough traction to cause me to begin that process. I chatter towards Beauty as I walk, **"Hey Beauty. Are you going to get your food? I made it for you."** Beauty answers by sitting and I sense her telling me. *"You go. Shopkeeper closes door. Then maybe."* I grin, open the car door and swing my weight into the car. As I back, turn, and drive towards the street my mind and ego finally accept that there will be no treats given today.

As I drive home I feel the connections Beauty and I share within me. My mind begins to consider what we will say to Ute and Chery. Sensing no openness to call my mind shifts to reviewing the next steps.

Connections with a Neighbor

$\mathcal{B}$eauty is absent the next day. Somehow my sorrow at her absence is a bit deeper. As I retrieve her bowl, mix her food, and then place 'her' food in the enclosure I sense her laying somewhere nearby, out on the edge of the field. When I step out of the enclosure I notice a fellow stepping out from behind the fence that forms a yard for the apartments close to the shop. The apartments seem to have been a motel built back in the 50s, single story, several buildings creating a courtyard for parking. I remember vacations with my family, an old Ford station wagon with six kids pulling into a motel just outside a small town. I remember my father saying, "I will get keys so you can check the rooms before I pay." As soon as my father has stepped out of the car the other doors open and us kids tumble out as my mother reminds us, "Don't go out of sight! We may not be here very long." As my older brother and sister walk over to the Coke Cola chest vending machine my bother and I race towards the trees almost too far away to be within sight.

As the fellow and I walk towards each other I grin noticing how each of us is measuring the others energy and intent. "**I notice he is getting closer to you now. He used to play with the dog I had.**" His words open space for us to share and having negotiated boundaries we both relax into sharing. I am pleased by his expression of liking my feeding Beauty, a quiet acknowledgment that we both want her to have a home. I share that I suspect he is a she and he simply nods. During the five minutes we talk we come to agreement to be friends working to see that Beauty is safe and has a home. His opinions are different than mine in several ways and that is fine. We agree. I will continue feeding her and the fellow will support me and her with his friendship.

It is a pleasant day, a bit of sun providing gentle warmth so I decide to walk the field. My mind and ego have a sense of 'establishing a presence' and deeper within I sense that somehow I am claiming the space as territory for Beauty and I to share. As I stroll I notice more details, blackberry bushes, car tracks forming a dirt road, bushes separating the field from a house's backyard, a horseshoe pit recently used. An easy, relaxed stroll taking me back to my car. A drive back home that seems to lock Beauty and I into each others futures.

The next day right after morning coffee and meditation my mind anchors itself to figuring out 'better treats'. My ego grudgingly sits back waiting for a time when it can grab a bit of energy and offer it's judgments. As I putter through my morning there is a constant undercurrent of my mind working with occasional thoughts coming together in 'mini presentations'. At the end of each presentation, after a few seconds pause, there is a 'not good enough' from my mind as it drops back into 'figuring it out'. Finally my mind settles after deciding I should always have both a roasted chicken and kosher hotdogs with me to offer Beauty. Yes, try other treats with chicken and hotdogs as the mainstay. I am a little startle as I notice my mind seems to want my 'inner knowings' approval. Without thought I quiet, relax my shoulders, notice my feet, and relax into the spaces within my lower belly. I notice a gentle warmth, open relaxed space, and a slight pull towards 'chicken and hotdogs'. As I relax a bit more warmth and pleasure flows to my mind and it seems my mind 'smiles' at being acknowledged for it's solution. I notice myself sensing swinging off the path to feed Beauty, turning the car towards Costco to pick up a fresh chicken. I have a plan.

Early afternoon, driving to visit with Beauty, as I realize I am almost at the turn to Costco I also notice I have already turned on my car's right turn signal. Something within me is grinning as my sensing turning to Costco earlier blends with what is actually happening. My ego doesn't seem to know whether to be pleased or alarmed and seems to 'shrug' with a 'Weird. We are safe'.

As I am checking out at Costco I share with the checker that the chicken and kosher hotdogs are for a stray I have been feeding for three months with hopes of gaining her trust. Her **"That is wonderful. I hope it works out."** seems half admiration and half *'Fool'*. I grin and allow my mind and ego to offer, "**I have made some good progress. I suspect that she will take the last of this chicken from my hand. I may get to touch her next week.**" The checker smiles politely and as she offers an honest "**Well, good luck with that.**" I sense her being uncertain, a cognitive dissonance playing within her. She relaxes as I pick up the chicken, smile and offer, "**Thanks**".

Back to the car, back to the route to Beauty, the familiar flow allows me to relax, to open, to allow myself to notice the energy connections Beauty and I share. My mind and ego wonder whether we will see Beauty. Within it does not matter, we are doing what is to be done.

Bravely Building Trust

*A*s I drive past the shop onto the pavement behind the shop I am scanning for Beauty. I sense her and I do not see her, she seems further away and yet close by. I park and get out of the car, whistle and scan the field. Finally I let go of spotting her and turn towards the enclosure. As I take my first step I spot her and feel confusion spread through my body. It is my turn to experience cognitive dissonance. Beauty is laying inside the enclosure, under the deck, perhaps 10 feet from her food and water bowls. None of the familiar patterns apply now. My mind and ego are busy with 'Crap, what now?' as I very slowly walk towards the enclosure. Within there is a simply a quiet, relaxed, openness, making moving towards the enclosure the easiest thing to do. I whistle and chatter to Beauty. **"Hey girl. This is a surprise. New interactions."** Time is marked by each step, my weight shifting from one foot to the next somehow reflecting, marking the shift in relationship Beauty has chosen for us. I notice the energies shifting as Beauty lays watching me, allowing my movement to 'trap' her within the enclosure. Five feet from the opening I sense Beauty drawing her energy to herself, under the deck. As I step up into the enclosure it seems that Beauty and I negotiate an agreement, she will hold her energy back and stay where she is if I keep my energy back and quietly retrieve her food bowl. I am puzzled as I slowly walk around the deck to her food bowl. It seems as if I am in a hallway, on a single, narrow path to get her bowl and then retreat. I bend to pick up her bowl, pause a moment to look at her, connect with a '**Hi girl**." One moment and in the second moment my legs fill with energy and I almost jump to a standing position. Beauty has cloaked her energy, I sense her watching me step out of the enclosure and walk to my car. A few steps from the car and I sense her uncloaking her energy and getting up. When I pop the trunk and turn to begin preparing her food I see her moving towards the opening. Her movements are fluid and purposeful, she is escaping into open spaces.

With a bit of effort I relax into preparing her food, my view collapses to the car trunk. As I scoop dog food from the can Beauty comes into view off to my left, perhaps 25 feet away. I turn my head to her, offer a *"**Hey girl**."* and smile as she relaxes into sitting, facing me and I sense a *"That was scary, and good"*. She is watching me prepare her food, relaxed, ears forward, mouth open, her tongue in view for the first time. As I straighten up she tenses a bit and watches as I walk past the hood of the car and turn towards the opening. For some reason with my back to her I raise her bowl and call out, "**This is for you, girl.**" I grin as I sense a warm, grinning energy from her and feel her relax further into laying down. As I step up into the enclosure I glance back at her and see she is indeed laying on the ground facing me, watching my movements to place her bowl. I have the sense of her standing next to me, watching as I bend and place her bowl. As I stand and turn back to see her laying out in the field I notice a *'that was strange'* floating within myself, a signal that my inner knowing understands something not yet within the awareness of my mind and ego.

As I get to the opening I wonder if I should offer Beauty treats. She provides an answer by getting up and wandering over to our spot. As I walk back to the car I hear myself saying, "**Okay girl. Treat time.**"

Offers and Acceptance

At the car trunk I cut open the hotdog package and transfer 3 hotdogs to a plastic bag. Next I tear off pieces of still hot chicken and add them to the bag. The smell of the chicken and warmth on my fingers lure me into feeding myself. Suddenly Beauty's energy is right with me, sensing the heat on my fingers, the smells in my nose, the watering of my mouth. She seems to sense with me the flavor that bursts in my mouth, the texture, taste, and smell all blending in pleasure and satisfaction. I look up at her and notice her ears are fully forward and up, she is leaning towards me, her mouth is opening and closing making a smacking sound. I sense *'I want some.'* floating to me, it seems she is within me sharing her desires, whispering within me. Two more bites, the pleasures shared with her, and I notice I am closing the trunk.

As I step from the pavement to the field Beauty sits up, glances both directions, and relaxes seeming to open and invite my approach. I grin enjoying the warmth of her inviting me towards her for the first time. I am more relaxed, more open, enjoying being with her. She is laying perhaps 15 feet from our spot and sits up as my knees meet the ground at what has become my spot to be. As she shifts her weight I sense her eagerness, feeling a pull as she seems to be saying *'Well. Come on.'* As I draw the bag of goodies out of my pocket she stands and takes a couple of steps towards me, linking she and I together in what is happening. I select a piece of hotdog and toss it three feet from me. She calmly walks forward, bends, sniffs, picks up the piece, and chews. It is my turn to sense her experience, the smell, the desire, the pleasure, the taste and texture combined. As her head comes up from chewing I sense her withdrawing her energy and then choosing to remain where she is and

Bringing In Beauty

wait for a second treat. With a second piece in my hand I reach towards Beauty. Beauty is all attention as she senses my intent to reach to her. Time becomes molasses, oozing ever so slowly. Each inch of my hand moving takes several moments and includes Beauty's hopes and fears. Beauty tenses a bit when my hand reaches the end of my arm's extension and I begin to lean towards her. Time thickens and slows again and then stops as my hand stops a couple inches from Beauty's mouth. Beauty's energy withdraws as her body remains frozen. As her energy flows back to me her head comes forward, my fingers stretch towards her, her mouth opens, and she ever so daintily takes her treat. As the treat settles on her tongue she slowly backs up two steps before relaxing into enjoying her treat. I am suspended in warmth and awe.

I eagerly get out another piece of hotdog and as I look up sense '*give me time*' from Beauty as she balances where she is in between withdrawing, waiting, and returning closer. Her choice seems to take many moments and yet only a few seconds, she sits. My arm stretching towards her seem unimportant to her, my leaning forward seems equally unimportant. My left hand moving towards the ground so I can stretch further gets her full attention as she pulls herself to balance at a decision point. Every so slowly my hand travels to the ground and takes weight as I lean further. My right hand stretches closer and closer to Beauty's head and then runs out of stretch three inches from her mouth. One second, two seconds, three seconds, Beauty's nose twitches with the smell of her treat and she stretches her head forward the four inches needed to take her treat. The treat transferring to her mouth seems to tip her balance to withdrawing and she backs two steps, turns slightly, moves back six feet, finally sits and looking at me as she enjoys her treat. As I smile at her I receive a clear sense of '*enough for now*', mixed with a bit of snootiness. I watch myself continue by tossing a few chicken and hotdog treats to Beauty knowing what I am doing is just for me, a silly gesture to Beauty. After sniffing the first treat Beauty watches without responding and my ego worries. She is amused by my efforts.

I settle back on my haunches and wait. I can't leave yet, it is not done. A minute, maybe two of just sitting, noticing my legs are stiffening and Beauty bends, sniffs the treats, sits down and seems to whisper, "*I am done.*" Before my mind notices I am standing, enjoying the pleasure and pain of stretching my legs. Beauty just watches as I stretch and then steps backwards before turning and walking to the car. With the car door open I look back and notice with some confusion Beauty is sitting there calm, contained, regal. Our time together is done, I am to leave. Beauty has chosen to be by herself, today's visit is over.

I am on automatic as I swing my weight into the car, close the door, start it, drive to the street, and begin my 11 mile trip home. Normal time and space slip back to me as my car descends down to Airport Way. A few miles later I find myself smiling as I enjoy the pleasure of knowing we are one step closer, Beauty has taken food from my hand. I grin and relax further as I understand I will be quiet this afternoon and evening. Deep within stirs an understanding that only quiet will allow the deep connections of Beauty's energies with mine to strengthen and form connections into the physical within her, within me.

As I drive home I sense Beauty with me watching the road, noticing my response to traffic. It is not until much later that I realize her curiosity and desire to know more of my world, what may become her world. As I turn into the driveway her attention seems to increase and as I get out of the car I sense a time when I will reach back to open the backdoor of the car for her. As I open the gate into the backyard I sense her energies expanding out into the space of the backyard. And I sense an acceptance as if she has whispered, *"This space is for us."*

I open the back door to Fawn barking an excited greeting. Within seconds, without thought I pick up her harness and leash. We walk. A long walk. I need the physical movement away from the house with nothing for my hands to do. I need to spend time with Fawn. Beauty's energy is with me and with Fawn. I grin as I notice the first sensing of Fawn, Beauty, and I, a little pack in our territory.

Later that night I consider what other treats I might try.

Settling In

The next day Beauty is nowhere to be seen when I get to the field. I sense her energies partially connecting, partially cloaked. There is a quiet acceptance that everything is fine. I am smiling and as I walk to the enclosure my mind offers, "I am doing well." Immediately from within comes a sense of *"Beauty and I are doing well."* My mind and ego stage a minor protest, "Beauty and I? Together? What is this 'our' project? I am doing all the work. Beauty just responds or doesn't." *"Yes, and allow yourself to notice. Her energies are working with ours. Our energies are deeply intertwined."* In that moment I sense my 'inner knowing' opening a space and showing my mind and ego the deeper truth, the intertwining of Beauty and I's energies. My ego is happy with the recognition. My mind is accepting and unhappy with being shown it was 'wrong'.

The flow of retrieving Beauty's food bowl, mixing her food, and replacing her bowl is easy and pleasurable. I am doing what is intended. As I step down from the enclosure I sense an urge to walk the field. As I step from the pavement to the uncut grass of the field something primitive stirs within. My mind is startled to realize we are claiming territory for Beauty and I. We are marking the area as Beauty's and mine. I loop off to the left towards the spot where Beauty and I first met. When there I stop and remember back to that time. Without my mind noticing I begin the process of gathering the energies of the last four months, linking them into a timeline, a flow of shifts and changes. Next I walk to the rise and as I stand quietly I sense how the rise has shifted from a needed exit route to simply marking one boundary of Beauty and I's space. I notice the two stray Siamese cats hurrying away from me. Beauty had been like them in her lack of trust of me.

Malcolm Pullen

As I walk along the 6 foot chain link fence separating the field from the two story apartments I notice two children come out the sliding glass door from their apartment. One turns back and shouts something into the apartment. To my delight the little girl smiles and waves at me as her mother comes out the door. Her mother is wearing Arab attire and I am surprised and pleased when she looks in my direction and offers, "**Oh, you feed dog?**" "**Yes**." "**She your dog?**" "**Not yet**." "**Oh. You help is good**." Before I can answer the woman who never looked directly at me disappears into the apartment saying something to the kids as she retreats. The older boy jumps up in pleasure and the two of them begin to play. My "**goodbye**" is rewarded with a hesitant wave. Many energies are stirring within along with warmth and pleasure. I had been a suspicious stranger. Now I am with Beauty, a person bringing kindness into the neighborhood. At the blackberry bushes I sense how Beauty has used them to protect herself from me and as an escape route. I had seen her come out of them a few times early in our process. The bushes are no longer a barrier between Beauty and I, some of her hiding places are no longer hidden from me.

As I walk further and turn the corner along tall bushes that separate the field from a large backyard of a house my attention is drawn to an opening in the bushes I had hardly noticed before. I notice a metal frame with wire about the size of a baby gate that is pushed aside, an attempt to block the entry into the backyard. My world becomes surreal as I have a sense of the opening being a portal into another reality. The large field I am in is public, exposed, without boundaries to separate it from the jumbled energies of the area. As I step to the edge of the opening I sense a space that is separate, protected, honored, enjoyed, a place of sharing for the family living in the house. As I extend my energy into the space hoping to sense Beauty my mind and ego repeat what I was taught as a child, "Be respectful, don't enter other people's yards unless invited." The make shift gate reinforces my sense not being invited and I draw my energies back to me. As I stand there my mind is registering what it can notice, body sensations, ego warnings, physical boundaries, a block from stepping forward. With a shudder I step back and turn to my right. One step, two steps, three and then four. With each step the opening seems to close as the backyard disappears behind the tall hedge.

As I glance out to the street and at the 50s motel appearing apartments to the right life becomes normal. My mind scoffs at the recognition that somehow the backyard has room for magic. "How silly and childish!" A resonance within whispers, *"childish and true"*. A thought of Beauty draws my attention away allowing both realities to remain. As I walk along the hedge towards the street I sense Beauty, not here in the space we share but in a space she keeps separate from me. My mind carefully avoids the sense that Beauty has been chased out of 'our space' by teenage boys who are testing their ability to impact the world. I remember back to my years as a teen grateful that the need to push myself out upon the world had faded with marriage and children.

With a turn back towards the battery shop I am closing the loop and each step takes me further back into 'normal life'. As I turn back to my car I notice my attention is already on the drive back home and some cleaning in the kitchen that is long overdue. As I unlock the car door, open it, and begin to swing my body in I sense Beauty. It seems she is whispering, *'Perhaps when it is dark I will eat. If feels safe.'* As I start the car I sense myself offering her, *"I will be back tomorrow."*

BRING OUT FAWN

The next morning as we are walking the last block of Fawn and I 's morning walk I sense something stirring deep within and wonder what understanding the the stirrings will morph into. As Fawn and I turn into the driveway and I see the car I sense Fawn coming with me when I drive out to feed Beauty. My mind responds by offering the possible reasons I should do it and then reasons I should not do it. "Minor risks, no additional resources used, will see how Beauty and Fawn react to each other, attention with Beauty will be split, Beauty could run, Beauty may get idea of being in the car, could scare her" And finally, "Okay, good balance of risk and reward, limited resources burned." By the time I walk past the car the plan is accepted.

After lunch Fawn is a bit surprised when I pick up her harness and call her. In a moment her surprise changes to eagerness and I am clipping her leash to her harness. As we drive my mind and ego offer what might go wrong while within there is a calm and easy *We will learn.* It is only when I turn into the final left turn lane that I shift into a worried alertness and I catch myself hoping Beauty is not there. As I roll onto the pavement behind the shop I see her and suddenly what I am doing is important to the process of bringing in Beauty.

Beauty is relaxed, sitting in the field about 30 feet from the pavement. I park perhaps 50 feet from Beauty and before opening the car door carefully get hold of Fawn's leash. As I open the door Beauty stands and Fawn lets me know she is eager to get out by fidgeting. Fawn has not seen Beauty. Remaining eager and mostly calm as I step aside to give her an opening to get out of the car. Her front feet and then back feet hit the pavement and she is sniffing, happy and eager. A couple moments later she looks up and sees Beauty. Her reaction is immediate and violent, as she begins strident barking and lunges towards Beauty. I set my urge to pay attention to Beauty aside so all of my attention can be on dealing with Fawn's reaction. I am too busy to be disappointed. Fawn is fixed on driving Beauty away. Fawn ignores my attempts to get her attention and lunges time and again. Space seems to open to my left and I notice myself turning left and pulling Fawn with me. As we swing behind the car Fawn finally quiets just a bit. As we take a slow walk around the car her attention shifts away from Beauty to the paved area. We walk along the passenger side and Fawn is busy scanning the area. The turn at the front of the car, back towards the field brings Beauty into sight and Fawn back to barking and growling. Fortunately the lunging is less violent. At the back door on the driver's side I pull out treats and try to get Fawn engaged with me. A wisp of disappointment and acknowledgment I have work to do quickly disappears as I refocus on managing Fawn, working to interrupt her focus on Beauty. Two treats and I know it is time for me to put Fawn back in the car. I glance up and see Beauty standing there, very relaxed, unworried with Fawns displays. With the back door open I have to insist and physically turn Fawn away from Beauty. With her head just inside the opening and both of my knees pressing against her butt Fawn finally jumps up onto the backseat. Before Fawn can turn around I have the door closed and hear my mind's sarcastic understatement "That did not go well." With concern I turn towards Beauty and am surprised to see she is sitting there, seeming unaffected by Fawn's aggressive response to her. My mind is filled with cognitive dissonance, no thoughts, no logic, just awareness filled with the contrast of Fawn's frantic and aggressive reactions along with Beauty's 'Oh well' response. I don't know if it is a few seconds or a couple of minutes before I shrug and head to retrieve Beauty's food bowl. The walk is filled with wondering what is going on and how I can help Fawn past her fear of Beauty. As I walk I notice how even with Fawn's aggressive reactions towards Beauty I have no fear in physically guiding Fawn. That realization somehow brings me to notice how Fawn had separate responses to me and to Beauty. I smile as I notice the bond of trust Fawn and I share.

As I walk towards the enclosure I hear Fawn's barking intensify and without thought turn to see what Beauty is doing. Beauty has gotten up and is moving towards the enclosure as I do. Now it is time to notice how separate my connections with Beauty are from my connections with Fawn. I only half notice my mind wondering, "How do I bring the connections together?" A whisper from within informs me, *"It will happen. More visits to get ready for when Beauty and Fawn are at the dome."* I am surprised when I seem to hear Beauty saying in a happy, playful voice, *"Yes, when you take me to be with you."* Surprise gives way to startle when I notice myself sensing Beauty in the dome with us. Fortunately stepping up into the enclosure and noticing what Beauty is doing in response takes my attention.

From that point things are fairly routine except Fawn's less and less insistent barking at Beauty. Beauty waits at the enclosure entry and backs away as I return from within with her bowl. She seems to smile when I lift her bowl and prattle, **"Yes, this is your bowl. I am doing this for you."** Was that my imagination driven by my ego or my sensing Beauty sharing her pleasure with me? I chuckle as I sense a whisper from within, *"Or both?"* My mind seems pleased with that possibility, more room to play.

As I move to the trunk of the car Beauty moves to a spot only 20 feet from me where she can watch and be mostly hidden from Fawn. Fawn is mostly quiet and seems curious about what I am doing. As I pick up the food bowl I hear Fawn bark and sense her wanting to drive Beauty away from me. What I sense is very similar to what I had sensed times when female friends had inserted themselves into a warm conversation I was having with some other woman. My mind and ego seem to laughingly insert, 'Man. You better not share that with anyone. Bitch behavior! Good, clean instinctual choices, claiming and protecting resources.' With that bit of understanding I smile as Beauty follows me from 30 feet away to the enclosure entry and waits while I place her food. As I jump down, out of the enclosure Beauty seems to smile in response to my, **"Your food is there, girl."** Fawns bark claims a bit of my attention as Beauty seems to declare to me in a whisper, *"We are together."*

As I walk back to the car my mind and spirit play with perceptions around having two females devoted to me with one vying to keep her claim exclusive. Those thoughts remind me I have not been on a date for almost three years and I wonder when the urge to have a lover will return. I sense a playful jibe of, '*Dogs for now.*' from within. In the car Fawn's barking finally subsides as I pull out onto the street. A couple miles later Fawn is happily watching scenery flowing by and enjoying 'us doing together'.

MOVING TOWARDS TOUCH

*E*arly afternoon, as I drive out to feed Beauty, about half way there, I experience what I can best describe as being 'struck by a worry'. It seems both my mind and ego, and my inner awareness are insisting I pay attention. With my energies I open 'space' to work within. Several questions tumble into my awareness. "How do we get to touching?" "How do we move to her accepting my hands moving over her body?" "How do I trust her to not bite me?" "How do I introduce her to a leash and get her to walk with me?" "How do I keep both of us safe while pushing beyond her comfort and mine?" I sense and 'picture' where she and I are now in the processes. I sense and picture where I want us to be. Each question seems to represent vast chasms between the where we are and where I intend us to be. I have no ideas, no awareness of the paths we might take. My ego is on the verge of overwhelm. My mind is confused, unsure of where to start. A deep breath and choosing to notice my lower belly, keeps me from surrendering into misery. From within comes a quiet certainty that we will get there from here and I sense a future with Beauty nervously enjoying my touch, with she and I walking together in the field, with her allowing herself to be in the back seat of my car, with me closing the car door, closing the door on our current reality of separate homes.

The possible paths from here to there is a complex web of possibilities, too complex, too faint and expanded for my mind to contain. With that awareness comes a prompt, *"What is closest now? Next one or two steps only."* It seems I am receiving a smile and warmth from within as my mind and ego step in. "We need to touch her, head first, then shoulders. Then we need to get a leash connected to her collar." An attempt for my mind to picture beyond that brings no results. Understanding from within allows me to accept that searching beyond connecting a leash to her collar will steal the attention and focus needed for navigating through touch and leash.

As I notice passing by the furniture shop and then Wendys my mind and ego begin to tackle both touch and leash. Within moments my mind is in confusion and my ego is on the edge of panic. A deep breath and on the long slow exhale I sense a whisper of *"Touch only."* My ego's panic fades to worry as my mind makes one more attempt to contain both steps and then lets go of 'leash'. My ego relaxes a bit as my mind recognizes the 'size' of the journey to 'touch', the many, many little steps that will be needed.

By the time I turn onto East Burnside my mind has narrowed the immediate problem down to touching her muzzle after her taking a treat, then her being closer, then moving my hands to the thick, red mane on her neck. I grin as my mind relaxes and plays with 'Oh yes, we will touch the lion's mane.' As I turn into the parking lot and head to the back of the shop I sense Beauty and seem to receive a quiet, nervous, *"Yes, touch first."*

As I park the car I am encouraged by her sitting on the pavement in a place where I will walk within 20 feet of her. As I get out of the car I whistle 'our whistle' and watch as her ears come up and her tail wag just a bit. She watches, remains sitting. Just before I make the turn towards the enclosure opening she stands, tail and ears, down, turned slightly away from me. She turns a bit more away from me just as I shift my course. My **"Hey Beauty, I am getting your bowl**." and my turn cause her to pause. One more step, then a second, a glance back shows she is sitting again. With the next step the breath I was holding pours out of me and I relax into a smile. When I return to the enclosure entry with her bowl she has already moved to a place about 25 feet from the car trunk where I will fix her food. My choosing to swing behind the car to the trunk causes me to notice how I am avoiding challenging her and my mind plays a game of 'more or less challenge'. Rounding the car to the trunk brings Beauty back in sight. She is sitting, facing me, ears up as I pop the trunk. A glance at her treats brings the question of 'How to get to touch?' forward and I slip into imagining ways that might happen. I grab some chicken and a couple of hotdogs and head to the enclosure to place her food.

In contrast to a few moments before I easily swing around the side of the car closer to her. Before she can react I have turned to walk next to the car. Her ears shift back then forward, she stands, and I grin as she turns to walk with me back to the enclosure. She is following me, almost walking with me! I am filled with a warmth, walking becomes easy, relaxed, a bit playful and I begin chattering to her. **"Hey girl! Are you coming with me? Yeah, we need to get your food in place. Your a good girl."** Beauty seems to almost prance, head high, ears forward, tail wagging. When I am 10 feet from the enclosure she stops, watching my step up into the enclosure. Two steps into the enclosure and her energy disappears. A glance back shows she is walking off to the right. My spirits drop and I wonder if she is leaving. My playful mood returns when I stand up from placing her bowl and notice she is now sitting within 15 feet of the place I kneel to give her treats. I hear myself saying louder than planned, **"Hey girl. Waiting for treats? Good for you!"**

Two in a Row

*A*s I step down out of the enclosure I measure the 50 or so feet to 'my place'. I am nervous as I notice I will be walking almost directly at her. Take a breath, let it out, smile, notice how she sits there, ears up, watching me. With each step towards her it seems my steps are slowing. With 15 feet left to my place time has become molasses. And yet my steps seem to slow even more. As I step off the pavement, before my forward foot touches the grass time has disappeared. The final two steps to my place are filled with noticing a thousand little changes in my movements, in Beauty's movements. Each millimeter of movement of her fur, each millimeter of movement of her ears, is noticeable in a flow of motion. As my final step ends and I begin the downward motion that will bring my knees onto the cold, wet ground Beauty begins to stand with a turning movement. I am saying, "**It's okay girl.**" as the wetness soaks into my pant legs and the cold wetness encloses about me knees. As my butt moves towards my feet Beauty turns back towards me and her ears come up. By the time my butt settles on my feet she is facing me, ears up, tail with a slight wag and I have a sense of, "*Well... where are my treats?*"

    My hand does not move as quickly as I want as I reach into the pocket with Beauty's treats. I feel rather slow and clumsy under Beauty's intent attention. As the treats clear my pocket Beauty shifts her weight forward and as the treats arrive at the front of my body she is taking her first step towards me. My pleasure and awe seem to slow my clumsy movements even more. As Beauty comes to a stop, standing a mere 5 feet from me I fumble with opening the ziplock bag for the fourth time. Finally the bag opens and I look up from breaking off the first piece of hotdog to see that Beauty is leaning towards me. As my hand floats up and stretches towards her she takes a final step so she can take her treat from my hand. As my hand floats out I sense having only one treat and sense how if I had three treats I could invite her to stay close for a second and then third treat. As Beauty takes the treat from my hand I sense myself rolling a second treat out, her taking it and waiting as I roll out a third treat. As my hand floats back for more treats my mind notices I have just been given my next move in 'getting to touch'. Beauty takes a half step back as I reach inside the bag and my mind notices I am tearing off a second, third, and fourth piece of hotdog. As my hand comes up Beauty steps forward and I sense in the moment my hand takes to drift to her muzzle reaching out with a finger as Beauty waits for her second and then third treat. It is only as I roll the first treat out of my hand to my finger tips that I realize I had not kept the treat in sight as I had before while my hand floated towards Beauty. As Beauty takes her treat my mind and ego suddenly understand the path to touching Beauty.

I keep my hand up and Beauty's ears shift back a bit as her weight shifts back giving her perhaps eight inches between my hand and her muzzle. I sense her being uncertain and curious at the same time. With the sight and smell of a second treat she understands my offer and pauses, no movement as she decides how to respond. It seems she is whispering just loud enough for me to hear, "*He offers. He wants me to take. I want, smells good, okay.*" Her pause and my hoping end as she leans forward and ever so daintily and cautiously takes the second treat from my hand. My building elation ends quickly as I watch her immediately back away a full step and sit before enjoying her treat. From within floats, "*Good, now try again.*" I do try again but with no success. Three time Beauty takes one treat and backs away. Then when I raise my hand a fourth time she just sits there. She is done. As I toss her pieces of the third hotdog she just sits and watches. My mind kicks in. "Is that slight disdain I sense? No. Dogs don't have... Oh, maybe they do." And I notice my ego is certainly generating disdain. I smile and tell Beauty, "**Good girl. Enough for today. I guess it is time to go.**" But my body doesn't move, something is undone. A whisper of "*open, connect, smile*" causes me to chuckle, pause a moment and do just that. Perhaps

Bringing In Beauty

two minutes later Beauty gets up, pauses with ears forward, seems to say goodbye before cloaking her energy, turning and meander away. I sit and watch, no desire to move. 20 feet from me I sense her reconnecting and watch her turn and look towards the enclosure.

As my body registers cold, wet knees and stiff legs time returns and within a moment I am standing, turning, and walking to the car. As I swing into the drivers seat I notice Beauty walking to the enclosure in a relaxed, easy way. She doesn't turn as I start the car, nor as the car begins moving in a turn to take me towards home. My last view of her is her jumping easily up the two plus feet into the enclosure and I find myself saying in my head and heart, "See you tomorrow, Beauty."

Allowing Protection

The next day when I arrive having imagined enticing Beauty to take three of four treats in a row I am disappointed when I don't see her out in the field as I drive past the shop. My disappointment deepens as I drive and park the car scanning the field, enclosure, and blackberry bushes. I am aware something is going on as I notice each little movement, turning off the car, removing the keys, reaching for the door handle, looping a finger in, feeling the the latch release, sensing space opening to my left as the door swings open, swinging my legs out, shifting weight, my feet and legs engaging my weight, a slight push to move my body over my feet, my legs engaging and enjoying stretching into a standing position. As I straighten my eyes raise and scan along the six foot wooden fence that forms a backyard for the 50s style apartments. "There she is." floats in my mind as I notice Beauty laying against the fence. Without thought I notice Beauty has placed herself close to where people gather, protected by the fence and having her view of the field limited. As I smile, whistle, and offer, "**Hey Beauty.**" I am flooded by a sense of her wanting to be safe with people, her wanting to belong, the sorrow of her fear still holding her back, her careful sensing of her own struggle to step beyond her urges for the safety of separation. As I look at her, her posture, her slight movements, her ears partially forward, her holding her energy back, pressed against the fence I have a sense of her purposely wedging herself into a place that forces her and at the same time allows her to be a bit more vulnerable to me. In those few moments we seem to negotiate a new agreement, she will trust me a bit more if I become her protective fence from what she has suffered in the past. My mind knows something is happening, there are energies stirring within me it has noticed. Curious and uncertain my mind relaxes as I think, "Progress, more trust."

Within a few moments I notice the world just beyond the space Beauty and I have formed, drop away. As I think, "Wow!" Beauty and I are once again within a process, within a field, one step closer to each other, not yet home. The world drops back into my focus one area at a time, the fence first, then a bit of the field to the left, then the apartments, then the Quonset hut, then the physical distance between Beauty and I. As I take a step towards Beauty her ears go back, she gets up and seems to press herself back against the fence. As I stop and take a step back without thinking she relaxes takes a couple steps forward, walks along the fence away from me. As she clears the fence and her energy opens out into the field I sense sorrow and disappointment floating within and my mind and ego being disgruntled. I hear myself saying to Beauty, "**Hey Beauty. I make your food now. You can relax. Thank you.**" I turn right and step towards the enclosure.

After filling Beauty's water bowl I pick up her food bowl and head to the car. Beauty is sitting out in the middle of the field, further away than she has been as of late. I am disappointed by the distance and at the same time grateful she did not leave after allowing herself to be closer to me. She watches me go to the trunk of the car and does not stand and walk closer so that she can watch me fix her food. As I stir her food energies of pleasure, worry, disappointment, gratitude, and wonder all stir within me. Not wanting to be left out my mind begins to offer 'reasons' for my emotions and Beauty's behavior. Before heading for the enclosure I put three hotdogs into a sandwich bag. Fortunately my mind quiets as I step up into the enclosure to place Beauty's food bowl. As I bend and place her bowl I sense that somehow placing her bowl is more significant now, a signal of my accepting and honoring her new trust, verification that her new trust is merited. As I release her bowl to it's place I seem to be releasing some of the doubts I have been carrying about the wisdom of my efforts. As the bowl settles into place it seems my commitment to Beauty settles into place within me. As I stand I turn and look for Beauty out in the field. A smile signals my pleasure to find her sitting closer, now at the edge of the pavement and the field. As I move towards the entrance she steps onto the pavement and moves towards me and the entrance. She is moving slowly so she is half way to the entrance when I step down out of the enclosure entrance. I grin when my sense of her being nervous is verified by her turning left and walking about 20 feet from my path back to the car. There she sits, facing me, watching me, ears mostly forward, tail still. I have a sense of her whispering, "*I stay. You go. Food later.*"

When I get to the car I realize I still have hotdogs in my pocket and turn to look at Beauty just as she is jumping up into the enclosure and heading towards her bowl. I relax and watch unsure why I don't just get in the car. When Beauty reaches her food she turns, looks to see if I am watching. Suddenly time, the field, the car are mere wisps of vapors. The moment is filled with Beauty and I and our dances of connection. As Beauty turns back to her food bowl it seems she has drawn my energy into her body so I may witness her signaling her choice. The best I can do to express what I experienced is Beauty's energies whispering to me, "*I accept the food you provide, I take the food you offer into my body just as I take your love into my soul. The food you offer sustains my body. The love you offer sustains my soul's expansion into our life.*" I stand there, numb, filled with emotions, a deep warmth flows into my lower belly expands up into my heart. I sense the same happening for Beauty. I have no mind, no ego. All there is to do is experience what I have never known before. Time begins to filter back when I sense Beauty's mirth and amusement with my responses. A moment or two later my mind and ego begin to protest that I might just be going crazy, that I best begin acting 'normal' and never share what has just happened. Within I smile in recognition that my mind and ego were not denying what I experienced and sense a whisper of, "*Well, that is progress.*" and experience deeper warmth stirring in my belly.

I lean against the car and watch Beauty eat for a minute while 'reality' returns. In a single, fluid motion I push away from the car get my keys from my pocket and push the keys into the lock as my body flows back towards the car. A pause and I turn the key. Opening the car door feels like opening back into reality. Soon I am driving the 11 miles back home. I gratefully notice there is very little traffic. Within the traffic of energies flow and dance shaping new sharings with Beauty.

Doggy Intimacy

The next day Beauty is sitting at the edge formed by the pavement and the field, positioned so she can watch me make her food. She stands as I park and turns partially away as I open the door. As I stand I whistle, a long single tone, low to high. Before I am fully upright she has turned back to me and as I close the car door she sits, her ears come up and forward, her mouth opens a bit, and to my delight her tail wags gently. As I speak to her her head swings both directions checking to see that no one else is around. I retrieve her food bowl and return to the car where I pop the trunk. A glance at Beauty provides a surprise. She stands and saunters towards me. As I begin preparing her food she locates herself behind and to the left of the car where she can watch me prepare her food. I am both nervous and pleased as I sense her expectation that I 'do what I should do for her'. My ego protests that a dog certainly has no business judging my actions. My mind observes her relaxed certainty of our connections. And from within flows a quiet warmth and openness, *"all is as it should be"*. With her food prepared I head to the enclosure, surprised that she gets up and moves so she can watch me step up into the opening and place her food bowl under the deck. As I move back to the opening she meanders out to 'our spot' in the field, just beyond the pavement and sits facing me, waiting for me. This time walking towards her is easy, slow, deliberate, relaxed. She seems to be inviting me to join her. As I reach the edge of the pavement I notice she is about 12 feet from my spot. With my step onto the grass her ears go back slightly and her body tenses. I find myself chattering to her as I take the last five steps towards her, **"Hey Beauty. Are you ready for some treats?"**

I grin as I notice her ears come back forward as soon as my feet come together and I begin to kneel. As my knees meet the ground she relaxes and her mouth opens. Her tail begins to wag as the baggy of treats clear my pocket and come into view. As I open the bag and begin breaking off pieces of hotdog she stands and saunters forward and then waits about four feet away. With three pieces of hotdog hidden in my hand I stretch my hand towards Beauty. She takes one step forward and waits, one second, two seconds, three seconds, her ears go back. I hear myself saying, "**Here it is**." as I roll a piece of hot dog out into view. Her ears come forward and it seems she whispers, *"Oh, hiding game."* A half step and she stretches her head forward to take my offering and chews it while watching my still outstretched hand inches from the side of her muzzle. As she swallows her head goes back a couple inches. I don't wait, I roll the second piece of hotdog out into view. Time shifts and stretches as she pauses on the edge of choice. "**This is for you, girl.**" seems to help her decide for she stretches her head forward and daintily takes her second treat. My pleasure expands as I notice she stays close waiting for her third treat and immediately reaches for the third treats when I roll it out. As she chews and swallows I open my hand showing it is empty. When she does not move her head back without thinking I playfully wiggle a finger close to her muzzle. That is enough. She steps back one step and sits.

As I reach into the baggy and break off more treats I notice I am also chattering at her. "**You are such a good girl. Are you my Beauty? Yes, my Beauty to love and enjoy being with. Not my Beauty to own. Almost ready. Here we go.**" And I reach towards her with treats hidden in my hand. As my hand reaches I am pleased that there is no withdrawal and I am puzzled for there is no response. Beauty just sits there. By the time my mind reviews the situation I have a sense Beauty wants to be invited. "**Here you are girl.**" and my hand moves up a down a couple inches. I am suddenly surprised as I realize Beauty has opened her energies even further to me. A breath, relax my body, let my heart and belly open to Beauty, sense the earth and the grass, let the distance between us seem to disappear. As I sense warmth and pleasure shared with Beauty fill me, I notice myself and Beauty smile. My mind is confused, my ego chimes in "Oh no. Crazy talk."

and my mind offers, "The corners of her mouth did go back and her mouth is open further. She has leaned closer to us. Her ears are peaked up." My ego grunts, "Well, okay. That feels safer." As my eyes focus on Beauty once again I have the sense Beauty is amused by my silliness.

With the openness between us a small part of me rolls a treat into my fingers. My mind and ego seem far away as Beauty stands, steps close enough to take her treat without extending her neck. I have the sense of Beauty and I being in a dance, as she chews her head remains almost touching my hand. An invitation? The world becomes her head, her muzzle, my hand, our blended energies. I straighten a finger and extend my hand a couple inches. Beauty's eyes seem to soften telling me, "*You may.*" As my finger moves slowly up and down my hand drifts two more inches and I sense my finger brushing the fur just above her muzzle. Beauty holds herself still and I sense fear, pleasure, desire, self challenge coming from her as my finger goes up and down once, twice, three times. With a quick movement Beauty moves her muzzle just out of reach. As a "**Thank you, girl.**" floats up from deep within me Beauty swings her head further away, draws her energy back, and pauses on the edge of choice. As a sense of "*Need space.*" from her floats into my awareness she turns away from me, takes two steps, turns back facing me and sits. My mind and ego return and struggle with what I should do while my hand tosses each of the two remaining treats to Beauty. Beauty bends, sniffs each treat, raises her head, looks at me and settles into sitting facing me.

Time opens further, there seems to be nothing for her or I to do, energies suspended awaiting a choice. Ten, perhaps fifteen seconds of relaxed uncertainty and suddenly I sense Beauty getting an idea, my mind and ego begin to protest '*nonsense*' but stop as they register that her head has come up perhaps two inches, her head turns just a bit counter clockwise, her ears come fully up and forward. "Same movements I see when people get an idea. Okay, the body movement and energy match. Unexpected for a dog. New understanding." I become nothing other than an observer waiting to see what she will do. She leans forward to stand and moves easily into a step in my direction. In those moments I simply watch as she walks to my left, my body movements have been suspended, my head does not turn to track her as she moves past my left side only three feet from my side, then behind me she turns in an arch to face my back. *"What?"* I sense rather than see her step towards me and bend her head to sniff my butt. I am in awe as my mind and ego attempt to sort out what my body and energy already know. An act of trust, acceptance, and intimacy. I sense her tension shift to curiosity. She sniffs my butt again and then my back, and then my neck. I sense her step back and she seems to disappear. A slow careful turn of my head verifies she is still there, her head a foot from my back, curious and relaxed. Five seconds, maybe eight, I wait a bit worried about what she will do next. Then she is done, she turns and steps into completing the circle to return to a spot in front of me only 10 feet away. As she sits her ears are up, her mouth is open and I have a sense of the warmth of her energy telling me, *"Friend now, almost family."* My body is full of a warm flowing energies that seems to be cycling within the space we share, energies that warm and connect us. We are there for perhaps 30 seconds before Beauty stands and as she turns away looks back at me seeming to whisper, *"enough for now, connections forever"*.

As Beauty walks calmly away I simply breath, allowing myself to notice the connections, the acceptance she has initiated. As the physical distance increases, the warmth and ease of energies connecting us remains present. Within I gratefully accept the quiet knowing that she and I have acknowledged timeless connections we share. In the background, far away, my mind and ego are quiet, unable to coalesce their protests. Getting up, walking to the car, driving home occur in a smaller reality than the one Beauty and I share.

That evening I have to call Ute excited to share what has happened, eager to get her view and hopefully her agreement. As I dial I relax into my chair, as I lift the phone to my ear my body settles. Without a thought my energy opens to notice the energy at the other end of the line. First ring, little noticeable, second ring, disturbance, third ring, tension, fourth ring, maybe not, fifth ring and I hear the phone being answered followed by Ute's voice. We begin the amenities, the 'How are you?'es. Ute's voice verify what I had sensed and I wonder whether to share or not. As she tells me what has her tense I am both concerned as a friend and hopeful my news will cheer her up. Instinctually I connect with the warmth and wonder that fills me, with the news I wish to share.

Bringing In Beauty

I am surprised to sense that Beauty seems to be encouraging me. Over the next three to four minutes I sense Ute relaxing, connecting, sensing I have something I wish to share. I am grateful and offer, "**Beauty did something new!**" The warmth of Ute's, "**Tell me.**" removes the last bit of reservation I have. As my mind and ego attempt to craft something clever I hear myself saying, "**Beauty sniffed my butt!**" as I allow my pleasure and excitement to flow out. I am rewarded with a flood of warmth and Ute's excited voice saying, "**Oh Malcolm, that is huge!**" We continue with my sharing details. I am delighted as I sense Ute following the energy of what I experienced tucked within each factual detail I provide. My offering, "**Beauty has accepted me.**" brings what I hoped. I sense Ute opening and tracing out the energies and smile as Ute offers, "**Yes she has. She trusts you a little now.**" There is more but somehow the space for sharing has closed and we shift to discussing what remains to be done. Then we discuss other things going on in our lives. As I say goodbye and hang up the phone I sense a regret in not having the space to talk about the timeless connections Beauty and I had reopened.

As I sit there my mind turns to 'managing' what needs to be done. As strange as it seems my inner wisdom seems to smile at me ego, at my mind. My mind and ego relax a bit and I notice my inner wisdom gently guiding my mind and ego, acknowledging their 'good ideas' with warmth, letting 'okay ideas' float unopposed, causing 'bad ideas' to seem heavy and sticky. Beauty is very picky about what food she will take as a treat. Pieces of hotdogs, chicken, Ute's suggested bacon, dog biscuits are ignored. Hotdogs are cheap and chicken works better. Kosher hotdogs work better than Ball Park hotdogs. Whatever we use needs to have enough draw to get Beauty to come even closer. I get up and go to the storage closet with a plastic bag. I take a few of each type of dog treat there and set a plan to go to the pet store to buy other treats to try. After all Fawn is happy with any treat I offer her so the test treats will not go to waste.

TOWARDS A PACK

The next day as I get ready to go feed Beauty Fawn looks at me and with her eyes seems to implore me to take her with me. I pause to consider, to sense what choice will serve Beauty, I, and Fawn best. My choice becomes obvious as I easily reach down for Fawn's leash. Fawn is delighted, happy to be going with me.

As I turn to drive to the back of the store I sense Fawn's excitement. Beauty is sitting in the field, close to 'our spot'. Fawn begins to bark and I tense and open to what both Fawn and Beauty are feeling. Beauty's calmer curiosity and interest contrasts Fawn's alarm and uncertainty. Thankfully Fawn is a bit less strident than on the last visit. A deep breath and letting go while I say to Fawn, "**You stay here. I will feed Beauty.**" seems to help Fawn relax just a bit. After retrieving Beauty's food bowl and returning to the car trunk Fawn notices Beauty walk closer to watch me make her food. With Fawn growling and barking I pick up Beauty's food and move to the back car window so I am between Beauty and Fawn. Without thinking I link into Fawn's energy, take a deep breath, relaxing myself as I tell Fawn, "**Yes, girl. She is here. This is her food. She is your sister.**" Something changes in Fawn, her alarm has shifted to worry, her hostility becomes more rivalry, her bark shifts from aggressive pushing away to warning of 'keep your distance, I don't trust you'. Beauty seems almost amused as she begins to follow me towards the enclosure. When I stand from placing Beauty's food bowl I notice she is sitting at our spot, Fawn is quiet. At the car I break up almost a whole package of kosher hotdogs and carefully put the open bag in my coat pocket so I can get treats with one hand. I have plans for the other hand. I carefully open the back car door and grab

Fawn's already attached leash before stepping back so she can get out. In the first few moments Fawn busies herself with sniffing the grass as we walk closer to 'the spot'. Beauty getting up and moving captures all of Fawn's attention and she begins 'get away' barking and growling. I am surprised, pleased, and proud that Beauty seems more amused than worried. I stop and grip Fawns leash so I can keep her within 2 feet of me. Beauty stops and waits perhaps 20 feet from Fawn and I.

I grin for a moment or two as I notice Beauty's energy seems to be intent on helping me with the introductions. I toss a few treats about six feet from Beauty and quickly reach into my pocket with my right hand as I struggle to keep Fawn with me with my left hand. As Beauty walks forward I keep Fawns busy with the one thing more tempting than Beauty, treats given by hand. To my surprise Beauty chooses to stand and wait for more treats. As I reach into my pocket to get more treats and struggle with Fawn with the other hand my mind and ego offer, "Crap! This is really hard. Can't we quit." Fortunately they quiet as soon as my hand with treats clears my pocket. I am very, very aware of the split I am maintaining between controlling Fawn and fostering Beauty's trust. One, two, three treats to Beauty. One, two, three treats to Fawn, struggling to quiet her. Beauty makes the choice to stop by turning and walking perhaps 40 feet away. I turn away and partially drag Fawn to begin our walk around the field. As we walk Beauty follows us perhaps 50 feet behind us. Fawn often glances back, protesting with short bursts of barking and growls. My mind and ego suggest perhaps I am crazy. Finally after about 30 feet Fawn's cattle dog instincts kick in and her attention shifts to walking with me and eagerly sniffing all the new smells. To the apartments, along the blackberries, looping along the tall hedge, walking back past the 50s style apartments toward the car. Just past the apartments about 70 feet from the car Fawn stops, finds just the spot with her nose, and squats for a long pee. A few barks at Beauty and we continue back to the car. Fawn eagerly jumps into the car and I close the door, turning to see what Beauty is doing.

Beauty is just getting to the place where Fawn peed. Beauty sniffs, raises her head, looks right at me, takes two steps forward, and purposefully squats to pee where Fawn has peed.

I watch for a few moments, surprised, almost startled, to see her hunch her back in that unmistakable way of dogs taking a dump. She turns and looks at me, stretches, and begins scratching the ground. It seems she is showing off, making sure I notice, making sure I receive her message, "*I blend scents with you, with Fawn, we share this space.*" A minute later she looks at me and when I throw a piece of hotdog she begins running towards me, tail high and wagging. She pauses to sniff out what I had thrown and then trots closer and sit about 10 feet from me. As she sits I have a sense of Beauty whispering to me, "*I claim her, your dog, as part of my pack, as a sister.*" I am dumbfounded. My mind and ego are stupefied and struggle with reason after reason for why Beauty's choice makes no sense. I hear myself saying, "**Oh, Beauty. Fawn, you, me. Your pack?**" I sense a simple, amused, "*Well yes.*" in response.

Beauty soon gets up and continues on to the enclosure and jumps in, heading to her food. I reluctantly open the car door, get in and talk with Fawn to reassure her before starting the car and heading home. At the nature trail on the way home I stop. Fawn is agitated. I want to calm her, to reassure her she is still my dog, to relax the tension in our connections. A walk in nature with Fawn pulls me into turning off Airport Way so nature can sooth away the uncertainties, Fawn's and mine. It is only during that walk that I suddenly am struck with an understanding, Beauty's declaration included 'you, me'. Suddenly everything is different. Beauty is not a stray dog, I am her person and she is my dog.

Bringing Beauty Closer

*A*s I turn from 47th onto Prescott, just beginning my drive to feed Beauty, I remember that in the last couple of weeks in discussions with Ute the subject of Beauty allowing me to touch her had come up. As we chatted nothing we mentioned resonated with me, leaving me with a sense that it is not yet time for the next step. Now something is stirring deep within me. The combination of thinking about touching Beauty and a sensation that unknowable energies are stirring in my lower belly signal an answer, the next step is on it's way. As I write my mind and ego are unhappy, uncertain of the safety of sharing how I experience intuition's process within me. My mind reminds me that the few books that talked about someone's experience of intuition had been fiction. A thought or two and my mind runs out of 'shared information' about intuition. I grin as the question of how other people experience intuition shifts my mind into pondering mode. The question has been asked and I sense my mind taking hold of the question as worthy of attention. My mind is a bit startled to notice that paying attention to my and other peoples' energies offers rich possibilities in new understanding. But I digress.

As I start forward at the light at NE 60th my awareness returns to inner stirrings and how I will get Beauty to allow me to touch her. The question expands as I senses myself checking the collar she wears making sure it is not too tight. How will I get Beauty to let me 'handle' her? As that question forms in my mind I sense a grinning energy flowing into me and a sense of *"Yes... my people touch me, stroke me"*. As I turn onto 82nd, towards Airport Way I find myself beginning to explore different aspects of the question before me. Earning trust, developing trust, experiences that show both of us are safe, noticing choices she offers me, offering her choices to trust just a bit more. As I drive along Airport Way dozens of possibilities stir in me, some eventually forming mini scenes I sense in my body. Near the end of my travel along Airport Way it all comes together as if a map with several paths had been laid before me. As I drive the long arch transitioning Airport Way to 181st I understand my 'next step'. I sense placing treats on the ground closer and closer to me, luring Beauty in for her treats. Mixed in is having her take treats from my hand at each new 'closeness'. As I turn from 181st onto Burnside I sense Beauty taking treats I have put on my knees and later treats I have put on my thighs. "Hmmm, and treats placed beside me so she turns her side to me."

As I wait to turn into the driveway of the shop I remember back to Ute mentioning a friend using placing treats closer and closer. Handing Beauty treats with each 'closer' completes the path Beauty and I will use. Without thought I notice the many paths activate by choosing what I have just chosen. All lead in the direction I intend to go with Beauty.

As the car stops and I look out into the field I see Beauty along the blackberries bushes about 150 feet away. Before I unwind into a standing position I whistle 'our whistle'. Beauty's head and tail come up and she begins a lazy trot towards me. I hear myself saying '**Oh, girl!**" as she trots towards me and I experience her opening a warm flow of energy to me. Within a moment she seems to whisper, "*Walk to my bowl. I go there.*" Her message registers just as I take my first step towards the enclosure. As I step up into the enclosure Beauty is 20 feet from our spot. Glancing back as I head towards her food bowl I am surprised to notice she is coming closer, stepping onto the pavement. When I stand from picking up her food bowl I see she is sitting on the pavement perhaps 20 feet from the enclosure entry. With a bit of surprise, as I walk to the entrance, I notice I am not worried about having to walk directly towards Beauty. My jumping down out of the enclosure is a bit much for her and she stands, turns away from me and watches me as I walk towards her. I have a sense of her playing with me and grin. My mind chimes in with, "That is new. Maybe this will work." as it begins to wonder what 'this' is.

As I walk forward slowly Beauty moves easily out of my path. As soon as I pass she turns and follows me to the car trunk sitting about

15 away. I can almost hear her whisper, "*Good people, you do for me.*" and notice my ego scolding, "Crazy talk! Stop it!" with my mind offering, "And be quiet about it."

I fill a baggy with hotdogs and chicken, wag it in the air, and hear myself saying, "**These are for you, Beauty.**" As she gets up I notice her tail is up and wagging, her ears are fully forward and up, her mouth is open with her tongue showing. Her light step as we head towards the enclosure mirrors my pleasure in being with her. She trails behind me by a consistent 15 feet and stops to sit on the pavement as I step up into the enclosure. When I return to the enclosure entry she stands, turns, and trots to our spot without looking back. In a bold mood I walk quickly. She sits about 10 feet from my spot and then stands when she sees I am not moving slowly and carefully. "**It's okay, girl. I am just going to my spot**." With each of my last five steps she tenses a bit more. With my dropping to my knees she jumps back releasing her tension, takes a few steps away, glances at me, and loops back sitting a bit closer, perhaps 8 feet away. There is a playful, gently challenging energy flowing between us. I can almost hear her whisper, "*More fun, more fun. Scary good.*" I notice my ego is perturbed as I pull the treats out of my pocket and say, "**Okay Beauty. More fun challenges.**" With five pieces of hotdog in hand I lean forward onto my hands and knees. Beauty tenses, ready to get up, seeming to hang between flight and surrender. She stands as I reach out a hand, stretching towards her. She stops as she smells the treat and sees me roll a treat into sight. "**Well, girl. Still fun?**" She is on the edge. My mind and ego have slipped away and I notice I am turning my head away from Beauty, opening my neck to her. It is her turn to be suspended in time by confusion. In the next moment I lower my shoulders doing a play bow for her. She jumps up in the air and sideways, much further than I would expect of a dog her size. She spins around and runs 10 feet further away where she sits partially facing me. I am torn between work and play as I raise back up to my hands and knees. Without thinking about it I raise a treat up, say, "**This is yours**.", place the treat on the ground. As I move back to sitting on my heals I place several more treats each closer to me. For the last treat placed Beauty will have to step about six inches closer than she has been to take a treat from my hand.

Beauty waits, I wait. Finally she stands and walks to the first treat. Picks it up and eats it watching me the whole time. A pause and she goes to the second treat. As she steps to the third treat I sense a *"Too much."* from her and she backs away. She sits there about 10 feet from me, watching me, showing no intent to gather the last two treats. The next two minutes seem like days. Finally I offer, "**Okay girl, play time.**" Her head comes up and she stands as I lean forward onto my hands and knees. Her body is tense, ready to respond in flight or play. With a gentle growl I lower my shoulders in a play bow and bark at the bottom of my bow. She springs up and sideways, ears up, tail up. She scoots 5 feet and turns towards me, tail wagging quickly, mouth open, body tense. Without thinking I crawl towards her, carefully not directly at her and when she stands I do another play bow. She jumps in the air, runs 20 feet away and loops back within 10 feet of me. She stands there waiting, ready to spring. I do two play bows and charge at her on my hands and knees. Again she jumps high in the air, turns and runs away. This time she stays 20 feet away, facing away from me, her tail down, her ears up. "Is that enough?" I sense a, *"Too much. Want safety. Want play, need safety."* Beauty sits as I crawl backwards and then turn away from her. When I reach our spot I gather the last two treats, stand, and underhand toss them to her. "**Here you go. I like playing with you.**" warmth and pleasure flowing to her with my words.

In the three seconds before I turn to the car I sense a tumble of emotions within myself and flowing from Beauty. Desire for more, fear of what more will mean, yearning for play together, fear that it will not be safe, desire to end separation, need to have separation for a time. I turn slowly away from Beauty and walk to the car. When I look back she is still sitting there and I get a sense of *"You go now. I need just me."* As I drive out of the parking area I discover I am at ease. Somehow Beauty and I need to stir all the questions in our awareness and discover what the questions expose. That will take much more time than just this afternoon.

Cruelty Pushing Beauty Away

The next day Beauty is nowhere in sight and there is a feel of aggressive young men energies in the area. As I park I begin to quiet and open myself, remembering it is Sunday so kids were out of school and young men, apprentice warriors, had more freedom to roam in the evening. Anger rises in me blending with the indignation bordering on rage, my mind and ego feel that someone is violating Beauty and I's territory, putting Beauty in danger. By the time I reach the enclosure entry I am aware that staying in anger with others being who they are is casting my power away. At the entry I pause, sensing that my rage will contaminate the space where I provide Beauty sustenance, where Beauty accepts and enjoys my offerings. A few long, deep breaths, feeling my feet on the ground, connecting with Beauty and sharing the fear, sorrow, and confusion I sense her experiencing. I choose to focus on the task at hand, the love and acceptance I wish to express by providing Beauty food.

As I step up into the enclosure I have a sense of Beauty joining me, a bit of gratitude mixing with her sorrow. Deep within I have a sense of entering ceremony. Just inside the enclosure I spend a few seconds grounding my energy, sensing my feet, sensing the earth, accepting the pain that comes with opening to Beauty. My mind relaxes, my ego accepts it will have to wait to vent it's anger at others making 'us' unsafe. Within my body and energies I have a sense of Beauty being with me, finding relief in the contrast my acts of love provide against those who insisting on trying to hurt her. I sense their exploration of who they might become, testing their power in destructive, cruel ways. I wince remembering my own passages through those tests.

As I pick up Beauty's bowl I sense a warmth flowing from Beauty. Today feeding Beauty is a small part of what I am doing. Back at the car trunk as I prepare to mix her food without thought I draw her energies into me. It seems important that she experience the love and connections that cause me to spend my resources so she may have more. As I pick up her bowl she seems to step out of me and walk beside me as I return to the enclosure. She is first to jump up into the enclosure and seems to sigh with relief to be within the space protected by me and the shopkeeper. As I release the bowl to settle into it's spot a wave of deep connection fills me, holds me silent within time, and then releases me so that I may stand. At the entry of the enclosure I glance out into the field, scanning for anyone in view. An action to put my mind and ego at rest. I turn back facing inward, relax my mind, let go of my emotions, sense the earth, flow deep love into my belly, into my heart, and out to fill the space Beauty and I share. There is no time, I simply remain open, filling the space with love's energies until small energy tickles within releases me and time returns. I smile as I sense a *"Thank you."* from Beauty. I am done and soon find myself driving home. As I drive my mind and ego reluctantly accept a deeper knowing. Plotting against the young men tormenting Beauty will only weaken my capacity to shape what I hope to share with Beauty.

The next day there is no sign of Beauty. When I extend my energies out to sense her, she responds with a reserved, careful connection. I sense her sorrow, her confusion, abuse of the past magnifying the sense of rejection and the fear she feels now. What she shares with me awakens the energies I still hold from past torments. Anger rises in me and before it can build I sense Beauty withdrawing. My anger seems to fuel her uncertainty. Deep breaths, feet on the earth, relax my mind, let go of my emotions, notice my belly, the space there, and let it expand. The anger becomes a small part of my world, the connections I share with Beauty expand in my awareness as I sense her reconnecting. As I retrieve her bowl, prepare her food, and place her bowl within the enclosure I keep 'doing for her' forward in my heart and thus in my mind. At the car I open to Beauty and enjoy having just done something for her. Leaning my butt against the car I repeat the exercise of filling 'our space' with love. Five minutes later I am turning onto the street to return home.

That evening Ute and I talk about Beauty's tormentors. I am challenged to stay open rather than collapsing into anger. I choose to allow the anger to flow through me, to experience the anger's flow rather than turn it into rage by holding it within my body.

Getting Closer

As I unlock the car door for my trip to feed Beauty I sense her connecting with me. I relax and grin as a gentle warmth fills my belly and flow up to fill my chest and then my body. My sense is of Beauty resting in the place where we first met, laying protected partially within the 150 foot long hedge of bushes. A whisper of energy seems to carry *"Oh, good. I wait."* and Beauty seems to playfully withdraw her energies from me. The eleven mile drive is an easy pleasure. Traffic is light, there is only a trace of rain. With the slight warmth of early spring and early growth hinting at the tremendous energies of growth being released the world seems alive, tingling with anticipation. For several moments my mind plays with how the energy of plants beginning to awaken with new growth is reflected in the growing connections Beauty and I share. Both seem driven by deep, rich, powerful energies insisting on being allowed to flow after the withdrawal into winter.

    Parking in my usual spot and getting out I whistle and turn towards the hedge. My mind is surprise to see Beauty standing up from where I had first seen her and trotting towards me. My ego runs a litany of warnings of silliness drawing ridicule and a safety driven prohibition of ever sharing what we have just experienced. Without thinking of it I shout, "**Let's go girl**." and begin trotting towards the enclosure. Beauty follows perhaps 30 feet away and stops as I jump up into the enclosure. There she waits while I retrieve her food bowl and return to the enclosure entry. To my delight she sits where she is allowing me to walk within 15 feet of her before turning towards the car. She follows and places herself to watch me prepare her food. When I head back to the enclosure she gets up and follows until I am at the enclosure. I am grinning ear to ear with a sense of her following me like 'my dog'. As I jump down from the enclosure after placing her bowl she springs up, twirls, hurries to our spot, and sits about 10 feet from my spot. There she sits as I walk directly towards her, seeming to invite me closer. With me in place she gets up and moves closer as I get out her treats. I feel a strong draw to hurry my process and choose to carefully take my time to get four treats enclosed in my hand. Before my arm raises Beauty steps forward to within easy reach of my arm, and then takes each treat as I offer it to her. As I draw my arm back she sits only three feet from me. The pleasure that fills me is soon masked by my focus. I break a hotdog into five pieces and reach down placing one piece only two feet from my knees. Beauty stands and waits. I carefully settle back more onto my heals letting her know I will not be reaching out to give her treats. Beauty's ears come up a bit more as she seems to understand. With what seems to be an *"oh, okay"* she links with my energies, takes one step forward, and bends to retrieve her treat. To my delight she stands there, chews, swallows, and looks back at me.

Time slows, my hand moves like molasses as I reach forward and down to place another treat while Beauty stands and watches. I notice every twitch, a few hairs moving in the gentle breeze. Beauty's ears are partially back, she is not breathing as my hand places her treat less than two feet from her front feet. As her treat touches the ground I am critically aware that my head is less than two feet from and slightly below her head. She is a spring ready to launch. Something deep within me has taken over and I notice myself pause and then lowering my head and shoulders another six inches. I am looking at Beauty's feet on the ground and very aware her head is above mine. Beauty's energy carries puzzlement at my choice to trust her and be vulnerable. I whisper **"Good girl."** and a second or two later as I sit back on my heels my head shifts back to being above Beauty's head. Beauty's ears come forward and up and for a few moments she forgets her treat while she looks softly at me. All I can do is grin. A small wave of my hand draws her attention down and then to her treat. She bends and picks it up, steps back, sits, and then enjoys her treat.

With a playful quietness and a **"Want more?"** I place 3 more treats, 6", a foot, and 18" from my knees. As I withdraw my hand Beauty stands, moves forward, takes the furthest from me, raises her head and eats it, steps forward, takes the second treat, steps back while raising her head, sits and then enjoys her treat. There she sits watching my still form. In my body I have a sense of picking up the final treat and handing it to her. As I do what I sensed, reach for the treat, I glance at Beauty who seems to be grinning at me. Did she? My mind and ego insist, "Dogs can't do that!" As I reach out and she takes the treat we both seem to agree that she has just through her energies communicated her desires to receive from my hands and I have responded.

After receiving several treats by hand Beauty steps back a couple steps and sits. I have a clear impression that she is done. As my mind and ego register their dissatisfaction I notice Beauty shift her front feet from one foot to the other. Her playful energies stir with mine and before it registers I am leaning forward onto all fours and beginning a play bow. With delight Beauty jumps, spins, loops out and comes back to within 5 feet of me. As she sits I notice the curtains of a second story window fall back together and my ego moans, "Now they know we are crazy." Beauty is standing again and leans towards me. In response, with no thought, I lean towards her and bow. Jump, spin, run a loop out, come part way back and sit. I growl, crawl forward a few steps, turn slightly, and play bow. This time Beauty faints a rush forward, taking only two step before jumping, spinning, and looping. I smile as I watch Beauty's body movements become more fluid, more relaxed, and it seems more playful. Soon Beauty is sitting 20 feet from me, my pants are soaked, and I am done. Beauty seems to hope I am getting up to chase her but that is not my intent. I offer, "**That was fun, girl.**", turn, and head to the car. Beauty sits and watches me walk. At the car I yell, "**Bye girl.**" and soon I am on my way home. For the first several blocks of driving I am puzzled by my abrupt departure. From within floats a sense of, "*You leave her wanting more.*" My mind offers, "interesting", my ego offers, "dumb".

WORKING ON TRUST

*A*s I drive out inner awareness, my mind, my ego envision that over the next week we will work on building trust, my trust of her, her trust of me. Each session will ask Beauty to come a bit closer to take a treat from the ground and to allow just a bit of touch when she takes treats from my hand.

On this day's session Beauty takes a treat from the ground three inches from me and allows me to brush against the hair of her muzzle with one finger. I have no words to describe my sensations of connection and delight as my finger ever so slowly moves her hair. The next day I place treats just an inch from each knee and do not lean back to sit on my heals. I close my hands and place them between my legs, tight against my crotch. Beauty seems both perturbed and pleased by the challenges. As she glances back and forth between the treat and my head I offer, **"Hey girl, we need to build trust. Will you trust me?"** I smile and fill my belly with warm, loving energies. Beauty responds by standing and stepping forward to take the two treats closest to my right knee. She looks at the treats by my left knee for what seems a minute. Finally she steps back and sits. I sense she is waiting for me to hand her treats. Instead I take one treat and move it 6" from my left knee, leaving the other where it is and settle back to sit on my heals. Beauty does not hesitate and is picking up the treats before my butt has fully settled on my heals. While she is still standing close I reach out with a treat showing in my hand.

Suddenly the world shrinks and time disappears. Beauty is standing less than arms length away, tense and watching each millimeter of movement of my hand. I can almost hear her fears screaming at her to run as her desire for connection pleads with her to accept, to stay within grabbing distance, to experience receiving a gift when so vulnerable. With each millimeter of hand movement, with each choice of Beauty to trust, I fill with a bit more pride and pleasure. For the first time Beauty stays still and opens her mouth allowing me to hold the treat where all she has to do is close her mouth in acceptance. Her daintily closing her mouth stirs warmth within me. With her chewing and then swallowing the treat she allowed me to give her with my hand only an inch from her muzzle my chest fills with love and gratitude and my eyes begin to water with deep joy. As "**Oh, girl**" slips from my lips Beauty opens her energies a bit further and steps back one step. As she stands there just an arm's length away her and my emotions, hopes, and worries seem to tumble together while deep energies forged new connections of trust and acceptance. A moment, or five, or twenty and Beauty sits. Time slips back into my awareness remaining slow and unimportant.

    I break off more hotdog bits and while sitting on my heals hand each treat to Beauty. Beauty waits with open energies for me to give her each treat. My mind and ego are quiet seeming to accept that they will not understand what is happening until later. Within I am very aware of the change from Beauty choosing to take each treat to Beauty choosing to receive each treat, to allow me to give her each treat. After two more hotdogs Beauty is full of hotdogs and newness. With ease and grace she stands and steps back a couple of steps, pauses a few moments and then turns to walk away. I sit in awe and pleasure for several moments while Beauty heads towards the enclosure. Standing back up brings me fully back into the practical world. The drive home is a celebration of our deepening trust.

    The next two days Beauty and I fluctuate between her retrieving and receiving treats. Each day she spends more time so close I could easily grab her. Each moment of her staying close seems to be her testing my trust-ability. On the third day I sense it is time for more challenges. The first comes in the form of placing treats on my knees. As I place the treats on my knees Beauty is sitting about eight feet away seeming puzzled and unsure. Without thought I scan my body and notice my shoulders and chest are tense. A deep breath in and out allows me to relax and I sense a warmth spreading from my belly to my chest and out to Beauty. Beauty's head comes up maybe an inch, a pause, and she steps within arm's length. She pauses on the edge of choice, seems to scan my energies, and then she steps half a step forward and retrieves a treat from my left knee. With a bit of concentration I remain calm, feeling and not displaying the excitement stirring within me. Beauty steps back, swallows her treat, and steps forward to retrieve the treat on my right knee. I allow the warmth that fills me to flow to her. She seems pleased as she sits close enough that I can hand her treats. A first and then a second treat by hand while she sits there. Suddenly I notice I am placing three treats between my spread knees with a playful, impish intent. Beauty responds by standing, switching her tail several times, and then stepping forward to retrieve her treats. A half step back and sitting I would swear she is grinning at me as I sense playful energyies from her. Next one treat on each knee and one treat back six inches more on my thighs. Beauty surprises me by standing and taking the first two treats, eating them and then after a few seconds stepping forward to take the treats further up on my leg. As she reaches for the final treat I sense my ego protesting, "This is not safe, she can bite." With her head less than two feet from my head Beauty looks at my face and seems concerned, her ears have come down, her head is back a few inches. With a smile and chuckle at my own foolishness I hear myself saying, "**It's okay, Beauty. I am learning to trust too.**" As I realize the truth of what I have just said my mind and ego offer arguments about needing to be careful and about being right. Within my belly there is the tickle of amusement. Followed by a whispered thought of, "*Yes, we are crazy. And it is fun!*"

Over the next few days I place treats further up my legs as I kneel there sitting on my heals. I also place treats closer and closer to my crotch causing Beauty to put her muzzle and head more and more into a position where she cannot see the parts of me that might signal an intent to grab her. During the same time, each day I am touching her a bit more. She begins to wait for me to stroke her muzzle with the back of my hand after a treat. Each time I go a bit further back to her cheek, back and up to her ear, back to her neck. Sometimes it is okay, a few times she seems happy, sometimes she is not okay and she steps back, raises her head and looks right in my face. It seems I can hear her whisper in a clipped tone, "*That is not okay.*"

Lessons of Worry

As I drive out I am upset. One of my children, a young married adult, is having family problems. I am struggling with the desire to 'just fix it', the desire to honor my child's adulthood, my respect for the adults they have become, and my worry that things will not work out. When I arrive Beauty is laying in the field about 20 feet from where I park my car. Before I am parked she gets up and moves another 40 feet away. After placing her food I take treats from the car and go to kneel at my place just beyond the pavement. Beauty will not come any closer. It seems a response to my worries. While wondering why, I sense Beauty answering, *"Not safe. You're different. Not warm. Don't like."* In my body, in my energy it feels as though I have been slapped. As I notice it is simply a statement of conditions, no accusing, a second slap arrives with the realization of how cold, distant, and unavailable my worries have made me. I hear myself saying, **"I am sorry, girl."** as I take a deep breath, then a second, then a third. When I finally look back at Beauty she seem to say, *"Okay. Now I can sit here for a while."* As I drive away a few minutes later I find myself thinking, "Thank you for the lesson, girl. Wow. I had no idea how much worrying about a problem blocks me up." As I drive home I begin the process of exploring the impact worrying has had on my energies, on my openness to others, on my openness to my inner wisdom. I accept that I have a week or two of self examination ahead.

Sweetness of Surrender

April 19, 2012

Today is a rainy, drizzly day. I choose to leave Fawn at home. As I go out the back door she looks at me quizzically, *"What? I don't go?"*

When I get to the field behind the pool and spa shop I do not see Beauty at first. As I park I see her laying under a tree against a "rustic" red six foot wood fence. She watches as I get out of the car and go into enclosure where her water bowl and food bowl stay. As I step up into the enclosure I once again feel thankful that the store manager long before my arrival had afforded Beauty a safe space to eat and sometimes sleep. As I carry the food bowl out of the enclosure to my car Beauty gets up and begins wandering towards me. She comes within 20 feet, sits, and watches as I prepare her food. She sits there, relaxed, ears up, mouth open, tongue visible. Were she human I would say she is smiling at me. As I finish she moves around the old hot tub watching from between the tub and enclosure fence. I smile and speak to her, surprised and pleased that she is willing to place herself in a spot that limits her "escape" possibilities.

After preparing her food at my car I go back into the enclosure and put the now full food bowl in it's place. As I head back out of the enclosure I notice with delight Beauty has come to the enclosure entry. She backs away as I leave the enclosure, heading back to the car to get the hotdogs I have brought. As I walk from the car to the grass she delights me by scampering over close to where I kneel to give her treats. As I kneel down I feel the water from the grass seep into my pant legs. I look at a very wet Beauty and surrender to the rain, knowing I will become wetter and colder as I spend time with her in the cold, spring rain. As I look at her I notice that for the first time I am seeing her stand close to me with her tail up fully.

You see Beauty is a Chow mix, many reddish hues in her longish fur, about 75 pounds, black splotches on her tongue. For the first three months of feeding her I only saw her with her tail down, cautiously moving, usually away from me. It was only four weeks ago that I saw her walk to the food I had tossed to her with her tail out from behind her. Three weeks ago for the first time I saw her tail wag behind her as she trotted to get food I had tossed to her. Two weeks ago her tail began wagging just a bit higher than her back as she moved to me. Last week her tail began to wag just over her back. When she would sit close to me her tail would be partially up. Today it has that full curl, curling the tip all the way back down to her back. What a site! She is right there, a few feet from me, showing her beauty. There has been a change, one I find difficult to express in words. She seems more relaxed, comfortable and pleased to be close to me, trusting enough to share her beauty, her grace. I am smiling, a warmth within my heart and lower belly. What a joy to see and experience her open up, to sense her trust of 'us'.

Kneeling I place a few pieces of hotdog close to me. She steps forward to gather them and backs away. The second and third set go within inches of my knees. She hesitates and then steps in waiting a moment to see if I will drop more. After she backs away with her treats I offer her one from my extended hand. She takes a half step in to take her prize. When she steps in to take the fourth set from my hand I slowly move my hand back and gently move a finger so that it barely touches and moves the fur on her ear. As I carefully hold the deep pleasure stirring within me she hesitates and then steps back. She has allowed my hand behind her muzzle, allowed me to almost touch her. After five hotdogs she looses interest, sniffing the hotdog bits but not picking them up. She sits about five feet from me ignoring the bits of hotdog.

After a couple of minutes I get up and watch in surprise as she gets up and moves towards the enclosure with a gait that says she has a plan. My walk to the car parallels her movement. I get to the car, open the door, and look up to see her jump up into the enclosure and move to her food bowl. Surprise and delight mix within me. I watch with pleasure and satisfaction as she begins to eat. My movements are easier as I get in the car, back up, and turn to leave. When my driver's window reaches opposite her I roll down my window and shout "**Hey Beauty**". She stops eating to look up, in her gaze I feel as though she is saying, "*You can stay.*"

Back on the street, heading home, I am elated. As I drive I allow myself to sense what happened, what I experienced, to explore the subtle energies that are building and shifting. I enjoy a sense of accomplishment, my choices, Beauty's choices have brought us closer together. She is beginning to declare herself to me.

BECOMING FAMILY

April 20, 2012

When I get to the field Beauty is waiting for me, sitting right where I kneel to give her bits of hotdog. As I get out of the car I notice her open her mouth, lick her lips, and then open and close her mouth making a smacking sound. Do dogs smile? It sure looks like she is smiling, head up, ears up, looking right at me, mouth open, corners of her mouth pulled back a bit, tongue out. Most of all I sense acceptance of my presence, even a relaxed pleasure in my being there. I sense a gentle warmth within myself. After a few moments I head into the enclosure to get her food bowl then return to the car and begin mixing her food. Time to help her get more used to the car. I open both back doors and then split up a hotdog, 2 pieces on the edge of the seat, two pieces on the sill of the door, several pieces each about a foot from the other, stretching towards her. A last piece I toss close to her. I watch as she sniffs the hotdog and does not pick it up, sniffs it again, looks at me, sniffs again. A bit disappointed I head into the enclosure to place her food bowl. Once the bowl is in place I turn to watch her. She moves forward one piece of hotdog at a time, sniffing without picking it up. She get to the car, waits a bit, and then takes one piece and returns to the grass. "Well, not yet." I return to the car, get the blanket a friend loaned me and walk the fifteen feet to where Beauty is. Somehow it feels right to go directly to her for the first time.

    She gets up and moves six feet away and then sits, watching me put the blanket down and kneel. I toss her a couple of pieces one of which she catches. With a big grin on my face I recognize it is the first time she has enough trust to catch her treat! The next is about three feet

Bringing In Beauty

from me, one two feet away, another a foot away. With tail up she comes forward picking up each piece as she comes. Then she pauses looking to see if there is another. I reach out my hand and she gently takes a piece from me, then another, then another. Next I place several pieces inches from myself. She comes in eating each until she is six inches away from my knee. Again she waits for me to hand her a piece. A step back and sit. I pause and when she moves her head down and then up I offer her another piece from my hand. She steps forward to take it. Now for some work. I put several pieces in front of me all within six inches, one just between my knees. Without hesitation she comes in picking up each piece, takes one piece from my hand and retreats. Okay, again. My hands are resting on my thighs so one of her ears and the fur of her head touch me, one more from my hand and she backs away. Again, several close to me and as she picks the last one up I move a finger forward touching her ear, moving her fur. She hesitates and then steps back. A pause and I reach forward with an empty hand, fingers down. She sniffs my hand, I uncurl a finger and with the back of my fingers stroke the side of her muzzle, once, twice, three times before she steps back. I smile and with effort remain quiet, for the first time she has let me reach out and touch her without food. My elation soon turns to playfulness. I lean forward onto my hands, make a few play bows, and crawl a couple steps towards her. She jumps up and to the side, turns around and sits facing me.

She is playing and I want to keep playing. I fill myself with playful energies, stand, jump back and forth and then jump towards her. She jumps up and sideways again, her tail wagging, and moves back about twelve feet. I jump back, jump forward, jump back and forth several times and then run towards her two step. As I jump to the side she jumps back, tail at half mast, and moves away. My worry becomes relief when she stops at a distance of 25 feet, turns and sits down. She is watching me carefully. I jump back and forth a bit and then go back to the blanket and kneel. She waits, I wait. After about three minutes I notice my tension and relax and then smile as she gets up and wanders towards me stopping about five feet from me and sitting down. I am excited and thrilled within, careful to hold my movements quiet and measured. For the first time on her own she has 'come back to me'. After a few moments she gets up and saunters towards the enclosure. She seems to relax as I carefully take a deep breath and let it out. I get up and enjoy walking parallel to her, me going back to the car. She jumps into the enclosure and with relaxed movements meanders to her food bowl. There are two men standing at the back of the back door of the store, just out of Beauty's sight. Unsure what will be best for her I get into my car, back, and then move forward, roll down the window and stop to talk with her. As I look at her I want to stay a bit longer so I turn the car off and get out. Warmth fills me as Beauty rewards me by walking towards me. I have been sharing my progress with one of the men, the shopkeeper. After considering it I call to him and tell him Beauty is in the enclosure. He takes a step and bends over to see her. She notices but stays where she is, careful and watchful. As I wander over to the men she moves closer to the enclosure's entry then lays down within site of the men, partially facing us. Within I feel a sense of pride, my girl is staying close. I feel her watching me as I chat with the men. After a few exchanges and feeling pleased with their, "**Wow, she is doing better.**" I walk back to my car and the second man heads to the gate to leave. That was enough newness and closeness, Beauty gets up, slowly walks to her exit, jumps down to the pavement, and walks out into the field.

    I feel a deep satisfaction as I drive away. In the entire eight months the manager had noticed Beauty in the area she would leave the enclosure whenever he came out of the store. Today she stayed there, within 25 feet of him. So much growth! She is no longer feels a need to keep her distance from everyone. And yes, I am pleased and excited by what she and I are creating! Part way home I am struck with a realization. Somehow Beauty was showing the two men that she and I are together.

A Step Backwards

April 21, 2012

Today is a sunny and pleasant day. I feel disappointment and concern as I whistle for her at the field, a single rising note, distinct in it's simplicity. The grass in the field has become longer with spring and I hope that I will see Beauty raise her head above the grass. After a few seconds of scanning I turn to the enclosure and retrieve her food bowl. Back at the car I raise the trunk, put down the bowl and go through the process of mixing her food, canned wet food, supplements for her joints, and kibble. I feel a slight ache as I mix her food and look at the empty field. I notice the undercurrent of concern for her well being as I move to the enclosure. As I stand up from placing her bowl I sense her, in standing up my eyes seek her. I relax and smile as I see her 150 feet away at the hedge. I walk back to the car and get out the hotdogs and open my energies a bit more as I notice she is staying at the hedge. A calm puzzlement flows within me. I take the few steps to the grass, still no movement towards me. I kneel – no movement. After a minute or two I get up and cautiously walk towards her with her paying close attention to my movements. At about thirty feet I stop and toss her a bit of hotdog. She doesn't get up. Two more steps towards her, a pause, another toss. Waiting, waiting, one more toss and she gets up, moving towards the food. She smells the tidbit but does not pick it up. Okay, today is a day of her stepping back. As I allow myself to experience my worry, my sorrow, it takes several minutes for her to come closer to me and then a couple more minutes before she very carefully takes food from my out stretched hand.

It feels right to move the car closer to the grass and "invite" her closer to the car. Once the car is in position I open both back doors, put hotdog pieces on the door sill and in a six foot trail back towards her. I position myself a few feet away from the car on the side away from her. She knows the food is there and I must wait about three minutes before she moves to investigate. She follows the trail to the car, sniffs the tidbits on the car door sill, pauses a few seconds and then walks away. Hmmm... I feel myself being tempted to be despondent and carefully choose to relax and open a bit more to Beauty.

When I return to my usual place and kneel Beauty comes over and we go through a few rounds of my placing hotdog bits close to me and her coming forward to get them and then move away immediately. Her moves, my moves, seem mechanical, almost meaningless. I have a strong sense the only thing I can do that will help is to relax and remain open, to simply enjoy what she is able to share. Then she decides it is time to go into the enclosure, gets up and heads that way. With an undercurrent of sorrow I return to the car, get in, and drive to where she can see me from inside the enclosure. She turns and watches me guardedly as I say goodbye. As I leave the area I have a sense of disappointment underpinned with a sense of *"things are as they should be"*. Sorrow mixed with contentment.

Hiding, Then Returns

April 22, 2012

*W*ow, what a beautiful day, sunny, 78 degrees, the smell of flowers blooming as I drive to feed Beauty. I am full of expectations, eager to interact with Beauty. As I pull in I don't see her. Okay, not what I want, but okay. I get out of the car and whistle and whistle, hope fading with each repetition. Finally I surrender, fetch her food bowl, and bring it back to the trunk of the car. I whistle more as I fix her food. Before I begin mixing the wet food with the kibble I sense a whisper from within, *"Mix love with her food rather than sorrow."* With effort I choose to open to the love Beauty and I share and open to my mixing her food being an act of love. My ego snickers when it seems I hear her responding, *"Thank you. I need space for my confusion."* Closing the trunk I think with a bit of playfulness and regret, "Well, maybe it won't be a Beauty full day."

There are a couple of families with kids from the apartments playing on the pavement close by. One reason Beauty might not be here. It is Sunday. Last night was Saturday night so young men from the apartments across the way may have been chasing Beauty. After placing her food I walk around the field with no luck. It is early afternoon and I have not had lunch. I have a pull to stay in the area so I drive out into the neighborhood to find someplace to eat. While eating I take my time, sensing the bond I share with Beauty, hoping Beauty will be at the field when I return. No such luck. The families have returned to the courtyard of the apartments so it is quieter. Still no Beauty. In the car, on the way home, I am concerned and worried. This is the first time in two weeks that Beauty has not showed up. I find myself thinking, "I may need to come back tonight."

I chat with Ute, my rescue friend, that evening on the phone. She expresses concern that echos my concern. As she says, "Maybe you should go back out tonight." I feel my energies moving towards the car, opening the path. "Yeah, I am going back out." "Oh, good. Call me if anything happens."

I decide to take Fawn with me and as I drive Fawn sits next to me letting me know she would like attention. As I drive and pet her I have a sense that I am doing what is to be done, a sense of deep quiet within my belly. The flower scented breeze from the rolled down windows adds to my sense of well being.

I turn off the main road wondering what I will find. As my headlights sweep the enclosure and I see Beauty standing inside the enclosure my worry shifts to excitement. As I drive to park in my usual spot Beauty watches carefully. As I get out of my parked car I call to Beauty and am rewarded with the sight of her relaxing her stance, her head raising a bit, her tail coming up and wagging. In my energies I sense her relief and pleasure at my showing up. Still a bit unsure how open she will be I enter the enclosure carefully with measured steps. She is sitting as I walk fifteen of the thirty five feet that separate us. As I move forward I throw her a couple of pieces of hotdog. She sniffs but does not pick them up. I kneel and drop a piece about half the distance between us. She waits while I put a second piece a bit closer to me. My building uncertainty shifts to hope when she stands and moves in close to me. When she looks up I reach out my hand with a piece of hotdog, the love and concern that flows out to her is palpable to me. I sense her cautiously welcoming my love and concern with sorrow as she cautiously steps forward and takes her treat. Her staying close as I break off a second piece and offer it to her, her daintily taking it seems a signal of her surrendering to the deep connections we both yearn to share. One more piece and she backs up. I shift to my left hip using my left arm to support myself in a semi sitting position, carefully showing no intent to pursue her, only a desire to invite her. I smile as she comes in close and stays close as I break off pieces of hotdog and hand them to her. I shift my position a bit and playfully drop a hotdog in some lattice lying on the ground, she backs up and the comes forward again sniffing to try to find the piece of hotdog. I know she won't be able to get the piece and think to pull the small flashlight out of my pocket. When I turn the flashlight on she immediately backs away and slinks back under the protection of the deck. Her energy withdraws with her. Watching her uncertainty and sensing her causes me to realize that people have used flashlights when they tried to catch her at night. At the same time I feel gratitude for the understanding and regret for my causing Beauty fear. I hear myself saying, "**Oh girl, I am sorry**." as I retrieve the piece of hotdog and put the flashlight away. I am relieved I did not shine the light of the flashlight on her. I sit for three very long minutes before it feels okay to move where I can entice her out of her protective space. Two minutes and five pieces of tossed hotdog later she rewards me as she steps out from under the deck and forward for more treats. Perhaps you can remember a time when worry was gently eased by wonder, hope, pleasure, a sense you have done well, when you have allowed love and concern to guide your choices. That is what I am feeling in these moments.

Soon she is done. As she moves back under the deck and lays down I feel sorrow for her uncertainties, relief in her bit of recovery, and gratitude that she is showing me trust even as my actions trigger her fears. Something within me catches me before my intent to stand begins. A breath, two breaths, and I hear my tone and rhythm reflect my concern as I fill the air between us with words of support. As I whisper things such as, "**Oh, Beauty, thank you for trusting me. I am so glad we connect.**" and other things. I sense my ego protesting, "It sure is good no-one is around. Otherwise funny farm for sure!"

Within a couple minutes I sense Beauty's energy pushing me away, a request for space. As happily and quietly as I can I whisper, "**Okay girl. I will see you tomorrow.**" I get up, walk to the exit, and as I jump down I am surprised to sense Beauty's energies enveloping me and then flowing in to fill my body with warmth. My mind protests. My ego assures me I am crazy. And I grin and seem lighter as I almost skip back to the car. I sense Beauty with me as I drive to the entry for the business. As I turn onto the street she disappears. Several times on the way home I search for her, unable to sense her each time. I am worried and know I must simply give her space.

HER APPROACH

Wednesday, April 25, 2012

I didn't write on Monday or Tuesday. Now I don't feel much like trying to recall those two days. I feel sorrow and uncertainty after today's visit. Last night when I was chatting with a friend and wondering how to move forward with Beauty I felt it was important to have a leash with me and to show it to her. When I arrive I park my car and do not see Beauty. I whistle several times as I retrieve her food bowl and mix her food. I look up from the car to head into the enclosure. I am suddenly happy when I see her at the hedge. I place her food bowl and empty a bottle of water into her water bowl. I go back to the car, pop the trunk, and open the cooler with the hotdogs in it. I get a few hotdogs, close the trunk, and then get the leash from the passenger compartment. Beauty is about 140 feet from me and I head directly to her. She waits and watches. When I am about 30 feet from her I slow and shift my walking so I am not walking directly to her. At 16 feet or so I stop. When I kneel, Beauty gets up and moves towards me. I pull the leash from around my neck and she immediately stops, pauses a few seconds, turned her back and walks away. She does not stop when I call her name. Finally she stops. We both sit looking at each other. I throw a few pieces of hotdog which she ignores. After about 3 minutes I get up, pick up the leash and take it back to the car. I walk back to within 30 feet of Beauty and sit down. She does not move to the bits of hotdog I toss towards her. I get to my knees and move within 15 feet of her. There we sit for several minutes. Finally she get up and moves away, stopping just before going out of sight. The trust carefully built seems to have evaporated with my showing Beauty the leash. I get up and wander back to the car. Part of me wants to be anger to avoid the sorrow and disappointment I feel. Other parts of me want to make up a story about it being over. Deep within there is simply the sense that tomorrow will be another day of uncertainty. How will she respond tomorrow? Will I have to wait a few days to see her again? All I know now is I am tender and unsure of what success I might have. Tomorrow I will come again hoping the trust can be rebuilt.

WORK TO DO WITH FAWN

Thursday April 26th

I am unsure what I will find today. I have decided to bring Fawn with me. During the drive I listen to a lectures on CD and stay away from worrying by reminding myself I do not know what I will find. When I turn onto the pavement bordering the field I am surprised to see Beauty walking on the pavement right in front of me. As she hurries her pace I quickly rolled down my window hoping she will stop when she knows it is me. I whistle, she stops, turns around. As I turn to park I come into view in the driver side window. When I see her relax and lay down I relax, relieved she is there. She lays down on the pavement about five feet from the field. As I get out of the car she meets my gaze, head high, mouth open. I have made it a habit to talk to her and tell her I am happy to see her. As I head to get her food bowl I wonder whether she will stay where she is laying, less than 15 feet from the trunk of the car. She watches me get her bowl and return to the car, go to the trunk to mix her food. She watches me with her usual occasional look in each direction to check for activity. I feel both relief and warmth each time I look up, she is laying closer to me while mixing her food than she has ever been. I place her food and return to the trunk to get treats wondering how close she will come for them.

From the trunk I toss her a couple of pieces of hotdog and a couple of new treats I bought for her. She comes closer, sniffs each one but does not pick any up. I decide to take only one hotdog and watch her move to the right as I walk to the field. She moves about 10 feet ahead of me. Her 'taking the lead' pleases me in ways I cannot explain. When I kneel down at my usual place she walks to just in front of me and does a play bow, tail high and wagging, mouth open, tongue out. I chuckle with pleasure and play bow to her. She does one more bow and sits just five feet from me, facing me. In the back of my mind I recognize she is carefully being separate and connected. She finally eats the third piece of hotdog I toss to her. Game on! I lean forward and place a piece half way between us. As I straighten back up she comes forward, picks up the piece, and eats it. To my delight she stays close and takes several pieces from my outstretched hand.

Within a couple of minutes the hotdog is gone. She backs up and sits only four feet from me. Within I experience a conflict of safely enjoying the new firsts of today and continuing to challenge Beauty for more. I talk to her as I turn and get up. To my surprise she stays seated as I get up. Another first. As I retrieve the remaining three hotdogs in the package at the car she lazily gets up to watch me. When I return to kneel again she lets me walk within six feet of her. I am floating between wonder and worry as I place a couple of pieces close to me, she comes within a foot of me and stays to take several pieces from my hand. She then backs up and sits just within arms length. In the past she would not stay seated if I leaned towards her to hand her food. It feels like time to try again. To my great pleasure she waits as I lean forward and stretch out my hand. After a moments pause she stretches her neck slightly forward and takes first one, then a second, then a third piece. As I lean back she gets up, takes two steps back, and sits. Grinning I take out another hotdog and place two pieces close to me. She comes in and stays in as five times I break off a piece and hand it to her. Then she backs up and sit. After a minutes pause I repeat the same and feel warmth spread through me as she takes eight pieces before retreating. When I started I had both hands close to my body, just reaching out my left hand to give her a piece. With each piece I let the hand not holding the hot dog move closer to her. I place two more pieces on the ground, leaving both hands on my legs just above my knees. Without words her energy whispers, "*You challenge me. I will trust.*" and she comes in cautiously. As she raises her head from eating the second piece I roll my left hand over and out two inches offering her a piece. She take it and waits for another. I will never be able to fully express the wonder, the pleasure, the openness, the gently acceptance and love we share as she stays right there, inches from me, both of my hands inches from her muzzle, taking one, then two, then three, then seven more pieces before stepping back. With each piece I feed her I feel myself soften and open a bit more. In my mind I sense from within, *"Food and love, given and received, trust deepens."*

I am down to one last hot dog. Time to play. She is sitting only four feet from me, too close for a play bow towards her. I turn a little to the left, reached out with my right hand and patted the ground several times. She tilts her head slightly, curious and uncertain. When I bow and bounce back up she does the same, her feet coming off the ground at least two feet. As I bow a second time I realize she has an advantage, I lack a tail to raise high and wag happily. I turn back towards her, play bow and then crawl towards her one emphatic step, a pause, then a second. She scampers a few feet away, turns and looks at me expectantly. I jump back and forth, then towards her. She bows down, darts her head left and then right, jumps up and scampers further from me. Too far to crawl now, I get up, bend towards her, jump back a forth and run a few steps towards her. I have slipped beyond thought, each move seems guided by her wisdom and mine, by the love we wish to playfully express. She moves left, then right, jumps high, and runs a bit further from me. Then I jump back and forth and run towards her veering away from her after a few steps. She jumps back and forth and trots a bit further away. She is now about forty feet from me and I am breathing hard. She watches as I walk back and kneel in my usual place.

She watches me from afar. I wait, hoping she will come to me. After a couple of minutes I consider tossing some hotdog bits but then decide to get Fawn out of the car. As I walk to the car Beauty comes closer. I put Fawn on her leash and let her jump out of the car. Beauty is bit surprised, turns, and walks several feet away before turning and sitting. I smile noticing Fawn is carefully ignoring Beauty. Beauty watches as Fawn and I head out into the field. When Fawn and I are a couple hundred feet into the field I turn and see that Beauty is not in sight. Both worry and the possibility that Beauty went into the enclosure come into my awareness at the same time. Fawn and I head back to the car. When we are close to the car I see Beauty in the enclosure, under the deck. With a thought of 'Oh, good.' I relax a bit and notice how love and openness seems to flow between Beauty and I. As I put Fawn in the car I talk with her, pet her, reassure her she is still my dog. She remains connected with me as I go into the enclosure to share a few pieces of hotdog with Beauty. Beauty is cautious and will only come within three feet of me. Still it feels good. Suddenly I know it is time to end our sharing, Beauty has somehow let me know she is done, she is full. With both sorrow and certainty I return to the car, say goodbye, and drive off. As I leave the area, I am pleased with where things are, the fun of playing with Beauty plays in my memory as warmth dances within me. I am also relieved, less worried that I won't succeed in creating an environment that will allow Beauty to fully trust me.

I am concerned with how I will, how Beauty will, make the transition into coming home with me. I can sense something stirring within me, a method, a process to create the transition. My lower belly is relaxed, my heart is content. In contrast my mind and ego are busy raising questions about whether I will ever "succeed".

Three in a Row

Friday, April 27th

*O*nce again I am rewarded by the sight of Beauty on the pavement when I arrive. She seems to be wandering, looking for me. This time when I drive into sight she looks more expectant, less relaxed which cause me to smile. She watches me park with movements that seem to me both relaxed and expectant. As I get out of my car she positions herself about 18 feet from the back of the car and sits down. I happily do the usual retrieving of her food bowl, returning to the trunk of the car to mix her food. Beauty lays there seeming to watch with approval. Once the food is mixed I take out a hotdog, and from the trunk of the car break off a couple of pieces and throw them to her. As usual she sniffs them but does not pick them up. With her food bowl in one hand and a small ball of wet dog food I walk in her direction. About ten feet from her I slow, take one more step, turn and put down the ball of food. As I approach she tenses, sits up, and just as I turn from her she stands up. I smile as I walk to the enclosure and see her approach the wet food, sniff it, and after a pause, take it into her mouth. As I watch I notice intricacies that had not registered before. Gentle awe and pleasure flow within me as I notice that Beauty laid down with relaxed, accepting expectancy while I made her food. There was a feeling her 'being at home' while I fixed her food.

And as I stand in the enclosure watching Beauty I recognize what leaving her the lump of wet food had been about, that quiet wisdom had a purpose. Beauty has always received the food I prepared for her in the enclosure, under the deck. As her picking up the lump of wet food in the field plays in my body's memory I notice she is creating new possibilities in her awareness. She can receive her food in places other than under the deck. I smile as I notice how new possibilities now exist in her awareness. I can give and she can receive sustenance in places other than the enclosure. I also notice traces of worry within myself. Am I really ready for her to be in my home? Something is still pushing me away from allowing that to happen.

Returning to the trunk of the car after placing her food I get out the hotdogs and head to the usual place and kneel. She immediately comes over and sits about six feet from me. There is a warmth and acceptance about her and I wonder again if dogs smile as I look at her sitting close, mouth open, the tip of her tongue just showing. With her already close I break off a piece of hotdog and extend my hand towards her hoping she will take the tidbit without the usual gradual enticement to approach. I am disappointed but not surprised when she simply sits there watching me. So begins what has become the routine, my breaking up three or four hotdogs and giving her pieces in various ways. When the last hotdog is almost gone, she is sitting about three feet from me. She has already allowed me to lean over and stretch out my hand to give her a tidbit. The last time I break off three tidbits into my left hand. I lean forward and give her the first treat, leaving my arm outstretched after she gingerly takes the treat I offer. As she lowers her head to eat it I roll the second tidbit into my fingers as an offering. I hold my breath and carefully, hopefully hold my energy still. When she raises her head she is a little startled to find my hand close to her head. In the moment she considers moving back she smells and sees the tidbit, pauses, seems to relax a bit and then stretches her head the six inches needed to take the treat. Grinning with excitement I leave my hand in place and roll the third treat into my fingers. She raises her head, considers what to do and reaches again to take the offered tidbit. I lower my hand as she enjoys her treat and I sense within myself what seems her whispering to me, "*scary good*". I find myself grinning as I sense myself floating an energetic, "*And you like it.*" to her. My grin broadens as I notice her ears come forward a bit more, her mouth opens a bit more, and I sense "*I like*" from her. Once again I find myself wondering, "Do dogs smile?"

Having fed her four hotdogs it is time to play. As I have before I lean forward onto all fours and do a play bow. I am rewarded by her tail coming up and beginning to wag as she jumps away. Our play is very much like yesterday's play except she allows me to crawl a bit closer before jumping away from me. For the first time I have the sense of playing with my dog. My mind grudgingly accepts my sense that our efforts are succeeding. I seem to sense her intent before she moves, it seems she want to give me a chance to get closer. As I become tired it seems Beauty is inviting me to keep playing and so I push myself to play a bit longer. Within a few moments I am surprised to realize we are playing now based on her invitation. With the realizations come a flood of warmth that somehow opens new bonds between us.

After play I get Fawn out of the car and take her for a long walk in the field. I am pleased and relieved as I noticed that Fawn is much less focused on Beauty. I am also pleased to see Beauty come over to where Fawn has peed and carefully sniff the ground. Back at the car, with Fawn already in the car, I put the treats back in the trunk. I notice the leash and decided to show it to Beauty who is about twenty five feet away. I lift the leash into Beauty's view. Concern sweeps through me as I see Beauty's posture stiffen and her urgent turn to get away the instance she sees the leash. With my whistle, she glances back at me just as I toss the leash into the trunk. Connecting with her movements I sense curiosity mixing with her barely controllable terror. Deep sorrow and concern flood through me as I realize there is much more work to do. As I get into the car I have a sense of Beauty being restrained on a leash, a man's hand locked on the leash where it is clipped to her collar as in rage he strikes her rump again and again with the other end of the leash. I feel anger at the person, sorrow for her suffering, and love's warmth flow to her with the hope she will open to things being different with me. It is almost a year later when due to what is happening at the moment I realize that somehow the man's rage had clamped into Beauty's energy. With concern I find myself wondering how many times during my earlier years I had clamped my rage into someone else.

In sitting with Beauty's responses and in talking with my friend I come to recognize that Beauty is only comfortable with what she has already experienced. Any change in our routine causes her to be more cautious and more tentative in her movements towards me. With that realization I also recognize that I need to carefully extend how and what we do, always changing in small increments. If I want to have her allow even one new behavior I will need to park the car in the same spot, and kneel in the usual place, move with the same movements when mixing her food and placing it. My mind carefully ignores a gentle warmth with the feel of Beauty that flows into my belly.

Tomorrow I will make a change. I have been initiating play after the hotdogs are gone, when Beauty has little remaining appetite. At the end of each play session Beauty has been forty or more feet from me with no motivation to come closer. Tomorrow I will initiate play after she has had only one hotdog. Hopefully after play she will choose to come close again for additional treats. Also I will work on training her to accept treats other than hotdog bits and chicken. I have strange sensations as I recognize that my mind, ego, and inner wisdom have just blended together to create our 'next steps'.

HIDING FROM YOUNG HUNTERS

Saturday, April 28th

*A*s I drive to spend time with Beauty I sense that today I will not see her. She is hiding in one of her other areas, areas she has kept hidden from me. I sense that she has chosen to retreat with the first signs of the young hunters' energies the night before. She will wait until the dark hours of Sunday morning to return to the field and enclosure.

As expected she is not at the field and does not respond to my whistles. As I place her bowl my mind protests when I experience a whisper of *'thank you. I will wait. It is less scary here.'* As I drive home my mind and ego busily inform me I am not to ever share what I just experienced.

Startled into Flight

Sunday, April 29th

*W*ow! What a visit! I will do my best to share what occurred. Please know that much of what I experienced is beyond what words can carry. Hopefully my words will provide a starting place, a pointer you can trace with your energies. Perhaps as you read you will notice stirrings within.

As I turn into the paved area I can not see Beauty and feel a bit of disappointment thinking, "perhaps not today". As I get out of the car I whistle and as I turn towards the enclosure I notice Beauty standing inside the enclosure her head extending from under the deck. As warmth flows through me I hear myself saying, "**Well hello there girl**." Her response is to take one step out from under the deck. Yes, I use 'girl'. It feels much better than 'bitch'. (grin) I hesitate, not sure how she will react to my approach. A deep quieting breath and I begin walking to the enclosure opening. As I round the hot tub sitting just outside the enclosure Beauty comes towards me a couple of steps. Surprised I slip into that space of extended awareness where things are not quite real, where time no longer matters. As I step up into the enclosure she takes another couple of steps towards me, stepping up onto a wood platform between us, tail up and wagging, head and ears up. "**Oh girl, yes.**" I take a couple more steps towards her bowl, not towards her, and she starts to take a step towards me. The world disappears, all that exist is Beauty, me, and the few feet around us. The draw between us is palpable. As she does a step forward, then a step back I hear her whimper. With quiet excitement I turn partially sideways to her saying, "**Good girl**." She takes another step forward, steps back, a moments pause, her head lowers. Still sideways to her I extend my hand, palm towards me, fingers down. She shifts her weight left and then right and sits down. I feel a strong, almost urgent, desire to reach beyond the fear that separates us, to touch her. "**You're so beautiful. Thank you girl.**" A few seconds pause, an eternity dancing on the edge of change . "**Your incredible.**" Then the spell is broken, she draws back her energy and seems unsure whether to stay or retreat under the deck. A couple of breaths as trust seems to be replaced with gentle fear and I gently, without thought, move towards the bowl. Energies and emotions tumble within me, joy, pleasure, wonder, gratitude, worry. I pick up her food bowl noticing it will not need to be cleaned. A glance to her water bowl shows I will need to give her more water. The practical decision of carrying the water bowl back to the car shifts me more into the practical world. I pick it up and head to the car. With each step I sense Beauty and I's connections shifting and changing. There is less need and more choice. There is less fear and more hope. What we do now no longer involves other people's expectations. My mind and ego worry as they realize Beauty has chosen me as hers and I have dropped the expectations of others and have taken her as mine.

The raising trunk blocks Beauty from my view as I begin mixing her food. Halfway done with my task I shift to look over the trunk lid and see she is still in the enclosure, she is standing facing me. "**Hi girl.**" She moves towards the enclosure entry as I go back to mixing her food. One step from completion I look over the raised trunk lid again and see her jump down out of the enclosure and come towards me between the enclosure fence and hot tub. She stops at the edge of the hot tub, a couple of feet from the front right bumper of my car. When I look at her I sense, "*waiting here.*" from her. As I finish the food and then pour water into her bowl I wonder how she is going to respond as I move towards her to get to the enclosure entry. I step to the right side of the car from behind it and begin walking right towards her. She slowly gets up. As I pass the front passenger door she turns back to the enclosure. Her movements, her choice fill me with quiet wonder. As I reach the hot tub she turns and gracefully jumps into the enclosure. As she jumps my wonder turning to awe. As I step up into the enclosure warmth fills me, "*She waited for me and led the way into the enclosure.*" Somehow the reality she and I share has shifted far more than I can understand. It will be a few days before I sense all that has changed. Deep, deep within I sense that the future has shifted, she is no longer guardedly allowing our bond to deepen, she has begun leading the process. In the still, silent moments that follow, I sense her invitation, her request, her sharing of her yearnings for us to blend our souls' love, for there to be her, me, and us. As warmth fills me I notice 'us' has always been my desire. With a gentle jolt I also accept 'us' has always been my soul's intent.

As I return to the car I realize that "sharing of the treats" is going to happen in the enclosure. My mind offers, "That will be different" At the trunk I take four hotdogs and a couple of each of the treats I have bought hoping Beauty will like them. Back in the enclosure I lay down and put a piece of hotdog on the wood platform laying on the ground. Beauty watches from under the deck staying back just under the deck, a couple of feet from my offering. I toss her a tidbit which she sniffs and finally eats. There is a net for cleaning swimming pools close to Beauty, in the way of her coming forward. I reach over, pick it up and watch in surprise and regret as Beauty crouches, slink backwards, turns and heads out of the enclosure. I call to her. As she continues her retreat I sense from her, "*Too much new. Too much new.*" With regret and resignation I watch her move 40 feet, then 50, then 60, my worry growing with the growing distance between us. Seventy, eighty, ninety, "Is she slowing?". I holler to her. She turns her head but keeps moving away. As I step out to the enclosure, 120, 130, 140, and she finally turns and looks at me, standing, ready to turn away. I am encouraged by her staying where she is as I walk across the pavement to the field. I wave a hotdog in the air and talk to her, **"How about me moving here?"** as I take the few steps to where I usually give her treats. She is watching, body ridged, all but her head turned away from me. I kneel, take a deep breath, relax my body posture. She responds by turning towards me and sitting, her body still tense. I gratefully engage all the training I have had on how to relax, open, shape an empty space within, and flow love energies into that space.

As I sit there hoping she will relax I marvel at how she has gone from signs of needing to be close to signs of complete distrust. After a couple of minutes she relaxes her body. A few seconds later her mouth opens, she shifts to face me directly, and her ears go up. I watch her, waiting for something that will let me know she is ready to approach me. I can't say how much it is the energy I sense from her and how much it is the shift in her body and her tongue coming out, I just know it is time. I tear off a chunk of hot dog that I can toss much of the distance between us. "**Here you go, Beauty**." I toss the hotdog underhanded and am rewarded by her staying seated and watching the chunk's arc. The hotdog hits the ground, she does not move. Okay. A minute later I toss a second chunk. This time she stands and moves towards the chunk and me. As she sniffs around I holler to her and toss a third chunk about twenty feet from me. I smile as I see her trot to it. Game is on! Cool!

What follows is tossing, handing, and laying out of pieces of hot dog much as has occurred before. At one point I put four pieces of hotdog inches from myself and add one each of four different treats. Beauty comes forward. Quickly eats the hotdog pieces and then spends a couple of minutes sniffing one and then another and then another treat. Finally she picks up one treat and eats it. One more sniff of the remaining three and she retreats. As she retreats I sigh with relief, finally she has taken something other than hotdog or chicken! By the end of the four hotdogs Beauty is more relaxed and comes in within inches of me and is taking pieces from my hand.

As I drive away I wonder at the scope of response during the visit. Such expressions of trust, so many choices to be close. Then near terror, Beauty quickly walking to get far, far away from me. Her stopping 2/3rds of the way across the field. Her waiting, choosing to release her fears, and finally deciding to cautiously come to me. Finally as the fear dissipates, replaced by guarded trust, her coming in and staying within five feet of me. I am deeply touched that she has allowed me to hold loving space for her, supporting her in shifting from her fright to trust and connection. There are stirrings deep within my belly, some group of awareness is rearranging and filtering itself so my heart, mind, and ego can understand the small bits they will need. I grin as I wonder how many moments, minutes, hours, or even days it will be before those small bits are in my consciousness.

As I drive home I sense within my body the energies playing when Beauty was in the enclosure, shifting from one foot to the other, and

Bringing In Beauty

then whimpering. I sense her urgency, her desire to be touched. As I notice the energies that were dancing within me I wince. Within I knew she was inviting me to touch her yet my mind and ego were unwilling to surrender to her offers. I sense my fear of exposure, my fear of the flood of energies surrendering to what she and I both want would bring. In quiet dismay I accept that I do not yet fully trust Beauty, accept I am avoiding the pain, sorrow, and joy opening fully to her will bring. I am curious and uncertain as I sense the simple truths with no need for judgment, mostly a desire to understand.

ROLLER COASTER OF FEELINGS

Monday, April 30th

In the last 24 hours I have visited Beauty three times, last night about 7:30, this afternoon at 2, and tonight at 7:45. What a roller coaster it has been. A week or so ago I had a sense that it was time to begin visiting Beauty twice on some days. After yesterday afternoon's events it felt right to make a second visit. I drove out still feeling pleasure from the afternoon visit.

As I get within a mile of the location I feel some doubts. As I turn into the parking area I see Beauty laying in the field over a hundred feet from the pavement. She watches as I park the car and get out. I take a few hotdogs out of the trunk and turn towards the field. As I cross into the grass she gets up, stretches, pauses, and then lays back down. That concerns me. For more than two weeks if she was out in the field she would get up, stretch, and then walk towards me. My concern deepens when after I have taken a few steps towards her she gets up and turns away from me. I stop and holler, **"Hey girl, what is going on?"** She stops, pauses, and turn back towards me. It feel like we have slipped back four weeks. Her distance, both physically and energetically, bring forth sorrow, yearning, and uncertainty in me. Like a hunter I set my feelings aside and key into how to create what Beauty needs. **"Hey girl, want some?"** I tear off a larger piece of hot dog and toss it towards her. The hotdog travels less than 1/3 of the 80 feet between us. She watches but does not move. Okay, a second piece makes it half way to her. Still no movement. It is not working. Okay, careful, deliberate steps towards her watching for any signs. After 8 to 10 steps she gets up, turning slightly away from me. I stop and talk to her. I break off another piece of hot dog, holler "**Hey girl.**" and swing my arm as if tossing the piece. She turns back and watches me. She takes four steps sniffs it and backs up two steps. Three more pieces have the same results. Discouraged and uncertain of what to do I decide to head home. I am discouraged and feel empty. With effort just before I get into the car I turn and holler to Beauty that I will see her the next day. On the drive home part of me wants to be angry, at her, at myself, at the people who destroyed her trust in people. Part of me simply feels empty and resigned, a vast nothingness. Deep within I sense that things are okay, like before Beauty has stepped back after making progress. I am careful to choose sensing that things are okay again and again and again. As I make the final turn close to my house I simply accept the empty feelings, the uncertainty. At home I consider calling my friend. It does not feel right. For whatever reason I am to be with the emptiness and uncertainty.

The next day when I head back to the area Beauty lives in I am aware that I have no way of predicting what I will find. As I turn into the parking area I am pleased to see Beauty, discouraged that she is about 80 feet out into the field, better than last night but still far from the pavement where she has recently been waiting for me. She stays where she is, laying there watching me as I retrieve her food bowl and mix her food. As I head towards the enclosure to place her food bowl she sits up to watch. Back at the car I get a couple hotdogs and a few other treats. I cross the pavement to my usual kneeling spot and am rewarded by her getting up, stretching, and walking part of the distance between us. She sits down 60 feet from me. I toss three pieces of hot dog but she does not move. Frustrated I get up and slowly walk towards her. When I get about 40 feet from her she gets up and backs up a bit. Without thinking I stop and kneel down, she stops and sits down. Over the next ten minutes I throw a dozen pieces of hot dog. She comes within 20 feet of me before stopping and sitting down. She remains seated as another 12 pieces decorate the ground between she and I. Okay, breath, relax, let go, open up, wait, shape space for her to respond into. After five long, long minutes I get up and return to my car. Once again different aspects of me offer their view of how I should react. From within I sense a *"respond, stay open, notice, allow what is"* within the emptiness, the sorrow, and the uncertainty.

In the evening I respond to a gentle pull to go back to the field. Driving out I wonder just why I am going and find only reasons that bounce along the surface of my awareness. One in particular makes me smile, "It is better than watching TV."

When I turn into the parking area the sun has set, darkness is overcoming the faint light. I don't see Beauty in the field or under the deck in the enclosure. As I turn to park I roll down the window and whistle. As the car rolls to a stop the driver's window faces the field, the windshield faces past the enclosure opening and the Quonset hut just beyond. A bit discouraged I get out of the car, whistle again, and turn to look into the enclosure over the roof of the car. I am almost startled, there she is, sitting on the deck as close to the car as possible, her head slightly higher than mine. Surprise turns to pleasure as I sense her presence, she is displaying herself to me, more exposed than she has ever been.

For many seconds I lean on the roof of the car, seeing her, feeling her, sensing her openness. She is sitting, head high, mouth open, tongue out, looking right at me. Were she a person I would have expected to hear, "I am here."

I turn to the trunk, get a couple hotdogs, and head to the enclosure opening. As I stand at the enclosure I say, "**Hey there**." and wonder whether she will stay where she is or back away. I am pleased and a bit awed that she stands there as I step up into the enclosure and walk the 10 feet to the platform just below the deck. She is within 5 feet of me. I am flooded with warmth and pleasure as deep from within floats the realization, *'new trust! I am standing close to her, she invited me!'* Time slips away as she and I seem to shift into ceremony, the inner changes being reflected in the physical and energetic worlds we share. I break off and place one, then two, then three hotdog pieces, my offering. She steps forward to sniff them, acknowledging my offer, my request that she accept. After a brief pause she eats each one, once, twice, three times she accepts my offerings.

With her standing on the deck the top on her head is just below my chin level. I sense how our physical positions reflect her choice to be in front of me only slightly below my authority. I smile, close to tears, as I sense her energy whispering, "*Yes, I choose to have you stand before me, a part*

Bringing In Beauty

of my life." I hold a piece of hotdog out, an offering. She pauses, seems to whisper, *'choice is mine'* and then stretches her neck a bit to take it, *'I move to accept your offer'*. Another piece accepted and she retreats, *'only when I choose'*. After I place a couple pieces on the deck, each closer to me and sense within my body, *'come closer, my love'*, she comes forward eating each *'I take your offering within'* and then sitting four feet from me, *'I relax into being close'*. Five time I break off a piece, stretch my hand towards her. Each time I sense myself accepting more of her offer of more intimacy, more trust, more of herself. As she takes each piece while sitting close to me I sense her and my energies blending shaping an 'us' that reaches into the future. When I extend my hand towards her the sixth time she backs up a couple feet and sits again. Her energies whisper, *'I will choose'* within me. When I stretch to hand her another piece she gets up and backs a bit further away. And so it goes, we have begun a dance of discovery. Sometimes she easily responds to my lead. Sometimes she retains her choice. At one point, when she is within 4 feet of me I raise my hand and playfully, slowly wave my empty hand in front of her inches from her muzzle. She stays where she is, curious and relaxed and just a bit playful. Beauty's ears come up as our first intimate play fills me with warmth and tenderness. When the second hotdog is almost gone I place pieces on the deck within 18 inches of me and keep the five final pieces in my hand. Our dance is suddenly more intimate as she comes forward and staying within 2 feet of me takes four of the five pieces from my hand. She back up two feet sits and takes the final piece from my outstretched hand. Her energy seems to whisper to me, *'the dance has ended, the intimacy is just beginning'*. Two, perhaps three minutes later time slips back into my awareness. Suddenly I am very aware of Beauty sitting less than four feet from me, us within the enclosure after business hours, the sounds from the street. 'Time to go' filters into my awareness from deep within. As I carefully take a couple of steps backward it seems that Beauty is claiming herself, claiming her right to be who she is, where she is. Deep within I sense myself acknowledging her claim with a bit of awe. In those moments she is Beauty. As awe fills me I barely notice my return to the car. As I swing my body into the car I reenter the 'normal' world.

As I start the car my mind and ego take over as deep, deep energies play within. I feel great. The setback has been resolved and new territory has been explored. I am delighted that Beauty met me in such an open and exposed way. The sorrow is gone, the emptiness filled with wonder, the uncertainty has but a little sting. I enjoy a relaxed drive home. My ego is delighted with what it calls success.

Others Want Her

May 1st

It is the first day in May. As I drive out to feed Beauty I reminisce about May Day celebrations I had seen in various films and news broadcasts. Days are warmer and kneeling to interact with Beauty brings only a cool wetness to my knees. As I think about the improving weather slipping into Summer I sense Summer days when Beauty will live in the dome with me. Oh, I live in a geodesic dome I designed and built thus the reference to 'the dome'. Sensing Beauty with me in the dome draws me into a semi-meditation where I sense subtle energies stirring within my lower belly, within my body. What I sense is end of May at the earliest, probably not, middle of July, probably, mid June, maybe, mid August, yes. From within come body sensations of new activities that will be important. First full touch, first petting, sitting with me as I pet her, handling her collar, first time on leash. Suddenly I am in the middle of considering how I will transition to Beauty being in physically connection with me. Her terror when she first unexpectedly saw the leash plays through my body and I know I will not be able to use a leash. As I wait at the left turn signal to turn in to feed Beauty the problem slips into the background, my focus is now, is with Beauty.

As I drive past the enclosure to park I notice Beauty's energies and do not see her. As I get out of the car and look across the car roof my energy jumps as I notice her energy drawing my eyes to her. She is in the enclosure sitting at the end of the deck, away from the entry I use. I grin as I notice that the railing around most of the deck will be in between she and I as I retrieve her food bowl, make her food, and return it to it's place under the deck. As the awareness completes in my body I seem to sense Beauty's energies showing me that she expects just that to happen.

As I stand with her food bowl and head towards the entrance Beauty surprises me by getting up, jumping off the deck and following me towards the entrance. I jump down out of the enclosure, take a few steps to get beyond an old hot tub and glance back as I turn left towards the car. A smile fills me as I see Beauty step up on the platform just inside the entrance to the enclosure. My pleasure deepens when Beauty with tail up and wagging sits and then lies down on the platform. I notice she is close to the deck, furthest from the entrance. Without thought I assess her easy access to slip under the deck, away from me. As she watches me I have a sense in my body of her whispering, '*trust more, want more, risk more, need safe*'. I quiet further as I sense her slight surrender, '*towards you my people*' gentle warmth filling my chest as her yearning blends with my hopes. As I take the last steps and reach to pop the trunk my mind and ego come forward and scan the area for possible threats. Within I sense how with her invitation I have expanded my energy to shape a space we share, how I carefully monitor for any possible threats impinging upon 'our space'. A thousand subtle stirrings are shaping changes within me, between Beauty and I.

With the food mixed and the closing of the trunk my attention shifts and a new exploring of boundaries begins. Beauty is laying where I must step up into the enclosure directly towards her. I am aware of my mind and ego tussling with my instincts for control. As I raise my left foot to step up into the enclosure the space shrinks to the 20 feet between Beauty and I. Both of us are tingling with tensions that somehow link us together. As my weight begins it's upward movement Beauty sits up and turns slightly towards the underside of the deck. As her head turns back to look at me she seems to be grinning at my caution. I relax a bit and loop to the right, swinging out and back in to lean down and drop her bowl just under the deck. When I turn back towards Beauty and the entrance I notice Beauty has turned to face me. My mind and ego scramble for 'an approach' and in slight confusion surrender to an inner whisper of, '*relax and see what happens*' followed by tension draining out of my body. As this is happening I notice Beauty has closed her mouth and drawn her ears back. As I relax so does Beauty. Is that a playfulness I sense? Her ears come back forward and her mouth opens.

As I round the end of the deck Beauty and I seem to negotiate how it will happen. I walk past Beauty to the end of the platform nearest the entrance. This cuts off Beauty's exist from the enclosure and gives her full access to slip under the deck. With kneeling being impractical I simple turn a bit and sit on the platform. I get a couple hotdogs out of my pocket and grunt with a bit of confusion as Beauty lays down making it obvious she does not plan to come to me to get her treats. Barely noticing what I am doing I match her move and lay down myself stretching my head and shoulders towards her. With two bits of hot dog in my hand I roll onto my side and stretch my hand towards her. Carefully filling myself with playful energies I wave my hand gently only four inches from her muzzle. With her tail wagging she reaches out and takes her first treat. As I begin to break up the second hotdog an impish, playful energy slips into me. I grin, roll onto my back and reach towards putting two treats only a foot from my head. I hear myself saying, **"Well, girl?"** I sense Beauty's energy, *'Too new. New risks.'* All I can do is wait, 10 seconds, 15 seconds, 20 seconds. Just as I am giving up Beauty stands, shakes herself, and steps forward to retrieve her treats. I am surprised and pleased that she stays close to receive the rest of the hotdog from my outstretched hand. I am very, very aware of having my body fully exposed and below her. My mind, ego, and instincts are warning me 'NO, not safe.' Gentle warmth and playfulness from within somehow make it okay. As I take out the third hotdog a car comes from around the Quonset hut. I sit up noticing Beauty slip under the deck. Our space has collapsed. As the car turns towards the street two people from a house nearby step from the field onto the pavement. Beauty retreats further under the deck. When I stand the people see me and shift their path so they can say hello. 20 feet from me they ask about Beauty and smile when I offer, **"She is here, under the deck."** **"Oh. You sure seem to be set on getting her."** **"Yes, I have made progress. I am retired so I have the time."** They laugh a bit and offer, **"Well, good luck."** Their 'good luck' seem to contain a good natured *'Silly old fart.'*

Beauty has retreated and cloaked her energy. With a **"Hey girl."**

she uncloaks just a bit, just enough for me to know she is too worried for more. I allow myself to feel warm acceptance and say, "**I am going to go see the shopkeeper.**" and head out the enclosure, around and into the shop's front door. The shopkeeper greets me with a smile asking how things are going. He seems a little surprised by my smile and, "**Beauty is under the deck now. She is taking treats from my hand.**" His body relaxes and with a slight tilt of his head he asks, "**When do you expect to touch her?**" He smiles as I grin and reply, "**Well, it should happen soon. She ran when I showed her the leash so I have to figure out how I can get her to walk with me.**" "**Why would you do that?**" "**Well, I need to build her trust. I want her on leash to get her from the car into the backyard.**" As his body tenses just a bit, "**You are sure going slow. But then is seems to be working.**" "**Yeah. As long as I make progress I will keep feeding her.**" As my voice fades at the end of my sentence the front door opens and a well dressed man in his 20s walks in. Shane's facial expression and body language inform me we are done talking. As we say goodbye the shopkeeper seems to be considering something. As I step away from the shopkeeper the new arrival says, "**I wanted you to know I would be coming after that dog tonight.**" The shopkeeper becomes tense and uncertain, looking at me while he answers, "**Oh, okay. Thanks for letting me know.**" My ego is not happy and yet I return the shopkeeper's look with a slight smile and a nod. He understands my message and relaxes turning his attention back to the fellow. I am out the door in a blink.

Confusion, uncertainty, a sense of betrayal, stir within me. As I turn the corner of the shop towards the field it all flushes away with a knowing that somehow everything is as it should be. By the time I am half way to the field my energy is with Beauty and I hear myself repeating 'our whistle' every other step. With the third whistle I see Beauty trotting towards me from 120 feet away. I slip into an easy trot towards her and begin wondering what will happen as the distance reduces. With Beauty 40 feet away I stop, plant my feet apart and begin shifting my weight back a forth between my feet. Beauty charges towards me. 20 feet from me she veers off to the left a bit. When she is 10 feet away I lunge my weight towards her and she veers running away from me, tail high and an energy of 'wee'. My weight settles back and I give chase. Beauty is much faster. When she is 30 feet away she turns and faces me, does a play bow, shifts her weight back and forth, charges two steps towards me and veers off in glee. It only takes me two or three minutes to tire and bend over panting. Beauty stops perhaps 40 feet away and watches. As soon as my breath returns I whistle for her. She sits and watches giving me a strong sense of *not done, want more*. I respond by kneeling. She waits and watches as I break off several pieces of hotdog then lean forward placing them on the ground in front of me. As I sit back down with an 'I am resting.' attitude she gets up and slowly, slowly walks to the pieces, eats each, and retreats. With each set of treats she stays closer. I am grinning. We are doing a playful dance, playful testing of boundaries, little bits of surrender. With the last four pieces she is sitting two feet away from me. She tenses a bit when I notice I could reach out and grab her and for a moment consider the possibility. I breath out and think 'No' and Beauty relaxes watching my hand float up to offer her the last treats. I keep my hand extended and she takes a treat, looks me in the eyes, looks down to eat the treat and does it again until they are gone. As I lower my arm I sense the warm, playfulness enveloping Beauty and I. I show her both hands and offer, "**All gone.**"

Ten seconds of quiet and it is time to go. During the quiet there is only Beauty and I sitting in a small patch of grass. Deep within energies are stirring and Beauty and I seem to be agreeing that our play was indeed 'our' play, something we both wanted more of and more importantly somehow needed more of. As is my usual move I turn to the left, away from Beauty, and shift my weight to get up. My movement is suspended as she gets up and I feel her energies pulling me to turn back to face her. As my weight settles back sitting upon my heels time opens, there is nothing to do except observe, to be still in allowance of Beauty's request for a chance to choose. She steps past me only 18 inches from my side. I notice a strange blend of curious and quiet with only stillness within me. With my head slightly turning to watch her Beauty steps behind me and turns back towards me. Every cell of my body is in relaxed awareness as she comes in from behind me and ever so daintily stretches her head out and sniffs my arm just above the elbow. With her simple movement comes a flood of openness, intimacy offered and accepted. My body, her body are motionless one moment and then two as energies stir within her, within me, between us. Deep, deep within my lower belly I sense her, sense new connections we now share. I am still as she steps back two steps and cloaks her energies. Time slips back as I stand and turn to face her. A pause, a moment or two, and she becomes separate. The separation deepens as she walks away from me. Deep, deep within there is no separation, the increasing distance has no meaning. In a semi-trans I walk back to the car, unlock and open the door. I turn to the field and see Beauty sitting there, facing me. A breath, two breathes, three breathes and reality returns, what is within becomes veiled as I turn and swing my body into the driver's seat. As I plug the key into the ignition I seem to plug back into everyday reality. As I start the car I wonder what Beauty and I just started. A quiet whisper from within notifies me it will be a week or two before I begin to understand.

A Bold New Move

Wednesday, May 2nd

I drive out to visit Beauty today after stopping to check on how my friend's dogs are doing with their recent family addition. Fawn has not come with me for a couple of days and somehow it seems important that she come with me. It is a cloudy day with occasional sun and thankfully no rain. When I first turn into the parking area I don't see Beauty in the enclosure. The sorrow beginning to form within me is quickly replaced with warmth when I see her sitting on the grass just beyond the pavement. When she hears the car she turns, sees me and watches me park. By the time I get out of the car she is sitting about 20 feet away at the edge of the pavement where she has a direct view of the driver's door and the back of the car. I get out, turn to face her, and say my hellos. She is relaxed, ears up, tail up, mouth open facing me directly. With a smile and light step I walk to get her food bowl from inside the enclosure. For most of the walk back to the car she is in view, laying there, watching with her head high. She seems to approve of what I am doing for her. At the trunk I start to prepare her food and decide to do something a bit different.

    I get out a hotdog and break off a piece which I toss to within a couple of feet of her. She gets up and sniffs it but doesn't pick it up. I toss a second and third piece with the same results. A bit disappointed I turn back to the trunk and finish fixing her food. On a whim I take a bit of the wet food and walk directly towards her. To my surprise she stays where she is, her body tensing a bit. I stop just six feet from her to put the food down, turn and head to the enclosure to place her food bowl. As I walk I glance back, noticing she is sniffing the food, licks it and then turns away. As I return to the car I see that Beauty is laying where she had watched me while I made her food. She is relaxed, head high, mouth open, a regal sense about her. I get out three hotdogs and put a few of several types of treats in a baggy. As I load the baggy I glance at Beauty and smile as I notice her head is higher, her ears up, her mouth open more, and her tongue hanging out. She gets up, finds each of the pieces I tossed earlier and eats them. Time to be a bit bolder. Rather than walk to the place where I usually give her treats I walked directly towards her. When I am 20 feet from her she trots towards me. My smile deepens as I am filled with a playful warmth. A couple more steps and I stop. She continues towards me and then trots back and forth 4 to 6 feet from me, tail wagging, jumping playfully, and making a whimpering sound. During her 30 seconds of display my body is filled with her bouncy, playful energy and deep within I surrender to deeper bonds with her. When she stops and moves back a bit I kneel and toss a piece of hotdog about six feet from me. She runs to it, tail high and wagging quickly. One sniff and she picks it up, chews and swallows. I notice how much my attention is fully keyed in on us. Without thinking I break off another piece, stretch out my hand and offer it to her. To my delight she pauses only a second before stepping forward to take her treat. She stays there for four more pieces before stepping back and sitting. I hear myself saying, "**Wow, this is really cool**." as within I register Beauty has come to me when I am standing and stayed close while I am standing. The warmth of new trust floods from deep within, fills my body, flows out to Beauty who returns her pleasure with a teasing, "*Well, yes!*"

    I kneel and I place several pieces inches from my knees. She comes in to take her treats and backs up a couple of feet. Once again I place treats, this time Beauty will have to allow her muzzle to touch my knee to get her treat. She stands, looks at my face, steps forward and ever so daintily takes the piece almost against my knee. I grin as she raises her head and looks at me while she eats it. She backs a bit to retrieve the other treats and then sits within arm's length of me. Somehow things are different now, Beauty is relaxed and accepting when close to me, she seems to be seeking, surrendering to, enjoying the space of acceptance we now share. As warmth flows out to her I sense her whispering, "*Now we are within each other.*"

At that point I hear the voice of the fellow from the nearby apartments who I had chatted with a couple times about Beauty and a dog he had that played with Beauty. Watching Beauty I acknowledge him with a shout and watch a plastic bag fly over the fence he is behind followed by ""**This is for Beauty. "Cool, thanks.**" is my reply. "**She will enjoy it.**" Beauty is so close that when I get up to get bag I have to turn to avoid leaning into her. I am standing and have taken a few steps before it registers. Beauty stayed close with something new happening, something new involving another person. I notice Beauty just as she is catching up to me, going with me to investigate the bag. I am busy with my surface project and do not notice the energies stirring, creating new bonds as Beauty and I do our first little project together.

As I pick up the bag I notice it is filled with scraps of chicken from a cookout. Without thinking I return to 'our place' and kneel. Beauty sniffs the spot where the bag landed and follows me. I open the bag get two pieces of chicken and toss them towards Beauty. She picks up each piece as she comes closer to me and sits to watch me get three more pieces out and lay them close to me. I am a bit concerned and curious how Beauty will respond to the newness of what is happening. Beauty comes in and surprises me as she step a bit to my left and reaches down with her muzzle to daintily take the plastic bag laying on my left, next to my leg. She lifts the bag, turns, moves eight feet away, and proceeds to tear the bag apart. As she eats each extracted piece of chicken she rewards me with glances. As she does her work my mind recovers from it's surprise and begins trying to figure out what will need to change now that Beauty is confident enough to take the package of treats rather than wait for individual treats. While my mind and ego struggle with their new problem an impish energy dances within me celebrating Beauty's courage and choice to be more familiar. We almost feel like family now.

I get a hotdog out of my pocket, break it up, put two pieces close to me and keep the others in my hand. As my hand comes up off the ground she steps in and takes the two and then looks at me with an expectant gaze. Easily, naturally I reach out and give her each piece, leaving my arm extended, my hand inches from her muzzle as she eats the treat. While she chews the last treat I open my hand and turn it upward. She sniffs my hand, backs two steps, and sits. Wondering how she will respond I break off a piece and lean forward towards her. I grin as she remains seated, pulling her head back a few inches with my approaching hand. A moment after my hand stops she allows her head back forward and takes her treat. My grin broadens as I settle back on my heals and break off another piece of hotdog. For three treats she remains relaxed as I lean into her, extend my hand within an inch of her muzzle where she takes her treat.

Tired of kneeling and a barely noticed desire to get her close to my head causes me to lay down on my left side. As I tear off a few pieces she walks to my legs and sniffs me just above my knees. Her relaxed bit of intimacy with me fills me with warmth and I notice myself shifting to a relaxed playfulness. Three times I place several treats close to my body, each group extending up my body, closer to my head. Beauty's movements become a bit less fluid as she comes in and retrieves the first two groups. The last group is placed within a foot of my head. Beauty's ears are down as she shifts herself so her butt is further away from me, leaving only her head close. I choose to grin and relax. Finally she steps in, lowers her head and quickly gathers and eats her treats, steps back and sits. Concerned I notice her ears are partly down, her mouth is closed, her posture is stiff. I grin and reach out my hand offering another treat. As I guessed Beauty backs away finally sitting several feet from me.

I very slowly roll and sit up facing Beauty. Beauty's ears coming up and her mouth opening brings a grin to my face. It seems she is not done yet. I stand up and return to the car to retrieve more hotdogs.

When I turn around she is standing, ears up, mouth open, body relaxed yet slightly tense in a playful way. I smile as I sense her playful energy within my body, sense her playing with me. She is inviting me to play! Without thinking I relax, let go of worrying about her responses, and walk towards her with a bouncy step. Twenty feet from her I spread my feet and begin clomping towards her, one foot lifted high and forward with an exaggerated stomp of my foot back onto the ground. Beauty begins shifting her weight from one front foot to the other, weaving her shoulders back and forth, showing me she is ready to jump away, ready to begin play. I am startled when I get ten feet from her and she jumps towards me. Without thought I respond in play jumping to the side. As my feet come back to the ground I am flooded with several realizations but don't have time to process them as I notice I am in the air, in the middle of jumping towards Beauty. It is Beauty's turn to jump sideways. Her feet come down and she spins around with her tail up, her movements quick and relaxed. I am in awe. We are playing together, our energies synchronized. As Beauty completes her spin she leaps away and half trotting moves a few more feet away. Though my mind and ego are unready to accept it I am playing with 'my dog', she is playing with 'her people'. We continue our play. Most often I faint a charge towards her and she leaps away. Occasionally she surprises me by charging two or three steps towards me. Within three minutes she is about 35 feet away, tail high and wagging, mouth open, tongue out, ears high. Panting I feel the stretching of the huge grin on my face as she stands there proud, happy, radiating warmth to me. She is indeed Beauty.

I have no idea how long we stand there enjoying being 'with' each other. Eventually I have an urge to move and find myself looking for a spot where the early May grass is still short. As I take the few steps to the clear spot and kneel my inner wisdom whispers to my mind and ego that there is no need to return to Beauty and I's spot for sharing treats. I break off a piece of hotdog and toss it towards Beauty, to a spot about 20 feet away from me. Beauty and I together watch the arch and seem to both feel the hotdog bounce on the ground. In the ten seconds before Beauty accepts my offer and trots to the piece, the energy of the toss and Beauty and I's energies seem to slowly settle into a relaxed, open, trusting space, our space, separate from the rest of the world. Beauty searches for the first piece and as she eats it I toss a second piece closer to me. While the piece is in the air Beauty trots to the place where it lands, sniffs it and scoops it up with her muzzle. As her head raises I toss a third piece just six feet in front of me. Without hesitation Beauty walks forward, sniffs the piece, and eats it. I grin as a sense of 'Game on!' washes through me. As I hold out another piece I am startled by Beauty stepping forward while my hand is still moving towards her. As my hand ends it's journey Beauty stretches her neck just a bit, sniffs the hotdog, takes it, swallows, and looks expectantly at me as she steps back one step. As I reach out with the second piece Beauty steps in to meet my hand taking the piece with no sniffing, munch, munch, and as she swallows her eyes look at me, then at my hand only inches from her muzzle.

Time drops away as ever so gently, ever so slowly, I extend my hand to the side of her muzzle wondering how she will respond. She tenses just a bit becoming very still as I reach back a bit more and then up. She stays where she is as her ears move back some and I extend one finger that meets and then strokes her ear. Each movement down and then up is the only marking of time. Finger down and Beauty shows me her fear, finger up and Beauty shows me her hope. One, two, three and Beauty turns her head towards my hand, letting me know 'enough'. I hear myself saying, "**Good girl**." as my hand returns to me, leaving Beauty empty space to reflect as she steps back. As she turns her head back to me I reach forward with the third piece. Again she comes forward, pauses a moment when I don't extend my hand completely, then steps in very close to me to take her treat. As I reach beyond her muzzle she steps back and sits clearly announcing she is done. I relax and enjoy the feelings of warmth and safety there in our own little world, safe from the outside. I cannot tell you whether we happily sat there for ten seconds or ten minutes. At some point the cold of wet May grass invading my knees brings me back to reality. For a few seconds I am fully aware of Beauty and I sitting five feet apart, open, relaxed, safe together. Pain in my cold knees finally wins and I let go of the space we share to stand. By the time I am fully standing Beauty has walked a few more feet away. There she sits and watches me return to the car. As I walk to the car I notice Fawn and decide to walk her at home.

At the car I turn back to her yelling, "**Hey Beauty, I will see you tonight.**" As I swing my weight into the drivers seat it seems Beauty is whispering, "*I want you here*." As I start the car I feel the pull between returning to the real world and staying with Beauty. On the drive home I bury my uncertainty with considerations of daily tasks still awaiting my attention.

From the Car

May 2nd, Evening

This evening as planned I drive out for a second visit. During the drive my mind and ego several times protest spending resources with no way to predict the return. Each time I simply connect with the feeling of doing what I am supposed to do and with a sense of Beauty waiting for me. As I make the final turn into the area behind the shop I tell my mind to go into observer mode and smile as I sense my body relaxing.

It is starting to get dark and I find myself noticing how much detail is still available in the fading light of dusk. As I pass behind the shop and begin my turn to park I note that I can still detect color differences. My sense is reaffirmed as I notice the red of Beauty's fur in the green grass just beyond the edge of the pavement I am driving on. I find myself smiling as warmth fills me and it seems that Beauty is connecting with me, letting me know she is happy to see me. I park, open the car door, grab the hotdog package and dog treats made from duck, and swing my legs out onto the ground. Beauty is watching me and seems uncertain. I hear myself saying, "**Hey Beauty. Do you want some treats?**" and my smile broadens as I sense Beauty relaxing and see her begin to wag her tail. She watches carefully as I make large movements to transfer treats to my jacket pockets, hotdogs on the right, duck treats on the left. I am surprised to sense texture and taste in my mouth. I look up to see Beauty smacking her lips which causes my mind to insist the taste and texture I am imagining can not have anything to do with Beauty giving me a message. The relaxing of my body and gentle warmth tells me otherwise. I grin when I notice Beauty seems amused.

Emboldened by Beauty's reactions to my showing up outside our normal time, her remaining laying exposed in the field right close to the pavement, I walk straight towards her with slow rhythmic steps. Her head is up, ears forward, mouth open. As I move through the 25 feet separating us she begins showing signs of being uncertain, ears lower a bit, tongue disappears, tail drops below her hips. I have a sense she is both pleased and worried. My pace slows as I get closer and bit by bit my awareness of the world around me fades. Ten feet away and my world becomes Beauty and the space we share. I seem to be moving in slow motion and as my foot moves down to meet the ground just six feet from Beauty she shifts her weight, beginning to get up. As my other foot comes forward my weight shifts as I slow while Beauty's body is raising off the ground. My foot swings a half step and as it lands on the ground Beauty springs the final inches to standing up. As my weight settles I begin a smile, Beauty's tail is up high as she moves two to three feet away from me. As the other foot comes off the ground I am beginning the downward movement to kneel. As I notice I am kneeling only three feet from where she had been lying Beauty moves a bit further away and turns to face me. Her tail is up and her ears are partially back. I have the sense she is playfully tense. Her ears come forward as my hand pulls the baggy with hot dogs out of my pocket. I am no longer thinking, Beauty and I have once again slipped into a dance. I toss two treats the twelve feet that separate us and as she sniffs the treats I lean forward onto my hands and knees, suddenly realizing I am doing play bows while she sniffs and soon begin grinning as she joins me in doing play bows, her tail wagging happily. As I sit back on my heals I flip the third treat just four feet in front of me. Beauty scoops up and eats the two treats closest to her and then steps in to take the treat close to me. Without thought I stretch my hand out with treats and feel rewarded as Beauty steps forward to take the treats from my hand with little hesitation. As Beauty steps back and sits I sense myself opening my energy to draw her in closer.

"Are you ready, girl?" marks me leaning forward and placing one, two, three, four treats each one closer to my body, the last inches from my knees. As I settle back on my heals Beauty gets up and moves forward taking each treat as she comes closer. As she munches the final treat she steps back from me a bit and looks at me expectantly To my surprise she does not retreat other than to gain a slight amount of room by sitting down. She is so close I have just enough room to lean forward and place treats by my knees. As my hand moves down to the ground Beauty tenses a bit, her ears going back slightly, she remains sitting. She seems to relax as I sense placing a treat on the ground as my hand moves towards the ground. As I open my hand and release a treat her ears come forward and she stands and watches me place a second and third treat by my knees. I grin happily as she immediately leans forward to take her treats from the ground. As she munches on the third threat, her head up, I reach out with another two and find myself a bit excited when I notice she is so close my elbow is bent when she takes the treats from my hand. My mind is suddenly busy, 'elbow half bent, her head about 30 inches from my chest, could grab her, oh... no, no, she seems to be offering herself to be touched, ears perhaps'. Beauty steps back, sits, and looks at me. I can almost hear her saying, *"No grabbing"* with her ears back. For reasons that confuse my mind I move my hands just in front of my chest, palms towards her and wiggle my fingers. Her ears come forward as her head tilts slightly and within a moment the tension is gone.

Twice more I place treats on the ground and then give her additional treats by hand with her head less than arm's length from my chest. Each time I let my hand float back towards her ears, stopping when either ear twitches. On the third set she allows my hand to float an inch or two from her ear. Every so gently I bend my wrist so my fingers move over and barely touch and stroke her ear. Beauty steps back before sitting with her mouth closed and ears no longer fully forward. Without thinking I begin wiggling and bowing forward. Suddenly Beauty is all attention, standing, ears forward, head high, mouth open, tongue out, tail up and wagging. As she stands a wave of warm playfulness wash over me and fills my with delight. As I retrieve more duck treats from my pocket Beauty steps so close that giving her treats with her head only 18" from my chest is easy and natural. Something beyond my mind registers that we have crossed a threshold and contentment fills me as I sense that Beauty has somehow opened my heart by moving her head into my heart space. Time and space have slipped away as I notice her look to my right and then shift her body to face in that direction. Suddenly my world shrinks. I am kneeling, Beauty is standing sideways to me as my attention shrinks to the fur on her shoulders and I feel myself drawn to that fur. I watch as some force causes my hand to float over to brush the fur, my fingers noticing each hair brushing against each finger. A bit of reality returns as Beauty turns her head towards me, moving so her shoulders six more inches from me and then takes two steps back. With the bit of reality comes the pleasing awareness that Beauty is more surprised than startled.

   I feed her one, then two, then a third hotdog. With each she comes in close and stands close as I tear of pieces of hotdog and hand them to her. As I hand her the last two pieces of hotdog she seems to be getting bored, shows no eagerness for more. Her attention returns when I reach into my other pocket and take out duck treats. Soon the treats are gone and on a whim I extend my empty hand towards her, palm towards me, fingers down. One step back and she sits, looking at me with ears forward and mouth open. She watches as I extend my hand towards her and wave it gently within six inches of her muzzle for a few seconds. As my hand floats back to my lap I realize I am not ready to leave. Beauty seems curious and remains seated as I turn away from her and stand to go back to the car where I get more hotdogs.

   I walk directly to where she is waiting for me and kneel only six feet from her. I smile and do an inner happy dance as I notice she simply waited for me, relaxed and expectant. I place one piece to get her close and enjoy watching her come in without hesitation, take a few pieces by hand and then back away a bit. With each round she stays in close a bit longer before stepping back. Before I realize what I am doing I reach out with both hands, one holding the hotdog, one tearing off a piece and offering it. Beauty does not back away. As warmth flows from my belly into my chest I notice that I am in a playful, slightly challenging mood. I am delighted as I observe Beauty intently, happily accepting my hands working only six inches from her muzzle to provide her treats. On the last round I switch to the more favored duck treats. I reach up with both hands closed stopping six inches from her muzzle. Her ears come a bit more forward and her head tilts a bit before she reaches her head forward and sniffs each hand. In response to her withdrawing her energy as her head moves back, I immediately expose the duck treat. It works. As I tear off a piece her head and energy returns to me. In the few moment gaps between tearing off each piece and giving it to her I wait for Beauty to look directly at me. I am smiling with contentment and I am a bit disappointed when I give her the last bit.

As I walk back to the car I experience the sensation of feeding her from the car. What the heck! By the time I get to the car I am experiencing a strong urge to try and so go to the trunk and retrieve a single hotdog. As I look up from closing the trunk I notice that Beauty has followed me back to the car and is standing about 10 feet from the drivers door. For reasons I will probably never know I am nervous. Somehow what I am doing is far more important than my mind can understand.

I open the car door and sit down so my feet are on the ground, my knees right above them. Beauty is standing about 10 feet away, ears mostly back while looking directly at me. There is a feeling of important work being done, something both Beauty and I need. With a "**Hey girl, here you go.**" I tear off four pieces and toss each in closer to me and the car. The fourth lands seven feet from me. Ever so slowly Beauty moves in closer and after eating the fourth piece looks at me and then backs away. Within I have a sense that Beauty is about done with new things. I notice I seem to have no choice as I tear off additional pieces and toss them with the last piece landing just on the pavement almost at my feet rather than on the grass of the field. Like me Beauty seems motivated by something unidentified. She slowly retrieves and eats each treat backing away once the final piece is consumed. Over several rounds of treats Beauty comes in closer and closer eventually picking up treats near my feet before backing away. When she takes the last treat of a round and is in close enough I bend over and offer her one from my hand. She backs away. I seem on autopilot, no thoughts, no reasons, just doing. I do a couple more rounds and then do a round with the last treat laying between my feet. I watch in awe as she steps in, picks up the treat between my feet, raises her head, looking at me, seeming proud, as she munches her treat. This time after eating the treat she hesitantly takes the treat I offer from my hand and retreats. With the next round she takes two treats from my hand before retreating. Out of hot dogs I switch to duck treats doing a few more rounds including Beauty taking treats from my hands.

When I first sit in the car I do not expected much, I simply follow an inner insistence. Beauty taking treats from between my feet and from my hand pleases me. At one point when she is in close she reaches her nose up and sniffs the door jam. I am delighted. As her nose twitches with each sniff warmth bursts deep in my belly and expands to fill my chest with deep contentment and pleasure. My mind and ego seem absent, buried beneath an undeniable inner urge to action. On the drive home my mind and ego return partially, just enough to register that they have no idea what has just happened. Within I sense a thousand, thousand stirrings of new possibilities being worked. In those moments all I can know is somehow Beauty's and my futures have changed.

BRIEF AND MEANINGFUL

Thursday, May 3rd

*L*ife is good! You might suspect my time with Beauty has once again boosted my sense of self, of well being. It is true. We seem to have turned another corner. Yesterday Beauty showed more interest in interacting with me, more interest than in just the food I offered. At least that is my sense of things.

When I arrive Beauty is laying in the field laying close to "the rock". The top of the rock sticks out of the ground about five inches. The people cutting the grass of the field have trimmed the grass short around the rock and perhaps applied weed killer around it. An attempt to make "the rock" visible when the next grass cutting is done thereby avoiding equipment damage. The rock is about 15 feet from the pavement and about 40 feet behind and to the left of where I park my car. If Beauty is in the area of the rock she can watch me open the car trunk and rummage around. She also can see what I take out of the trunk.

Beauty watches as I park the car and get out. "**Hey, Beauty, it is good to see you**." I notice she is sitting with her head higher, making herself more visible. I head into the enclosure and retrieve her food bowl. It rained earlier today so her water bowl has plenty of water. As I walk back to the car I am smiling. Beauty sitting with her head high, seeming more available to me, lightens my mood. As soon as I get the trunk open I take a hotdog out of the cooler and toss a couple of pieces towards her. She remains laying down watching. As I get about halfway through mixing her food I look over at her and sense a pull to walk to her, to be closer to her. She watches carefully as I approach. When I am half way to her she gets up and leans forward into a lazy stretch. As I watch her slow deliberate movements of stretching and sense her awareness of her body, I can almost feel my body stretching, and remember seeing pictures just such a yoga pose. As I cross from the pavement to the grass my senses open, a couple more steps and Beauty turns and unhurriedly walks, almost prancing, to the right. As I talk with her she stops and sits down facing me. I bend down, hand forward, as I step within 5 feet of her I kneel. I say hello, pause a bit, and lean forward onto all fours. She gets up wagging her tail, taking very small steps back and forth with her front feet. I sit back and extend my hand, she takes two steps towards me. I lean forward and slowly extend my empty hand, palm towards me, fingers down. Time slows as a part of me watches my hand extend in slow motion, watches, senses her responses. I feel a warmth of wonder stirring in my lower belly as I watch my hand move to within two inches of the side of her muzzle. She is still intently focused on my hand. I move my hand a couple of inches back and forth. She seems content, remaining still. I move my hand ever so slowly to gently brush the side of her muzzle. One, two, three strokes, she gently moves her head a couple inches away, I stop, leaving my hand motionless. She turns her head, sniffs my fingers, pauses and then licks my hand. As she draws away by sitting and I allow my hand to lower I hear myself saying, **"Oh Beauty, thank you."** The warmth of wonder stirring in my belly becomes more real and expands up into my chest. My mind seems to be observing from far away. After a few seconds pause I reach my hand out again. She draws back slightly and then leaps up, tail coming up and wagging. I am elated, awed, and want more all at the same time. I shake my body side to side, she does another play jump and turns. I lean forward onto all fours and faint towards her. Another play bound and she dances about 10 feet from me and sits.

I return to the trunk, toss her three pieces of hotdog and return to mixing her food. She meanders forward, sniffs each piece but does not pick any up. With her food ready I walk to the enclosure, step up and into the enclosure, walk around the deck and bend to place her food under the deck. As I stand I have a sense of Beauty being happy and grateful that I am 'being her people'. I smile, enjoying the warmth and sense of well being flowing within me as I return to the trunk. Beauty is watching me, relaxed, at ease, and even seems eager for us to do more. I get out some hotdogs and saunter towards her. When I get close Beauty does a play bow and then leaps into the air, spins around, and scampers away. I charge at her, she waits a few of my steps and then leaps into the air, spinning, and scampering away to where she then sits. As is usual after we "play" she is further away, in this case about 20 feet away. I kneel in the grass and toss the first piece close to her. She slowly, half heartedly sniffs for it, pauses, and then turns to check out each of the pieces I tossed earlier. She eats none of them. My mind guesses, "Her belly isn't feeling well or she recently ate." Finally I toss a piece of hotdog about three feet from myself, watch her pause and trot forward to it. I sense a, "*Okay, now I get to interact with you, here I come.*" from her and enjoy warmth flooding through my body. She sniffs the piece, picks it up, and drops it. I am puzzled, a bit worried, fascinated, and excited all at the same time. I carefully reach out offering a treat. As she steps in my body resonates with her deeper message. My mind registers that she is stepping in to accept a treat. Deep within my body resonates with a knowing that she is stepping into, she is surrendering into there being an 'us'. As she accepts the treat she is accepting my desire to be with her. As she chews it slowly, she is separating what we imagine into parts that can be assimilated. And finally she swallows taking it all within to be processed, to disperse within and become part of who she is. When she looks up at me I sense she is enjoying the same happening within me. With a deep sense of flowing changes I barely notice myself tearing off another piece of hotdog. She takes three more pieces, each time deepening and expanding our connections. As she steps back and sits it seems she is whispering to me, "*We have done what we must. Now is time to relax, to allow the energies to continue what we have begun, to continue shaping 'us'.*"

I am puzzled, concerned, curious, elated with many deep energies flowing within my lower belly. Unlike other days I have other concerns waiting for me, other things insisting on my mind's attention. My friend's dog is very sick and I have several errands to run for her, things to pick up to help with her care of her dog. I mechanically tear off pieces of the second hotdog. Helping my friend fills my mind, keeping it busy. My body and inner energies are busy with the possibilities Beauty and I have just opened. Some treats are handed to Beauty, some are placed on the ground in front of me. Twice I reach out my hand and moving it close to her muzzle.

With the third hotdog Beauty looses interest. She takes a couple more pieces and then simply sits about five feet from me ignoring my offerings. I sit with her, munching a couple pieces of hotdog myself. I would like to engage her in play and also feel the need to get errands done. As I get up and return to the car my mind is busily generating reasons that Beauty was less interested in food. Parts of me tries to go into worry. Quietly within I notice a sense of how she stayed to interact with me even while the food I offered held little interest for her. I notice a contentment within myself, what was to be done has been allowed. Now is time to busy my body and mind with helping others allowing inner processes to complete without my mind and ego interfering.

Empty Absence

Friday, May 4th

I am worried, I have an empty feeling of uncertainty. I have gone to visit Beauty twice, each time she is nowhere to be seen.

On my first visit I am concerned and disappointed. My mind runs through several conditions and scenarios. It has been raining off and on all day, sometimes heavily. Many of the days Beauty does not show up are days when the weather is rainy and cold. Perhaps yesterday's shift was enough that she is taking a step back and not showing up. She seemed less interested in hotdog pieces yesterday, I hope she is not laying somewhere sick. Perhaps she has been captured, oh, if so I hope it was by someone gentle and loving. Her building trust may make it easier for someone else to capture her. Perhaps she has decided to try to find her way to my home.

Time and time again I take a breath, relax, notice my lower belly, allowing an emptiness, and remind myself I simply can't know for sure. From that place of quiet I sense no messages, no actions I should take. I connect with Beauty, with my sense of her, and open to the connections we share. Only a bit of her is present and it seems trapped. I have no way of knowing the form of the trap, a cage, an illness, her fear, an injury. All I am sure of is that worrying will serve neither her nor me. As I leave I am quiet within while my mind works to create an answer.

I return to visit Beauty in the evening. This time I take Fawn with me. Again Beauty is nowhere to be seen. Repeated whistles bring no response. The enclosure seems void of her energy. I check her food bowl and see that the soft food has been eaten, the dry food is still in the bowl. Perhaps she has been here, but my sense is that the feral cats have eaten the soft food, leaving the bigger, dry chunks. Again my mind becomes busy. I don't sense her energy in the enclosure. Has something happened or is she simply cloaking her energy as she has in the past? Checking within I sense emptiness, concern, a gentle sick feeling, and a knowing that I can't know now and that I may never know. I get Fawn out of the car and walk her in the field. She eagerly sniffs and explores. I enjoy her eagerness. Ten minutes later I return to the car and drive home worried and yet at piece. Driving along Airport Way, a route I have driven dozens of time, for the first time I notice the red fire hydrants that show up every couple hundred yards on either side of the road. My mind is puzzled leaving more room for inner processes to occur.

TRUSTING AGAIN

Saturday, May 5th

$\mathcal{D}$riving out along Airport Way I am quiet. Part of me is sick with worry, part of me is content that I am doing what I am to do. From deep within I notice a whisper of, "*Allow, do. Things are as they should be.*" Driving takes just enough attention to keep me from withdrawing inward into a funk. My world is driving and allowing myself to notice each sensation, each thought as it comes up and then fades away.

As I turn off Burnside and drive behind the store the area seems to reflect the subdued yet quietly aware, quietly noticing state I am in. I notice my disappointment that Beauty is not in sight and then notice I had not expected to see her. As I get out of the car I sense the faintest trace of her, not far away, observing, avoiding interacting with my energy. I whistle 'our' whistle. A single long sound beginning with a low pitch and rising as high as I can manage. I sense no response as I scan the field and paved areas. My mood is too quiet to allow disappointment. As I walk to get Beauty's food bowl and return to my car to mix her food a slight glimmer of contentment seeps in. I am doing for another. As I mix her food I sense Beauty subtly connecting with gentle gratitude. Walking back to the enclosure with Beauty's bowl I notice some of the heaviness has slipped away and my legs move through space more easily. The effort I notice I must expending to step up into the enclosure tells me much heaviness remains. I bend to place her bowl and as I let go of her bowl I seem to let go of some of my heaviness. Standing is easier than I expect. I jump rather than step down out of the enclosure. I fall in slow motion, my feet impact solid ground and it seems that much of my heaviness continues on down into the earth. As I look up from the ground I feel relaxed rather than heavy. Without thinking I wander out into the field wanting to 'occupy' the space I share with Beauty. I loop off to the right. At the end of the large loop, as I move back towards the car I whistle once again. There she is! Moving slowly along the bushes at the far left of the field. "**Hey Beauty! It is soooo good to see you!**"

As I walk to the car to get treats I have the sensation of Beauty playing quietly with me. During my walk to the car I glance back and smile as I notice that Beauty is following me towards the car. As I pop the trunk and get out treats Beauty walks to a spot about 25 feet away and sits facing me. I have the sense that Beauty needs me to prove myself to her, needs me to prove her opening to me is safe. I am startled when I sense she is worried I will use being close as a chance to capture her and then beat her. A deep breath helps to begin diffusing and quieting the turmoil of emotions within me. Sense the earth, sense Beauty, sense the deepening connections we share, set aside the past and the future, allow quiet whispers within to guide me.

I take two steps towards Beauty and stop, hearing myself saying, "**Oh, it needs to be your choice to come to me. Okay.**" I feel Beauty watching me closely as I tear up a hotdog and toss several pieces towards her. Space and time become the world within which Beauty and I enter a delicate dance. Each group of treats I toss towards her is an offering, an invitation to trust me more. With each step towards me part of what holds us apart sinks into the earth. With each treat picked up a bit more connection is allowed, with each swallow the connection penetrates, becomes part of who 'we' are. As Beauty swallows a treat just three feet from me she looks up and shifts her front feet flooding me with playful energy. The game is on! I lunge towards her, she jumps sideways, twirls, runs several feet away, spins, and charges towards me half the distance that separates us. I turn away, quickly turn back towards her, and lunge. Again and again, each of us becoming more open, more playful, more certain of our trust, our bonds. Sometimes Beauty goes only a few feet away before looping back. Sometimes she goes 25 to 30 feet away. With the final loop she comes half way to me and sits.

I kneel and bend over breathing hard. As my breathing eases I notice Beauty is approaching me in a slow, still playful gate. She stops five feet from me and waits. As I get out treats and glance at her it seems

I can almost hear her say, *"Well? Treats?"* I am startled to notice in my mouth the sensations of her chewing and tasting a treat. When my focus shifts to her she seems to be grinning with excitement, *"Oh good. You finally notice my messages."* Two, three, four moments of confusion and suddenly my mind catches on to what my body already knows. Beauty is communicating with me by transmitting to me the sensations she experiences. Cognitive dissonance! Beauty moving brings my attention back to giving her treats. I grin and am filled with warmth as she steps forward to take a treat from my outstretched hand. A few treats later she is sitting close enough that I can touch her. In the moment I sense myself reaching out to touch her I have the sense of her getting up and stepping back. My mind is tickled now as I realize how quickly she and I begin to use our new way of communicating.

I suddenly remember the toy I had put in my pocket before leaving home. As I reach into my pocket I allow myself to sense wagging the toy in front of Beauty playfully. As the toy clears my pocket Beauty seems to be considering how she will respond. I hold the toy in front of me and when Beauty looks directly at me I wiggle the toy and bob my head back and forth. Beauty remains very still. I relax into stillness and then reach my hand out with the toy. I am pleased as Beauty relaxes into curiosity and extends her muzzle to sniff and then lick the head of the toy. I wiggle the toy and Beauty stands. I draw the toy back to myself and she sits watching as I dance the toy on the ground. I grin when her tail begins to wag. Somehow we both agree our time is done. I move the toy to a few inches from her muzzle, she reaches forward and sniffs it, and then it goes back into my pocket. **"Okay, girl. Time to go."** I am pleased that Beauty remains sitting, watching me walk back to my car. As I drive away I notice in the rear view mirror Beauty getting up and heading to the enclosure. I smile as I sense relaxed pleasure in her intent to accept the food I have provided for her.

Toy Time

*I*n the evening after dinner I drive out to visit Beauty again. Part of me would rather be in the backyard digging in the small vegetable garden I have started. Noticing blue sky with billowy clouds shifts me into looking forward to being outside with Beauty. I am very aware of the toy in my coat pocket and hope Beauty will play with me. As I turn into the parking area and drive behind the stores I am very aware of the stores being closed and find myself feeling like an intruder. Strange how a few hours makes that difference. As I drive to my usual parking spot I notice Beauty out in the field, sitting up, watching me. As the car stops she stands and turns away from me. As she takes her first step away I whistle and smile as I watch her turn back to me. "**Hey! You want some treats?**" gets her to turn back towards me and sit, ears up, mouth open. Once I have some treats from the trunk I head out towards her. As I notice she is about 30 feet away I grin as playful energy fills me and I sense playing with the toy with Beauty. Looking at her I wonder how much of what I just experienced was her energy and how much was my anticipation and think, "Oh well. Will never know."

By the fifth step I have the toy out and I am wiggling it back and forth at Beauty saying things like, "**Hey girl, do you want to play.**" A bit of movement at the apartments across the field causes me to wonder how crazy I sound. A glance at Beauty standing now with wagging tail and what anyone else thinks fades away. I slow my pace and begin shifting my shoulders back and forth, holding the toy out, wiggling it. Beauty seems both excited and a bit confused. Without thinking I stop and drop to my knees now less the 12 feet from her. Her ears come back forward and she begins a slow walk towards me watching the toy. When she is 5 feet away I put my hands in my lap and smile as she takes a few more steps and sits less than three feet from me. I hear myself saying, "**Well, this is nice.**" in a playful tone and with head movement. Beauty seems both uncertain and eager. I lean a bit forward and wiggle the toy on the grass just in front of Beauty. She watches, I stop moving, simply holding the toy on the ground two feet from her. As I hoped Beauty bends her head down and sniffs the toy. With my hand still on the ground I wiggle the toy inches from her muzzle. Beauty pulls her head back and up and I have a sense of, "*I am not so sure.*" As Beauty looks at me, her ears back just a bit I hear myself saying, "**It's okay girl. We can play.**" and wiggle my body slightly followed by a bit of a play bow.

Beauty's ears come forward and she leans just a bit towards me as I move the toy towards her muzzle, wiggling it slightly. Before I know it Beauty is stretching her head towards the toy in my hand. I stop breathing and watch in awe and delight as Beauty sniffs the toy. When I wiggle the toy a bit she licks it. I find myself pushing the toy an inch closer to her, almost inside her muzzle as she is licking it. Beauty begins to open her mouth and then stops and draws back. I have a sense of her wondering, "*What am I doing? Is it safe?*" Looking back I realize what I sensed was her wondering, becoming uncertain, holding her energy alert. I respond by moving the toy to the side of her muzzle and begin wiggling it gently. Beauty draws her head back a couple inches, her ears go back. As her ears come forward I reach in and once again wiggle the toy against her muzzle. A few more times and Beauty relaxes into my inviting her to play with the toy. I sit back and draw my hand back closer to my body. I wag the toy a few time acting like I am going to throw it. Beauty is standing, ears forward, weight shifting back and forth on her front feet. I let go of the toy and it floats to the ground five feet away. Beauty jumps up and lunges to the toy grabbing it with her muzzle. I watch as her head comes up in play and suddenly she is uncertain and freezes, dropping the toy. "**Good girl. Can we do more?**" gets Beauty moving again. She steps back. On my hands and wet knees I crawl towards the toy being very careful to not move directly at Beauty, being careful to focus on the toy. Beauty takes one step back and waits. I am stunned and excited. Beauty is trusting me to approach her, she is staying close to me as we do something new for us. As I pick up the toy Beauty leans in towards me. Again I wiggle the toy, then move it to her muzzle. After a few strokes against her muzzle Beauty lets her mouth open and allows me to move the toy just inside her mouth. After a very long two seconds I draw my hand and toy back and in a very controlled movement swing my arm tossing the toy about ten feet away. Startled Beauty jumps and as I hope her eyes follow the toy so as her weight settle back down she is instinctively moving to get the toy. She grabs the toy and spins back towards me and seems to relax as I move my shoulders back and forth inviting her to play. We play with abandon. Bit by bit Beauty accepts that it is okay for me to walk towards her to get the toy. Bit by bit I accept that I can trust Beauty. Each time I go towards Beauty to get the toy. Each time she is less guarded as I approach.

Several times I invite Beauty to bring the toy to me. Each time she waits where she is. After several minutes both she and I are done. Enough new for now. I toss the toy to Beauty. She bends, sniffs it, does not pick it up. "**Well, I guess I will see you tomorrow.**" and I turn and walk back to the car. I am pleased that Beauty looks at the toy and then leaving it there she walks back towards the car with me. As I swing myself into the front seat I notice the contrast of first being disappointed Beauty did not pick up the toy and delighted she moved towards the car with me.

Sunday, May 6th

In the mid morning when I let Fawn out I notice clouds filling the sky. As I wait for Fawn I think of my schedule for the day. As I stand there I can feel an eagerness to visit Beauty. My mind begins the process of selecting what I will do. I plan to visit Beauty twice like yesterday. A few minutes later before my mind has completed it's process I am in the car heading to visit Beauty. This first visit is occurring well before noon, the sky is partially clear. When I get there Beauty's area is sunny. After yesterday I am not sure what to expect and so I am pleased and relieved to see Beauty laying close to the hedge on the far left, the red hair of her back just visible. As soon as I get out of the car and whistle her head comes up. I immediately go to the trunk and take out a couple hotdogs.

Bringing In Beauty

The fellow who runs the spa shop is sitting out back on the stairs of the deck enjoying the sun while sitting so he can see into the shop. I feel it is important to share what happened the day before so I walk over to him. We have a brief and pleasant conversation. The conversation would have lasted longer except Beauty gets up and walks towards the car. Time to focus on her.

She moves within about 20 feet of the car before sitting. I go to The Rock, kneel, and toss a piece of hotdog. She stays where she is, not getting up. I toss a second piece, still no movement. After a few seconds pause I feel that I am going to need to approach her. I get up and walk about 20 feet towards her. When I am about 10 feet from her she gets up and begins walking away. A sense of worry washes over me followed by a sense of needing to walk away from her. I holler her name, turn back towards the car, and start walking. Glancing back I see she has stopped and is looking at me with curiosity. By the time I get half way back to The Rock she has started walking towards me. With a grin I stop, turn, and kneel. My mind notices I am on automatic as I toss five more pieces of hotdog. Her picking up each brings her a bit closer to me. The sixth piece brings her to within three feet of me where she sits. As she takes the seventh from my hand a gentle warmth fills my belly, flowing up into my chest. My mind is delightfully amused. When I offer her the next piece she ignores it. It feels strange and a bit scary to have her not taking pieces of hotdog. I pause, am quiet, and feel an urge to play with her. I lean forward onto all fours, play bow and she jumps and begins moving back and forth by shifting her weight from one front foot to the other. We play for about five minutes with her staying close. Suddenly she seems done playing. She moves to 3 feet in front of me and sits down. The next few minutes I spend placing hot dogs close to me and handing her pieces when she is close. Somehow what I am doing is both important and mechanical. Then, abruptly, it is time to leave for my friend's house. I stand and turn away before a now startled Beauty can respond. At the car I look back to see Beauty sitting where she had taken the last treat. Something is happening that my mind does not comprehend. Within I am calm. My mind is puzzled. I sense Beauty being equally puzzled.

SHE OFFERS HERSELF

*L*ater in the day, just before turning into Beauty's area I notice the car clock shows 2:00. The sky is nearly clear, the temperature is almost 70 degrees. I am pleased to see Beauty laying close to the spot she had been when I had left, her head is high, ears are up, mouth opened, tongue out. I get out and say hello to her as I head to get her food bowl. At the trunk when about half done mixing her food, I decide to toss her a piece of hotdog. I am pleased to see her get up and move to it. She does not eat it. Unsure I finish her food and place it in the enclosure. Given her limited interest in hotdogs I only get out two when I return to the trunk. I wonder how she will respond to me as I cross the pavement. She is about 40 feet out into the field, I tentatively walk about half that distance and kneel. When I do a play bow she gets up and stretches. With each of four pieces of hotdog she trots closer to me. And with the fifth piece she finally sniffs, picks the piece up, and eats it. After taking two pieces from my hand she seems to loose interest. I look at the hotdog and a half in my hand, look up to see her sitting three feet from me, and wonder how much more she will take with a thought of "Maybe play would get a better response." She is so close, showing little tension, the fur just below her ear seems so inviting. Okay. I reach out slowly with my hand and brush the fur just below her ear with the back of my fingers. Once, she stays put, not moving her head, twice, she moves her head away and then back as my hand moves away, three times, a couple of brushes and she steps back and sits. Warmth and satisfaction flow within me. I lean forward onto all fours, my head inches from hers and am surprised when she does not move away. A play bow and she jumps sideways, moves left, turns, and comes in close to sniff my head and neck. She jumps sideways again and we begin a series of her jumping away and towards me as I do the same with her. I am having great fun. After about 3 minutes she stops about five feet from me and sits. I toss her a couple of pieces of hotdog which she only sniffs.

Still on all fours I turn sideways to her and crab crawled closer to her stopping two feet from her. I swing my hips towards her and chuckle as she jumps and then bounds back and forth her body parallel to mine. With one bound close to me she pauses a moment and then bumps my hips with hers. I bend my head close to the ground and she does the same, her head less than six inches from mine. Then suddenly she stops, directly in front of me, facing me, less than two feet away. I feel drawn to touch her. I sit back and then reach towards her. As I touch the fur just below her ear she stays still, no tension showing. I reach forward a second time and am delighted when she allows me to press the back of my fingers against her in the same spot. Time slows and I watch myself slide my hand to the top of her head, one stroke, she leans her head ever so slightly closer making it easy and natural for me to turn my hand over and scratch her head. After a few seconds of scratching her head I move my hand away and pause. She stays right there and I have the sense she is inviting me to do more. I am amazed and delighted. I carefully hold the energies dancing within me inside my body. I worry my exuberance may startle her. I slowly reach my hand to just below her ear, stroke twice and then shift my hand to the top of her head. She shifts her body and head enough for me to pet a bit further down onto her neck. It seems like I pet her forever, shifting my hand from the top of her head to half way down her neck, back and forth. When I pause she does a play bound and we once again do faints and retreats with each other.

Then suddenly when I lean back onto my knees she is there, a foot away, standing sideways to me, her back directly in front of me, her head held high just beyond my body to the right. Her posture, her position, her energy all invite me to touch her. I scratch her head a few moments, slide my hand down her neck squeezing gently as I go, onto her shoulders. I pause there to scratch her shoulders then slide down onto her back for more scratches. As my hand slides past the middle of her back she answers my question of how much further by shifting her hips closer to me. I am in awe, deep pleasure and gratitude flowing within me. I slide my hand down to her rump just above the base of her tail and begin to scratch. I am rewarded by her arching her back to increase the pressure of my fingers. It is impossible to say whether she or I enjoyed it most. Her pleasure, my pleasure, our pleasure all blending and swirling and delighting both of us.

After what seems an eternity, probably 30 seconds, I shift my hand tail to head and back several times, petting her in the classic pattern. It seems that at the same moment she steps away and I sit back. My mind notes the synchronicity with confusion. We play a bit and then she stands about two feet from me, facing me. She seems to want more. I reach forward gently and soon find my hand on her head. A couple of minutes of that, then more play ending with her standing sideways to me once again. I spend what seems like 5 minutes petting her head, her neck, her back, and scratching at the base of her tail. Three times I touch her collar. The last touch includes enough pressure to move her collar. She does not object, no increase in body tension, no movement away from me. In those few moments it seems we both accept a future with each other, details to be discovered together.

With the task of getting Fawn and Beauty acquainted presenting itself I get up and walk to the car. Fawn, on her retractable leash, gets out of the car. She and I walk around the field with Beauty watching. Fawn indicates I have more work to do by either ignoring Beauty or pulling hard on the leash trying to get to Beauty. Thankfully frequent treats help divert Fawn's attention. After five minutes or so I return with Fawn to the car. Walking back to my car my plan is to put Fawn in the car and leave. At the car I look at Beauty and feel a desire to touch her before leaving. At first the feeling is but a whisper. As I consider just leaving the desire shifts to *"it's important"*. There seems to be unfinished business, the need to somehow verify our choices to be with each other. And so I head out into the field.

I walk to within 10 feet of Beauty before slowing and then kneeling. A couple of pieces of hotdog tossed close to her draw no movement. I lean forward onto all fours and slowly crawl within four feet of her unsure what she will do. At four feet I lean back on my knees and offer her a piece of hotdog. She ignores it. Okay. I lean forward onto all fours again and then lean even further forward stretching out my arm towards her head. She simply waits, allowing my hand to touch her muzzle and then slide to the top of her head. After perhaps 15 seconds I lean back onto my knees and wait for a sense of whether I should do more. A few moments pause and I know I need to move closer so that I am relaxed while petting Beauty. I shuffle forward on my knees to within 2 feet of Beauty. She waits, seeming to relax. As I reach out to pet her she shifts her body towards me so that I can pet her head and her neck. I am enchanted. I pet her for a couple of minutes. Each touch, each movement seems to work a bit of magic for both of us. A few moments of pausing and it is time to get up and say goodbye. As I walk towards the car I have the sense of stretching Beauty and I's connections over time and space, as if I am pulling a large piece of taffy that needs to be stretched and worked to be ready. As I drive away I start to review who I am going to tell and when. I feel a bit of regret knowing that telling one friend will have to wait until she gets home from work later. I decide I will give the person who told me about Beauty a call as soon as I get to my destination and I have parked. During the half hour drive to my friend's house I am filled with wonder and contentment and a sense of how I am about to announce 'Beauty and I' to the world.

Enjoying Attention

Monday, May 7nd

*A*nother beautiful day, or is that another day of Beauty? The sky is almost cloudless, a cool morning of sun warmed to the mid 70s. As with two previous days I have double duty visiting my friend's dogs to see that her dog in poor health is tended to. The plan is to visit Beauty each time before going to my friend's house. That means leaving my house by 11:45. As I am preparing to leave Fawn follows me closely, looking hopeful, letting me know she really does want to go. As I open the backdoor to leave I give in and hold the door open for her to go first. She barks with excitement as she hurries past me.

When I get to Beauty's area she is not in sight. I whistle a few times as I get out a hotdog. I spot the fellow at the spa shop unpacking items in the enclosure where I feed Beauty. I walk towards him, shouting a greeting. He response with a smile and, "**Oh, hi**". I tell him that yesterday Beauty enjoyed me petting her, that she let me pet her head, neck, and back, that she even let my scratch her back at the base of her tail. His reply of "**Oh, good**" seems a mixture of disappointment and pleasure. When I turn back to the field I fill with warmth seeing that Beauty has come through the hedge to the left and is walking towards my car. I holler to her as she stops and sits, about 60 feet away. With a big smile and some uncertainty I return to the trunk and get a hotdog.

When I turn back I find myself smiling, pleased to see Beauty is 20 feet closer and walking towards me. Each step seems to declare a tiny bit more trust. At about 30 feet she stops and sits. I close the trunk and wait and wait a bit more. As I wait I notice my mind trying to figure out why we are not taking action. She gets up and as she begins to walk towards me again my mind relaxes. In response I walk in her direction, not directly at her. Each step seems a declaration, a request, that she be mine, that I be hers. When I am about 20 feet from her she stands up, her tail raises and wags two or three times, then stops. I stop, shift my weight back and forth a bit with her just looking at me. Without thinking I kneel down and turn slightly away from her, sensing she is waiting for me . I feel as though she and I have stepped onto a dance floor, each of us unsure, we have not yet selected our music. She gets up and begins walking towards me, tail high with an occasional wag. Her ears are up and her mouth is closed. She stops and stands there looking at me and then allows her mouth to open. Gentle rhythms begin to flow between us. A tossed piece of hotdog invites her. She steps within 3 feet. She considers my offer with a few sniffs and signals her acceptance by eating the piece. Her looking up for more invites me closer. I stretch my hand out offering her a piece, she stretches her neck and takes the piece. Her ignoring the next piece offered invites me to be braver, to step closer. I pause a moment and then lean forward to gently reach out towards the space just below her ear. As I touch her she moves her head away. I sit back, pause, and she seems to whisper, *"You must offer more."* I offer another piece. This time she steps in a bit closer and takes it. She is standing so close to me, body a bit tense, head high, ears up, mouth closed, facing slightly to the right. I gently reach out and touch her just below the ear, she allows it. I stroke her slowly noting continued tension in her body, her mouth closed, her ears closer together. My strokes move down to her mouth and the back to below her ear. Four, five, six strokes and she shifts her face, turning her muzzle a bit further away from me, making it easier to stroke below her ear.

Watching her response closely I slide my hand to the top of her head. Her ears relax and she lowers her head towards me a couple of inches, the curtsy of a young maiden. As I scratch her head she lowers it another couple of inches, surrendering, inviting, giving me access to her neck. I slide my hand off her head, stroke her neck a few times and return to her head. As I withdraw my hand I hear myself saying, "**Good girl, you're so pretty.**" and realize how much that statement reflects what I am experiencing. I offer more hotdog, she takes the first and refuses the second. Unlike other times she refused a piece from my hand, she does not move back. She simply waits, a bit more relaxed. I smile, the theme of our music has changed from food to touch. I reach out and touch her muzzle and then move my hand to below her ear and then to her head. Her mouth opens slightly. After a minute of stroking her head I draw my hand back, turn slightly sideways, and lean forward onto all fours. I feel as though I have bowed to her offering her my hand. She bends forward, sniffs my head, and then licks the hair just above my ear. It is as though she has taken my hand and gently squeezed it in encouragement. I shift more sideways, placing myself parallel to her. Her tail comes up and wags, her mouth opens, her tongue comes out and we move forward together. Our dance has begun. After two steps I sense our movements linking, our pace and timing synchronizing.

At 15 feet I stop, she takes a couple more steps, turns towards me and stops six feet from me. I kneel there wondering how to move closer to pet her more. After a moments consideration, while she waits, I turn sideways to her and crab walk to within three feet of her. She remains relaxed, mouth open, tongue out. I shift my hips so that my hips move closer to her hips, so we face the same direction and I am only two feet from her. She is still. I reach and pet her on her head, then begin scratching. I scratch her neck, her shoulders, her back, and when I begin scratching her back at the base of her tail she arches with pleasure into my scratching. The warmth of her surrendering to sensual pleasure flows through me as we share. Two minutes or so and I stop, return to her head, and repeat the process. As the music shifts I bow my head closer to her, she responds with a playful jump to the side. We go back and forth, her jumping towards me, me jumping towards her. When she settles with her head inches from mine, I sit back on my knees and reach out to pet her head and neck. She turns so that she is sideways to me and I have access to pet her head to tail. As I shift my hand to scratch the base of her tail for the second time she takes a half step away from me, turning so her butt is facing me. She relaxes, stretches her back, arches her butt, and lifts her head slightly as I happily scratch the base of her tail. My sense of her acceptance, trust, and surrender fills me with gratitude and warmth. After about a minute and a half she steps away, turns towards me and sits. Being aware of the time and awaiting tasks I bend forward stroke her head and tell her I will see her again later. As

I get up and walk to the car she gets up and follows me, about 15 feet behind me. When I get to the car she stops and watches me get in. As I start the car she trots towards the enclosure. I find myself wishing I had not waited to mix her food.

After an enjoyable visit with Fawn and my friend's three dogs I head back to the geodesic dome I live in. It is getting too hot to leave Fawn in the car. I deliver Fawn home, pick up some cheese, water, and raw asparagus, my lunch, and head for Beauty's area. Once again Beauty is not is sight when I arrive. A couple of whistles bring her through the hedge. As I retrieve her food bowl she walks to the edge of the pavement. While mixing her food I toss her a piece of hotdog which she ignores. As I walk to the enclosure entry she walks towards the car. When I turn to return to the car I notice she is waiting at the car. "That is new." floats through my mind. She stays there until I exit the enclosure. Then she crosses the pavement and sits waiting for me as I take out hotdogs. I walk towards her, pointing to where I am going to kneel. She gets up, tail high and wagging, and moves to a spot about 10 feet from my target. As I kneel she walks to within 2 and ½ feet of me and sits. I offer her a piece of hotdog which she takes. She is sitting relaxed, her ears up and relaxed, her mouth open, tongue out. I reach out and begin petting her head. For a couple of minutes I alternate handing her hotdog pieces and petting her head. Then she startles me when she jumps sideways inviting me to play. We do fainting towards each other and jumping away for several minutes. She announces the end of our play by standing two feet from me her body arched sideways so her head, back, and tail are all close to me. Enchanted I reach up and begin petting her head, neck, and back. About then I notice the fellow from the spa place going to his car. I holler his name and smile as he turns to see Beauty and I together. With his return holler of "**alright**" my smile broadens. Though I want to stay, it is time to go. I get up and walk towards the car. Beauty follows. At the car I look back. Somehow it feels important to walk to her once more for a few parting strokes on her head. I turn and walk to her. Six feet from her I slow, take two more steps and kneel. She hasn't moved. As I reach out and pet her head I feel a warmth within myself, a connection with her, and her happiness to enjoy my attention. Reluctantly I get up, return to the car, and with gentle sorrow drive off.

HANDLING MY DOG

Tuesday, May 8th

Today is another double visit day. On the way out for the first visit I allow my mind and inner awareness to play with 'next steps'. What do I need to test? What steps are next? What 'flow' do I want Beauty and I to move through? I will need to get her on leash so some testing around her collar is in order. I will need to get her into the car so I will need to build her trust with the car. My mood sinks as I realize, "Oh... getting her on leash could be a major problem." I need to be able to get the leash off if she panics. I certainly won't want to reach in to undo her leash if she is panicked. An image of trying to undo her leash when she is panicking impels me to accept that getting her on leash will take some planning. I can include playing with her collar when petting her. I want her to be comfortable with me moving her body around with my hands. I will add that to our play bit by bit.

    My pondering ends as I turn into the parking lot and drive behind the shop and park. As I get out of the car and whistle Beauty's head comes up over the now long grass. Her long red hair makes it easy to see her against the lush green of spring. By the time I am closing the car door Beauty is trotting towards me, tail high, mouth open. A step away from the car and warmth flows into me with a sense of being greeted by Beauty. Without thought I flow warmth and happiness back to Beauty. My mind struggles with noticing that her tail begins to wag the instance I choose to flow love to her. With a shrug I holler, **"Hey Beauty! How is my Beauty?"** My mind protests "My Beauty? Since when?" The next moment my mind is wondering why we have not gone to the trunk for hotdogs. "What are we going to do?" Without thought I relax into

194

enjoying the warmth flowing between Beauty and I, and I sense an inner whisper of, "*No hotdogs, no treats. Just being her people!*"

When Beauty is about 15 feet away my energy shifts, I kneel and turn slightly away from her. My mind has slipped into observer mode, instincts and inner awareness are guiding my choices. Her pace slows slightly as I shift to my hands and knees and turn so she is approaching my left side. As she comes within 5 feet of me I begin crawling forward and allow myself to sense her joining me, walking with me. I grin as she does just that. We move together for about eight feet where I slow and then sit. Beauty sits down with me, together we are facing the apartment buildings across the field. With ease I reach over to stroke her muzzle with the back of my fingers. I smile as she turns her head towards me offering me her head. Soon my hand slips to her neck and then back. In a relaxed and focused way I turn towards her and stroke her back purposely not scratching at the base of her tail. I grin as I sense her acceptance of my being focused rather than playful. With a "**Your a good girl.**" I reach to her collar, brush her fur aside, and begin slowly rotating her collar to check for a tag. Beauty shows her uncertain acceptance by staying still, tail up, not wagging, mouth closed, ears slightly back, body alert, neither tense nor relaxed. I am now for the first time handling my dog. I wonder how far Beauty will trust me. I pull on her collar just enough to cause her to move slightly and stop as her ears go backwards. A deep breath in and then slowly out help me stay calm and alert. As the tension flows out of my body Beauty steps in a bit closer to me. I am delighted, mesmerized. I begin running my fingers through her fur and smile as Beauty allows me to pick at a couple of the many mats in her undercoat. With a "**Good girl**." my hand moves towards her head. I relax and smile when Beauty moves her head to meed my hand.

Without recognizing the choice I respond to sensations within my body that guide me to begin petting Beauty in the pattern I had used before. A minute later my mind protests the thought that I am responding to sensations Beauty used to ask me to pet her, sensations of her body enjoying my touch. Beauty shifting her hips towards me allow me to let go of my thoughts and I drop back into what my mind will only allow to be 'touch testing' with Beauty. My body and inner awareness know it is far more. As my hand slides from Beauty's head to her neck to her shoulders, instinctively I slide my hand away from me so it slips to the far side of her and on down to the base of her tail for a few scratches. Encouraged by Beauty remaining close to me I begin again. Hand on head, hand sliding down her neck slipping off her neck and stopping on her far shoulder so I am reaching over her. Very gently, very lovingly, with relaxed awareness I push my palm against the far side of her shoulder, pulling her towards me, causing her to lean towards me perhaps an inch. Her ears come back, her body tenses. In a playful voice I repeat, "**Good girl.**" several times gently pulling her towards me in time with my voice. Two, three, four times and Beauty swings her hips away and sits facing me. I grin, bow my head twice and reach slowly up to stroke her muzzle with the back of my fingers. To my surprise Beauty moves her head forward to accept my affection then stands and turns to offer me her entire body. My body is filled with a sense of her acceptance. Game on!

For the next ten minutes I pet Beauty allowing my hands to touch her in new places and applying just enough pressure to cause her body to move. In a playful way I am testing how much she will allow me authority, testing to find places she enjoys my touch, places she is guarded. I scratch the lower side of her neck and upper part of her chest. She tenses when my hand slide from her side to her lower chest and steps away when my hand slide to her belly. I smile and relax when she lets me reach over her side and pull her back sideways to me. I sense her choosing to trust me, to allow my guidance, to surrender just a bit to being 'my dog'. She allows herself to be petted, to enjoy my attention. I pet her with both hands, she protests when one hand is on her back and I slip the second hand to her upper chest. Finally she is sitting facing me about three feet away. Sensations in my body tell me she is offering herself as 'my friend', accepting me as 'her friend'. A bond of friendship opens with possibilities of more. I am enthralled.

With a "**You're such a good girl.**" I reach up with both hands, one on each side of her muzzle, pet her for a few strokes and then holding her head lean forward and touch my forehead to hers. One second, two seconds, three seconds and she pulls her head back. I sit back with a big grin, warmth flowing in my body, my chest swelling. My voice and warmth float to her as I reach out with one hand and stroke her muzzle. My pleasure deepens as Beauty's ears come forward, her mouth opens, and her tongue comes out. Our eyes meet, the warmth, openness, acceptance, pleasure flowing between us seems to deepen our agreement.

Reluctantly I accept I must go. Somehow going now is just what I need to do for both of us. Beauty seems uncertain as I get up and return to the car. As I drive to my friends house I sense Beauty and I both opening so our new connections stretch over the distance separating us, so our connections become timeless.

Showing Me Her Space

As I drive back for our second visit I hope Beauty will be around, waiting to be fed. As I drive behind the shop warmth fills me with the sight of Beauty's reddish glow in the lush green spring grass. Beauty is laying in the grass, close to the pavement. I grin as my mind notes she has chosen to be far more exposed than in the past. Her head comes up and she stands as I drive towards her. She turns and begins to walk away. As my mind and ego begin to panic I experience rolling down the window and whistling 'our whistle'. Before the whistle ends Beauty stops and turns back to face the car. As I turn to park I holler, "**Hey girl. I am back.**" As the door swings open Beauty begins to walk towards me, a friend walking to meet a friend. My mind and ego struggle with noticing she seems more relaxed and open than they feel. Within is simply warmth and pleasure. Beauty stops and sits about 20 feet from me and the car. Glancing at Beauty I have the distinct impression I am supposed to attend to the business of feeding her. With an "**Okay girl**." I head to the enclosure to retrieve her food bowl. I am pleased that Beauty remains where she is as I return to the car and pop the trunk. I grin as Beauty gets up and moves so she can watch me mix her food, standing about 20 feet away. Beauty watches as I return to the enclosure, place her food bowl, and then fill her water bowl. As I return to the opening of the enclosure I watch Beauty move to the edge of the pavement opposite the opening. I jump down out of the enclosure, Beauty stands and turns towards the field. What?

As I walk across the pavement my mind and ego struggle with my sensation that Beauty is going to share some of her secrets. When I am about ten feet from Beauty she begins a slow walk towards the hedge, off to the left, along the west side of the field. Following her seems easy and natural even while my mind and ego are uncomfortable with the lack of certainty. Beauty leads me to the spot in the hedge where she had appeared a few times. She turns her head, watching me as she takes the last few steps to our first destination. As she turns and looks at me I notice the grass is shorter here showing she uses the spot regularly. In a moment she turns back towards the hedge and then takes three steps into the hedge and turns back to me. Suddenly I understand. Beauty is showing my one of her 'hidy holes'. I notice how she is barely visible inside the bushes, protected from view and weather. I also notice the area just outside the bushes has the feel of a spot for Beauty to enjoy being out while close to one of her hideouts. When Beauty moves so her head and shoulders are outside the bushes all uncertainty evaporates, Beauty is sharing with me one of her places. My mind is puzzled and ego pleased with Beauty's demonstration of trust, demonstration of friendship. After a few moments of being with Beauty in her space Beauty heads towards the apartments. As we get close to the apartments I notice the two stray Siamese cats by the bushes near the rise Beauty used to disappear over. The cats are startle when they notice me and seem to relax when they notice Beauty is with me. I stop as I sense within my body Beauty whispering *'Wait here.'* Beauty continues towards the cats. I am surprised and warmed as I watch the cats 'lead' Beauty into 'their bushes'. A few moments later Beauty comes out, looks at me, looks back at the bushes, looks back at me. I have the sense of Beauty saying, *"Those are my friends."*

I am a bit surprised that Beauty walks back within 5 feet of me before continuing along the fence that separates the field from the 2 story apartments. At the end of the apartments the field side of the fence is filled with blackberry vines that extend 15 to 20 feet into the field. Beauty leads me to a gap in the bushes, looks back at me, and then at the gap. My eyes trace the gap into the bushes and I notice a gap in the fence at the other end of the bushes. It looks like a good escape route for a raccoon and as I wonder if Beauty could get through the gap Beauty answers by walking into the gap partway, carefully turning and walking back out. I hear myself say **"Oh, an escape route**." and smile when Beauty's tail begins to wag. Beauty interrupts my mind and ego protesting that possibility by continuing along the blackberry bushes. Another 20 feet along the blackberry bushes and I watch Beauty disappear into them. At the place she disappeared I find a small opening and crouch down wondering how far back Beauty has gone. I see Beauty laying down, back about eight feet, where the gap is bigger. Something is different. I see her... Oh... I do not sense her. I relax my body, take a couple deep breaths, put my mind in observer mode, and open my awareness. Beauty has her energy cloaked. Gentle breaths and quiet paying attention brings an understanding. Beauty is in an 'energy cave' she has created, a place where the physical barrier of the blackberry bushes has been blended with an 'energy cloak'. Puzzled, curious I step back and scan the bushes. The opening into the bushes seems to visually disappear, I sense no trace of Beauty. I few moments later Beauty physically and energetically comes out of the opening and continues along the blackberry bushes, waiting for me to follow her from about ten feet away. As I turn back to the bushes the opening, the space within are there, easily visible, just a trail for raccoon and opossums. Beauty moving on catches my attention and I step away, following her. Further on Beauty shows my another gap in the fence, another escape route. Turning and continuing along the edge of the field Beauty lets me know she does not trust the yard of a rundown house and work shed. We continue along a 12 foot high laurel hedge to a gap Beauty disappears into. It is an opening into a large, semi wild back yard. Beauty seems to have become part of the space. I have the sense that the space enjoys the way Beauty is within it. As Beauty trots in the backyard I wait at the entry, unable to enter. My mind and ego try to come up with reasons, private property, boards knocked out of place. With a deep breath I simply know I am not to enter. I whistle to Beauty and walk away, heading back to the car. Twenty feet and a second whistle later Beauty comes out of the backyard and joins me in my walk back to the car.

At the car I get out treats, open both back doors then walk towards Beauty sitting 15 feet away. She surprises me by getting up and swinging around me to the car. I simply watch and wait. Beauty goes around to the far door, paces back and forth, looks at me through the backseat and then goes to the backdoor and sniffs around the opening. I hear myself saying, "**Good girl**." as Beauty trots around the back of the car

Bringing In Beauty

to the backdoor closest to me. Her movements become tentative, small movements with frequent glances back at me. A few sniffs around the door opening and she backs away, turns and walks just beyond me. I grin as I understand. She showed me her territory, she just examined my territory. I am full. Beauty is full. Beauty begins to walk away. I can't let her go yet. I whistle and take a few steps towards her. She turns and stops as I sink to my knees. "**Come on girl, just a bit.**" I bend forward to my hands and knees and stretch a hand towards Beauty. I smile and relax as she takes the few steps needed for me to stroke her muzzle. Two seconds of stroking and she steps in offering me her side. I am smiling as I pet her being sure to move her collar during the process. I tense a bit with plans for an intimacy test. Beauty tenses a bit and turns her head to look at me. With my hand on her neck just behind the collar I dig my fingers in working to penetrate her undercoat. Beauty relaxes a bit and as I think "Oh, good." I begin to pull at the mats on her neck, close to her collar. I sense Beauty wanting me to do something. Disappointment flows into me as I seem unable to identify what she is hoping for. Twenty seconds and we are done. A few long strokes from head to tail and I stand, walk back to the car, get in, drive away. As I leave the area I know I will be processing what has happened for several days.

TAKING MY HAND

Wednesday, May 9th

Today is another day of two visits. The first about 1:00 PM on my way to spend time with my friend's dogs, the second about 3:30 PM after that visit.

When I arrive Beauty is in sight, laying at the hedge to the left, about 150 feet away. I park, roll down my window, whistle, and get out. Beauty sits up and watches as I go to the trunk and take a hotdog out of the trunk. As I turn towards the field Beauty gets up, stretches, and stands waiting. Mild disappointment wash through me as I sense that she expects me to show her I can be trusted. I walk towards her and she takes a few steps forward, that is better. At about 30 feet from her as I kneel, she begins trotting towards me. My smile reflects the warmth I feel as she approaches with her tail wagging. She sits down about five feet from me, head up, ears up, mouth open, tongue out. I pause, then sensing a bit of relaxed openness with her I knee walk towards her. Her mouth closes and her ears shift a bit higher, she remains relaxed and cautious as I reach to pet her head. As my hand approaches she raises her head, opens her mouth, lets her tongue out. I smile with a sense of her opening a bit further. She sniffs my hand and then licks it as I gently move my fingers against her muzzle. She stops licking and lowers her head towards me. I hear myself saying, "**You're such a good girl.**" as my hand touches her head. My words reflect the warmth, acceptance, and connection I feel with her. A few seconds of petting and she steps closer, looking at the hand holding the hotdog. I barely notice the sensation of chewing hot dog in my mouth. Without thinking I tear off a piece and hand it to her. She takes it (pleasure), drops it (worry and concern), then steps closer (warmth and pleasure blending). As I reach to pet her head she steps closer and turns a bit sideways inviting me to pet more of her. Warmth fills me and I notice that she and I are now in our own space, somehow separated from the world around us. Her tail is down, almost tucked between her legs. Over the next minute I scratch her and watch her tail. Bit by bit her tail rises, it seems to reflect her relaxing into being with me, into there being an 'us'. When her tail is level with her back I kept my scratching where my hand is at the moment. Once she raises her tail again I move my hand further down her body. As soon as my hand begins scratching the base of her tail her tail comes up and she arches her back in pleasure. She swings her hips closer to me and curls her tail even more. Her hips swing back and forth several times before she arches her head sideways, away from me and back towards her tail, once, twice, three times each time arching further, each time surrendering further into her pleasure. I feel her open mouth touch my scratching hand and she steps away. I am confused. Is it play? Is it protest? Is it both? She loops around bringing herself sideways in front of me and shifts her hips towards me. Her mouth is open, her tongue out, and her tail is high and wagging. As I reach out I think, "Oh, good." Inside I am delighted and in awe, such openness, such trust, such surrender. As I scratch at the base of her tail she arches her back in pleasure and again arches sideways bringing her mouth back to my scratching hand, once, twice, at the end of the third arching she swings her hips away pushing my hand with her mouth and head, then gently, playfully taking my hand into her mouth for a couple seconds. She is now facing me, tail wagging, and I notice myself gently moving my hand touching, almost caressing her muzzle. For about five seconds she follows my hand, pushing my hand firmly with her muzzle and licking. As she steps away it feels that we just became more intimate. Deep within there is no doubt. I sense the bending of us deep, deep within myself. Somehow by taking my hand in her mouth Beauty demonstrates she is taking my soul within hers. By allowing, by enjoying my caressing of her muzzle, by pushing against my hand for contact, by caressing my hand with licking, she expressed the connections we both desire.

As she turns back towards me she looks directly at the hand holding the hotdog and moves her head towards that hand. I smile, enjoying her directness. Clear enough. One at a time I break off several pieces and give them to her. With the last piece of hotdog in her mouth it is time to head to my friend's house. As I walk back to the car Beauty follows me at a distance of 15 feet or so. She stops at the edge of the pavement. I turn and tell her I will see her later. It seems important that I touch her again before leaving. I gently walk to where she is sitting, talking the whole time. I slow the last two steps, bend, and reach down and pet her head. To my pleasure and satisfaction she stays seated accepting the attention. Ten seconds later I am walking back to the car, 20 seconds later I am driving away.

INTIMACY AND PLAY

2nd visit

Driving back for our second visit I sense uncertainty, mine and Beauty's. As I remember our first visit and open to the future I sense that there will be many more days of showing I am trustworthy. I sense how over the last five months Beauty and I have opened little by little to each other. I am both amused and perturbed to realize that I have been every bit as cautious in choosing to trust as Beauty has been. I sense how bit by bit I am becoming 'her people' and she is becoming 'my dog'. As I sense the possible futures I understand both Beauty and I have more to do if we are to be together. I sense faint traces of her being in my home, of us being family. I plant the question of 'What must still be done?' within my belly. I notice I am in the left turn lane, ready to drive behind the store to be with Beauty.

It is a warm and sunny day. As I slow to park I notice the grass is fairly dry and I have a sense of Beauty and I rolling in the grass, a dog and her people playing together. I am smiling and relaxed as I open the door and stretch out into the warm spring, almost summer weather. With the stretch I am flooded with memories and sensations of what Beauty and I shared earlier. As I glance around the field I do not see Beauty. As I turn to scan the enclosure I whistle. No sign of Beauty. The worry of my mind and ego are interrupted by sensations within my body that cause me to begin walking out into the field. A cascade of thoughts, "What are we doing?", "This is silly.", and others cause my body to tense and disconnect me from the lush, green, spring beauty. A semi thought of "Observer mode now. We can figure it out later." quiets my mind and ego and once again I sense the flow of lush spring energy within me. One step, two steps, three steps and I am part of the field, time has shifted and the blackberry bushes are drawing me to them. As my mind seeks to locate the opening to Beauty's cave I sense a null spot where Beauty's blackberry cave is. Step, step, I sense deeper, step, step, the null becomes a barrier. Step, step, the barrier drops and I sense Beauty's playful energy greeting me. My mind and ego insist, "This is crazy." and quiets as I acknowledge, "Yes, it is." Walking the remaining 50 feet seems to take forever. I bend and glance into Beauty's berry cave. And there she is, laying there in her cave, head up, mouth open, tongue out. I have the sense of her smiling and laughing. Without choosing I kneel and then sit back on my heels and hear myself playfully saying "**What you doing, girl?**" Within I sense a whispered, "*Playing. Testing you. You passed.*" And with that Beauty stands and walks towards me. Suddenly I am in turmoil, "What do I do?" Beauty looks at me and seems a bit cautious. Before I can respond she is stepping past me, taking six steps before stopping to wait for me. By the time I am standing she begins a loop around the field, glancing back to make sure I am following. It is clear that Beauty is taking me on a tour. We head East. At the cluttered yard, the one that seems to scare Beauty, she goes closer and spends a few moments sniffing the trees. When she looks back at me I have the sense she wants me to sniff where she did. I walk to the spot and see nothing unexpected. I can almost hear Beauty asking, "*You don't sniff things?*" She turns and walks into the enchanted backyard that I am not permitted to enter. She goes in, sniffing here and there, several times looking at me as if to say, "*Well, come on.*" As she circles and sniffs a patch of dense grass and looks up at me I can almost hear her whisper, "*I sleep here sometimes.*" When I look at the house she seems to whisper, "*If no lights.*" Yes, I know. My mind barely accepts what I sense and offers, "Crazy! Okay, if you never mention it." A thought of the mystic I studied with ends the internal discussion.

After a few minutes Beauty trots out of the backyard and walks on. We loop along the fence towards the street circling back towards the enclosure past the dilapidated apartments that looked like they had been a motel in the 50s. When we get back to where the car is parked I retrieve some hotdogs and walk to where Beauty is sitting on the grass 15 feet away. I show my playful mood by bobbing my body back and forth. Beauty stands and wags her tail in response. In the last three steps I decide it is time to play, to be a bit aggressive and test Beauty's boundaries and mine. I drop to my knees, wiggle my body and fall over sideways. Beauty lunges towards me and I roll away from her. As I complete my roll I see Beauty jump sideways in play. Without thinking I roll onto my back and pat the ground. "**Come here, girl.**" Beauty cautiously, playfully moves to my feet, lays down, and begins sniffing them. A few sniffs and Beauty stands, seeming unsure what to do. I sit up, folding my legs under me and grin as Beauty's ears come down and she draws her head back. I wiggle a little and once Beauty's ears come back up I lean forward extending the back of my hand to her muzzle. Beauty surprises me by stepping forward offering me both her muzzle and her neck. After a few strokes of the back of my hand on her muzzle she steps in closer. Wiggling my body I begin petting her, playfully, gently pushing her away and pulling her towards me. Several times I push or pull with my hands putting pressure on her collar. After perhaps a minute Beauty takes a step back and I respond by playfully flopping on my side. "**What you gonna do, girl?**" Beauty immediately moves to my feet, sniffs them, I wiggle, she moves up and sniffs my knees. I wiggle some more and she move up and sniffs my hips. More wiggling and she just looks at me. "**Okay, girl.**" and I reach my hand down and wiggle it inches from her muzzle. "**Well girl.**" and I sit up slightly reaching towards her muzzle with the back of my hand. Beauty's mouth is closed and her ears are back. She draws her head back. "**Oh, come on girl.**" and I gently move my hand as if stroking her muzzle. Suddenly she steps forward offering me both her muzzle and her neck. I am elated. My pleasure expands when I stop stroking her muzzle and she steps in to sniff my chest, then allows me to stroke her muzzle and neck as senses of intimacy and connection flood through me. In that moment Beauty steps in closer, offering me her side. From laying on the ground, looking up at her it is easy and natural to reach and scratch her chest and belly. As I begin stroking her belly Beauty turns her head and looks at me with what seems a *"Did I say you could?"*.

I wiggle and roll partially on my side, reach under her and gently pull her towards me. As she allows it I roll my head aside opening my neck up to her. Less than a full breath later I feel her sniffing my neck.

On the next breath I roll my head back towards her and find my nose a couple inches from her nose. To my delight she sniffs me for several seconds allowing us to 'share breathe' for the first time. As she pulls her head back I reach up, gently push down at the base of her tail, and ask, **"Can you sit for me?"** She resists and as soon as I drop my hand away from her back she sits. I am delighted, perplexed, worried, and happy all at the same time. Beauty seems to sense my wondering and wonderment and confounds me by laying down next to me. My mind is gone, my ego is visiting some far off land. I reach over and stroke Beauty's shoulders and hear myself saying **"Thank you, girl."** and sense deep warmth and calm flow through me with a sense that Beauty and I have relaxed into 'our space'. I sense Beauty's surrendering a moment before she rolls over, first to her side and then to her back. Stretching my arm over to stroke her belly happens easily and naturally. So does sitting up part way so I have fuller access to Beauty's belly. I am quiet, enjoying her desire and offer for more touch. As I stroke her belly she surrenders into my attention. I feel an urge to hug her and am startled by her tensing up. I lay back down and watch with regret as she roles away and then stands. I am not ready to stop. Again Beauty surprises me by stepping in offering me her side and reaching down to sniff my neck. I roll towards her, onto my belly, and pause. She is inches from me. I push up onto my hands and knees and with my body along side Beauty's I bump her hips with my hips and hear a low growl come from deep within myself. As Beauty steps away I growl and do a play bow. Immediately she leaps away, circles around, and comes in parallel to my body and bumps bodies with me. We play in close with each other with frequent body contact. The sound of a truck door closing brings it to a sudden halt. Both of us turn towards the sound. As I sense Beauty's worry I find myself thinking, "He thinks I am crazy for sure." Still on my hands and knees I wave to him and then sit back on my heels. It is a truck delivery person who first suggested I talk with the storekeep about feeding Beauty in the store enclosure. We have talked about Beauty and I's progress a few times. My embarrassment fades as I see his expressive smile and he gives me a thumbs up before turning to enter the store.

 The spell is partially broken and yet when I reach my hand towards Beauty with a **"Come here, girl"** she does just that. In a few moments

I am petting her as she stands close to me. Within a minute she offers me her butt to scratch, arching her back in pleasure and then arching her head back close to my hand, inviting me to keep scratching. Two minutes later we are done. Beauty steps a few feet away and sits. My standing includes a "**Okay girl. Enough for today.**" A couple steps and I bend down to pet her. Her acceptance and pleasure delight me. A perfect ending for the visit.

So Much Grooming Needed

Thursday, May 10

Today there will be only one visit with Beauty. As I guessed while driving out she is not in sight when I get there but shows up as soon as I whistle for her. I park my car on the edge of the field rather than the usual spot so that I can start working to get her used to the car and possibly entice her to get in. As expected with the change she is a bit more cautious. Things flow pretty much as expected. One thing is new and puzzling. Now if I approach her and reach to pet her head she moves her muzzle to intercept my hand. I don't have a clear sense of why. Protecting herself, wanting a chance to approve touch, a bit of intimacy before other touch, all are floating in my awareness. I have a comb today. I place her food before I join her in the field and cautiously show her the comb before trying to use it. She sniffs it and does not otherwise react. I pet her for a couple minutes before I get out the comb. As I draw out the comb I notice that I am far more nervous than she. My mind and ego are unsure I should be stepping into responsibility for her grooming. Somehow it is a level of intimacy and commitment that makes me uncomfortable. She accepts my combing her back but will only stand in place for a few strokes of the comb. Four times she steps away after a few seconds of combing. With uncertainty I put the comb away. Her fur is a mess. I worry about how to encourage her to allow me to brush her. On to the next desired change, her becoming comfortable around the car.

I go to the car and gather a few hotdogs. Rather than going into the field I open the backdoor of the car and squat down there. I spend about five minutes squatting near the open backdoor of the car enticing

Beauty with treats. Beauty is very cautious and takes only a few pieces of hotdog there. I place another conundrum in my awareness, how do I get Beauty into the car and home? With that it is time to relax and just enjoy being with each other. Beauty and I spend a bit of time moving together around the field. I am pleased and warmed by the progress. Beauty accepts my affection, my reaching down to pet her while we are walking together. After about 15 minutes of interaction Beauty heads towards the enclosure. As she approaches the enclosure she slows, allowing me to catch up. I have a distinct sense that I am 'in tow', that Beauty expects me to follow her. At the enclosure entrance she waits until I am 3 feet from her before jumping into the enclosure. I am warmed with a sense of her wanting me to be with her, with her comfort of being in the enclosure with me. She waits for me just inside the entrance. I enjoy petting her a bit before she moves to check her food, and then retreats under the deck and lays down out of reach. When I bend down and talk to her I have the sense of her dismissing me, "*We are done. You can go now.*" As I return to the car I feel disappointed and worried to not have made additional progress. I ponder whether I should park in my usual place tomorrow or park where I did today, near the field. Plenty of time to decide. As I drive home I sense a whisper of "*Review what was good, what was new.*" Beauty accepting affection as we walk together and her waiting for me inside the entrance of the enclosure stand out, filling me with warmth and satisfaction.

OUR FIELD

Friday, May 11

A fairly uneventful visit. I park the car near the field again. Beauty seems more comfortable with the car being in a different place. Okay. What makes me say that? For one thing she came to me when I am close to the car, got attention, and played with me. Yesterday she preferred to be 25 to 30 feet from the car. Today she seems to be comfortable within 15 to 25 feet. Beauty shows little interest in hotdogs now. Three months ago when she first came to me it was to get hotdogs from me. Now we spend time close to each other, me petting her, she moving close to me, us playing. It is not until after she has moved around me offering/asking to receive attention for 10 or so minutes that she will take pieces of hotdog from me. Also she will only eat one or two hot dogs, far fewer than the four to six before.

Today I notice Beauty staying much closer to me while I am petting her. A common pattern is for her to face me at first. After a minute or two she will stand sideways in front of me. Soon she is standing with her side right in front of me, having moved her head to my side. With small steps she will move partially behind me placing her hips to my side, her head behind me. One more step and she is out of reach. Over the last three days her return circle to being in front of me has come closer and closer to my side. Today she circled less than six inches from my side making it easiest to reach over her head, her body between my body and my elbow. After several circles she circles in front of me and does a jump sideways, inviting me to play. After reflection it seems that when we first meet Beauty wanted me to only touch her with permission, permission consisting of my placing my hand in front of her, allowing her to sniff my hand before I began petting. That is what I did today and I noticed an almost immediate mouth open, tongue out when I first began petting her on the head.

On the second round of play Beauty scampers a bit further from me, turns and looks at me, does a play jump and heads to the hedge. Within my body I sense her invitation. When she looks back at me I am filled with playful energy and within a moment I am following her. She runs, leading me to one of the places she hides. I smile with the sensation of her desires to share her home with me. Only the sun on the other side of the bushes allow me to see where she is. I approach and as I watch her go from sitting to laying down I sense her invitation for me to join her. I kneel, find an opening and crawl to within three feet of her. She is laying, head up, mouth open, tongue out, waiting for me. As a sense of intimacy washes through me I lay down, reach out slowly, paying careful attention. My concern evaporates as she lowers her head a bit and I begin to scratch her head. I have the impression she is welcoming me into one of her "private spots". After perhaps 40 seconds of petting her I draw my hand back and laying there intrigued, a tearful warmth fills me as I sense the deep connections shaping us. A few seconds later I sense her inner whisper of '*Good, you understand.*', she gets up and as I draw back she exits her space.

Once I have backed out of her space and stood up she playfully runs from me looking back to see if I am following. When I catch up to her she pauses and seems to be considering what to do. Soon she starts walking forward towards the far side of the field. With her attention and mine linked we walk together, her head 8 to 12 inches from my knee. After a dozen or so steps she stops and I pet her head a bit. As we walk she checks to see where I am at and slows if I am more than a foot behind her. Occasionally she stops to sniff and move about and then moves back to me, glances at me, and begins walking. I sense that she is bringing me into her territory, shaping the energies so that it is 'our space'. After five minutes or so we wind up at the far right limits of the field. There is a large hedge with an opening into someone's backyard, the backyard I do not feel I may enter. Beauty pauses in front of the opening, looks at me, and starts to step through. When I do not begin moving with her she stops, turns back to me, looks at me and again steps towards the opening. After three invitations she steps through the hedge opening. I did not follow, the idea of going into someone's backyard without an invite seems disrespectful, something I attempt to avoid. Five feet in Beauty turns and looks at me. She pauses a bit, then goes in further. Halfway into the spacious backyard she stops, turns to look at me, turns away and sits. I watch her for a couple minutes. She sits where she is, faced away from me, not glancing at me. Finally I say, "**Hey Beauty. I am going.**" She does not turn to look at me. She is sitting in a relaxed manner, head high, with only occasional head movements.

Uncertain I head back to the car and get in. As I put the keys in the ignition I am surprised to notice her coming out of the backyard. She runs and then trots in my direction, a distance of about 350 feet. As she steps beyond the fence about 120 feet away I yell her name. She slows, her head at shoulder height, going back and forth. Filled with warmth I cannot sit still. I get out of the car and call her name again. Her head comes up and she begins trotting in my direction. At about 60 feet she turns and heads into the enclosure. What an incredible sight, her trotting, head high, shoulders up, bounce in her steps. I watch her jump into the enclosure and go under the deck where she lays down. Feeling a pull to follow her, in a mild state of confusion, I walk to the enclosure and step up into it. I go to her food bowl, kneel down, look at her, and tell her it is time for me to go. She looks at me from under the deck, not moving. When I sense, "*Yes, you go.*" from her I return to the car, a bit disappointed that she did not come out. As I drive away I see her at her food bowl gently nudging the food with her muzzle. In my uncertainty and disappointment I barely notice that for the first time she is allowing me to see her accepting my daily gift to her.

A Ritual of Connection

Saturday, May 12

The sun is shining, it is a hot spring day, I am turning into Beauty's area, eager to spend time with her. She is not in view so I whistle a few times. By the time I get out of the car she shows up by the hedge to the left and sits. I retrieve her food bowl, open the car trunk, and began mixing her food, half a can of wet food, some hip joint supplements, and a cup and a half of kibble. After mixing the supplements into the wet food I stop and without thought begin doing something different. I turn and walk towards Beauty. She does her stretching bow, walks a few steps towards me, and sits. When I am about half way to her I notice myself kneeling down. She immediately stands up and trots to within 5 feet of me where she sits. With my mind and ego far away I knee walk to her and when 3 feet away stretch out my hand waiting for her to indicate acceptance. This time acceptance comes in the form of sniffing and licking my hand. Space seems to open around us, for us, and we begin a new dance. She does her usual head towards me then sideways offering her neck, a step offering her back, and another step to offer her butt for scratching. She then circles behind me and comes forward on the opposite side. With the first circle her fur brushes against my side and I stroke her back as she comes forward. With the second circle I let my hand slide off her back, onto her side. With the third circle she presses against my side and pauses, leaning against me for a moment when I gently pull her towards me. As she completes the third circle she stays within a foot of me so there is no pause between ending of the third and beginning a fourth circle. I am delighted and amazed by her deciding to reduce the distance between her body and mine as I pet her. I sense how she is offering more intimacy, how I am easily responding with pleasure and warmth. There is a gentle, warm glow of shared trust. With the fourth circle I increase the pressure of my hands on her body causing her to step closer to me. With tail up and wagging she steps closer.

After a bit of her enthusiastically receiving butt scratches, with no thought I get up and return to the trunk. Beauty follows behind me by about 10 feet. At the car I mechanically finish her food and then head to place it in the enclosure. During my trip and return Beauty stays within 6 to 12 feet of the car. I notice I am in a quite mood, an easy flow with no thoughts. Back at the car I extract a hotdog from the trunk, put the scissors and comb in my pocket, and walk to Beauty. In the few steps to her I wonder what response my choice to groom her will receive. Surprisingly the idea, the impulse was so strong the night before I had placed the scissors and comb in the car before going to bed. This time I walk all the way up to her, bend, reach down in front of her, enjoy her licking my hand, and then pet her head. I kneel as without thought I pull the scissors and comb from my pocket and show them to her one at a time. She sniffs them with interest and watches me put them of the ground. Over the next few minutes of sharing she stays closer to me, sometimes stepping in to brush against me, and stepping even closer when I reach over her and pull her towards me. Her body remains relaxed the whole time. Her warmth and acceptance encourage me. A couple of times I pick up the scissors, reach to an area she had let me touch before and cut a dreadlock from her. When I show her the dreadlocks she takes them and plays with them. I am delighted and deeply touched that she is allowing, even enjoying, my efforts to remove tangles of her life as a stray. I put down the scissors and pick up the comb. Each time I begin combing the fur on her shoulders and back she is patient for a minute or so and then moves away with uncertainty. I can almost hear her whisper *"That's enough."* each time she pulls away.

At one point she is sitting sideways by me when my attention is drawn to her feet. Making sure she is watching my hand I reach down and stroke the back of her foot. Her ears come up a bit more as she remains still. I stroke the top of her foot a second time and then stroke the other foot. Her stillness as she watches along with her open mouth, tongue out let me know she accepts my advances with mixed concern and curiosity. After stroking her feet I praise her, also petting her back and head playfully. Without thought I bend down onto all fours, her response is to play jump, taking two steps away, laying down about 4 feet from me, rolling onto her back, and beginning to squirm. What a wonderful sight! I am grinning as I notice the warm playful energies weaving connections within us. After about 30 seconds she pauses and looks at me. Sensing her invitation I knee walk to her and slowly reach my hand to her belly. Her remaining on her back, moving all four feet signal acceptance and it seems to me pleasure. For close to three minutes I stroke her belly and chest as she lays there her back legs relaxed and open, her front legs relaxed and bent giving me full access to her belly and chest. I am in awe, enjoying her surrender, my surrender of mistrust, her reveling, my reveling in shared pleasures. I grin as I note that she is indeed female. A part of me notice with warmth that she is offering, surrendering her mysteries to me. When she has had enough she rolls away from me, gets up, and moves to stand sideways in front of me waiting for more attention. I happily surrender to her invitation. Cold, invisible boundaries that have separated us melt in the warmth and acceptance floating with the love connecting us.

Soon she steps away from me, standing still, body pointing towards the enclosure, her head turning looking at me. I get up and we begin walking to the enclosure. She walks with her head beside my knee paying attention to my position and movements. When I stop, she stops. When she starts walking her head turns to look at me until she sees me start walking. Ten feet from the enclosure she trots forward, turns her head to watch me, and when I am close to her she jumps into the enclosure, takes a few steps, turns, and waits until I step up into the enclosure before going on. She goes under the deck, sits for a moment and then moves to her food. Curious and happy I circle the deck and squat across her food bowl from her. I sense a shift in energy and notice we are in ritual, what we shape now will continue on into our future. She sniffs her food then lifts her head to look at me. I crawl forward, pet her head, and then lean back onto my knees. She bends her head and begins to eat. Her behavior reminds me of how both my cats and my dog will sometimes go to their food bowl and wait until I begin petting them to eat. With quiet warmth and reverence I allow myself to accept, she is now more 'my dog', I am now more 'her people'.

A Bit Surreal

Sunday, May 13th

I arrive at Beauty's area at about 2:30 when it is almost 80 degrees and the sun is shining. Beauty is not in sight when I show up. A few whistles bring her out of the hedge as I get a hotdog from the trunk. As I walk towards her she stays seated by the hedge. When I get 3/4s the distance to her she has not moved. With a bit of disappointment I walk ahead and kneel down. She gets up, stretches, and begins walking to me, her tail only partially up with but a few wags. Five feet from me she sits, head up, ears up, mouth slightly open. As she sits she moves her head to look around, checking her environment. I talk to her for a minute or so and then when her mouth opens further I knee walk to her, extending my hand, forgetting to pause for her to sniff my hand and lick it. As my hand passes above her muzzle she raises her head, her mouth closing as my hand reaches the top of her head. As I pause a couple seconds, waiting for her head to come back down, I have a sense of her whispering with an edge of scolding, *"That is not polite. Wait for my permission."* The moment I sense my own *'Oops'* flow through me her head comes down and I begin to pet her. I unhappily realize I have not brought the scissors or comb so there will be no grooming intimacy. I offer her some hotdog which she ignores. Usually after a minute or two of petting she will step so I can easily pet her neck and back. Not this time. I am concerned. Her ears are up but rotated back a bit, her mouth is only partially open. I gently knee walk to her side and when she let her mouth open a bit more I begin to pet and scratch her. She happily moves to offer her rump and then begins her circle around me. Unlike the day before she does not press into me. A few circles and she steps away from me, heading out into the field, and looking back at me. Obeying her signaled expectations I get up and follow. Finally her ears come up fully, her mouth opens, her tongue comes out, and her tail comes up, wagging. We spend several minutes walking beside each other, her sometimes stopping to sniff and then waiting for me to pet her head.

After following Beauty to the far right of the field behind the motel like apartments I return to the car by myself. Beauty wants me to follow her further but doing so will mean leaving the car with doors wide open out of my sight. When I get back to the car and as Beauty continues her walk I decide to drive to see if I can find where she has gone. I drive through the field to the far side but do not see her. Curiosity and concern tumble within me. I drive back out on the street and turn back into Beauty's area. Beauty is just trotting back as I turn in. I follow her in the car for about 50 feet. Her ears go back, her tail drops, her back lowers, and her gate becomes a slinking. With her movements I sense my concern becoming a deep sorrow, my dog does not feel safe. She pauses and then continues to the enclosure, walking fast, tail down. I park, get out, and enter the enclosure. She is under the deck as far back as possible. I squat down and talk with her. My worry eases slightly when her ears come up a bit, otherwise she remains still, hiding from the world. I go to where her food is and after a few seconds she turns, laying down facing me. After a very long minute she gets up, takes a couple steps towards me, then backs up and sits down again. I feel her turmoil, her struggle within myself. As I sense her being chased by young men, her fleeing aggressive, cruel energies, those energies flow through me. As anger stirs within me an inner whisper guides me to let the anger flow away, replaced with my wish for Beauty's safety and pleasure in life. A few moments later she lays down. I remain a couple of minutes, again and again setting aside my anger and worry so I remain open, allow myself to share Beauty's fear and pain. Then with uncertainty and concern I go back to the car, and soon drive away.

As I turn into the driveway at home I allow myself to experience my anger, so close to rage. I feel helpless, less of a man, unable to protect my Beauty. A part of me notices how unlike times before when I felt trapped, this time, connected with Beauty, I cannot go there. I simply must be with what is, filling the spaces within myself with connections Beauty and I share rather than filling those spaces with anger and 'figuring it out'. I allow myself to grin when I realize how I am choosing new possibilities, new behaviors. I am choosing beauty.

Towards Being on Leash

Monday, May 14th

Over the last few days I have been pondering what I can do to get Beauty and I past her fear of leashes. I have already shown her the retractable leash and was pleased when she had allowed me to bring the retractable to her and set it on the ground near her. I have imagined clipping the retractable onto her collar and know that she will allow me to do it. As I imagine us walking a sense of her getting spooked and beginning to pull frantically against the leash fills me. I would want to release her. And I know that she might be far too afraid to allow me to reach in close to her, to her vulnerable neck. I am very aware that she might turn against me in her panic. How do I arrange a method of letting her off the leash without reaching in close to her. I could tie a short rope to her collar and clip the leash to the rope. That would be okay but it would leave the short rope attached to her as she runs off. It would work but I should be able to do better. I set the problem aside. Well actually I transfer the problem from my mind to my belly. A couple days latter while driving out to see Beauty the problem returns to me. I sense something stirring in my belly. Suddenly I sense myself kneeling next to Beauty holding the clip of her collar with my left hand as I fed the loop at one end of a six foot rope through the clip of her collar. I bring the end to the retractable and clip it onto the retractable where the loop at the other end of the rope is already clipped. I now have a short rope looped through her collar with both ends three feet from her collar, clipped into the retractable. I imagine us walking, her getting startled, trying to run away. When it is obvious I cannot calm her I unclip one end of the rope from the retractable and release it. As Beauty pulls the freed end flies to her collar and slips through the clip. Beauty is free. With a sense of pleasure and competence I go to the closet, cut off six feet of rope, tie loops in each end, and put the rope in the trunk of the car with Beauty's retractable.

When I get to the area Beauty is laying in the field not far from where I park. She sits up as I drive across the pavement, watching as I park. I am in a business mode, want to test my rope loop out. As I get out and say hello Beauty stands and watches me go to the trunk where I get the scissors, the brush, a few hotdogs, and the rope with loops at each end. As I look up I drape the rope around my neck like a scarf. In my mind I am playing images of looping the rope through Beauty's collar clip and taking her for a walk. I am not paying attention to Beauty. By my third step towards Beauty I sense her fear, her uncertainty. I freeze as I watch her turn away from me and begin walking away. She is ten feet away before I realize I am far from being relaxed and open. I hear myself saying **"Oh girl, I am sorry."** and choose to shift all of my attention to Beauty. Within two seconds I recognize how far into 'doing mode' I am, how far I am from being open. A breath in, feet on the ground, relax my shoulders as I breath out. Beauty looks back over her shoulder and keeps walking away from me. "Oh boy, long ways to go." floats through my mind with a second breath in and out. With the third out breath I pay attention to my lower belly and drive my tension down through my legs into the earth. The fourth breath in is easier, deeper. With the fourth breath out I bend my knees sinking into a chi kung stance. Beauty looks back over her shoulder and pauses, now 50 feet away. Finally with the fifth breath out I sense my chest relaxing and opening. With the sixth breath out my belly opens. Beauty looks back over her shoulder at me, stops, turns towards me and sits. I have the sense of her whispering, *"Better, need more."* Three more breaths and I hear myself saying **"Okay girl."** and notice my knees are sinking towards the ground. I smile in response to Beauty standing and walking slowly towards me. She sits 25 feet from me. Five minutes of treats and carefully relaxing and knee walks and she is near enough that I can reach out my hand for her to sniff. Five more minutes and she is allowing me to pet and brush her. With my failures and lessons life becomes dull, I watch myself with few emotions. Beauty senses it and is guarded.

Frustrated and with an 'oh well' I decide I just need to to what I came to do. With my left hand I reach up, grab the rope, and toss it on the ground in front of Beauty. Beauty is scared and confused, holding herself very still. I reach over with my left hand and wiggle the rope allowing myself to imagine the rope attached to her collar. Beauty watches the rope move for two seconds and when I begin picking it up she hurriedly gets up, walking quickly away. I sit quietly and wait. Fifty feet away, with my energy quiet, she stops, turns, and sits. Frustrated and unhappy I lifelessly pickup the rope and play with it, wrapping it around my neck, around my arms, around my chest while Beauty watches. Soon she gets up and walks away. My mind and ego begin protesting, pointing out how many ways I had just failed. As Beauty disappears I stand a walk back to the car. I begin to go to the trunk and realize that fixing Beauty's food with openness and love simply is not going to happen. When I imagine her eating the food prepared in the foul mood I am in, my stomach churns unpleasantly. Another failure. I walk to the car, open the door, and swing my body into the seat. There I sit wrapped in frustration and regret. Finally I start the car and leave. Not wanting to expose Fawn to my mood I stop at the nature trail finally heading home after an hour of walking, the last ten minutes a walking meditation.

Effort Rewarded

My 2nd visit with Beauty occurs about 7:30 with the early evening sun less intense than during the day. A few times in the early evening I think of not going out. Simply remembering that Beauty has not been fed rekindles my willingness, a mixture of knowing the guilt I will feel if I don't feed her and the desire to ensure she has what she needs.

As I turn the last corner approaching her area I am not sure how much time I will spend. As I park and get out of the car I do not see her. After a couple of whistles bring no results, with a bit of relief, I think I can just place her food and head home to relax. I retrieve her food bowl then return to the trunk and after grounding myself and filling my belly with warmth I begin mixing her food. When I look up she is walking on the pavement towards the field. I don't know whether she was in the enclosure and I didn't see her or she came from a resting place I don't know about. She sits in the field next to the pavement where she can watch me. She is sitting tall, ears up, mouth open, tongue out, panting. Half way through mixing her food I feel a pull to go to her. I put down her bowl and walked towards her, just 20 feet away. Her mouth closes, her ears stay up, and she remains seated. I slow for the last three steps, bending and reaching out my hand. I politely extend my hand to just in front of her mouth. She sniffs my hand intently (I had just been mixing food), licks it twice, and lowers her head. Happily I begin gently, lovingly petting her. Her mouth opens, tongue comes out, she leans towards me. While I pet her head she glances at the hand holding the hotdog several times. One by one I break off pieces of hotdog, stretch out my hand and give them to her. The last piece I hold in my hand resting on my thigh. I wait, and wait, and wait (maybe a minute in all). Finally she steps forward and she takes it, but she does not eat it. After 30 seconds I move beside her petting her head to tail. A couple of minutes later, feeling greetings are complete with a smile I return to finish mixing her food. The thought of "Perhaps I will be here longer." shows me my mood has improved. I grin at myself. When I glance up at Beauty I have a sense that she is grinning at my recognition of grinning at myself, "*Silly people. Good you are learning.*" I sense some new awareness deep, deep within and wonder how long it will be before it has shifted and filtered into a form my mind can comprehend.

I finish mixing her food, get a bottle of water, and close the trunk. As I turn towards the enclosure entry I look at her and feel a pull to take the bowl to her. I pause one, two, three moments and then follow the only path my energies allow, I turn and walk towards her. She looks at me with ears cocked, mouth closed, watching very intently. I cross the pavement, kneel on the pavement, and place her bowl in front of her, just on the grass. She remains seated about five feet from me. I lean forward as she watches me, she glances down at the bowl and then raises her head looking to see what is going on around her. She repeats the cycle several times. Finally following a subtle urge from within I sit back on my heals increasing the distance between she and I. She stands, takes one step, and bends her head into the bowl. Soon she is taking small amounts of food, a few bites followed by raising her head and looking out to the left and right. A glance at me and she repeats the cycle. When about $1/3^{rd}$ of the food is gone I shift to sitting on my hip and shuffle over closer to her. When her head is in the bowl I reach out gently and stroke her neck. She continues taking bits of food so I begin to pet her neck and shoulders. Her posture relaxes a bit and her ears come up and forward. Memories of both Mystique and Fawn waiting for me to pet them before eating play in the back of my mind. Yes! Beauty is eating without raising her head to look around. With $1/3^{rd}$ of the food remaining Beauty steps sideways, turns, and moves about 10 feet away, standing still. I watch her for a couple moments, letting myself notice and enjoy Beauty's decision to trust me in a new situation. All the uncertainties about what I am doing here are replaced with a knowing and pleasure that I am doing as I must. A smile and I pick up the bowl, stand, and carry the bowl into the enclosure. As I walk to the enclosure I wonder why what happened is significant. A thought offers itself. What just occurred has begun separating Beauty's association of daily meal with the enclosure. She has experienced receiving her daily meal directly from me in a new place. I sense the shift in possibilities we have opened. For the first time I sense Beauty accepting her food in our home. I find myself smiling, filled with a gentle warmth as I wonder, 'How soon will I repeat this experience with her in our home?'

Beauty is waiting for me as I come out of the enclosure. I consider getting her rope/leash extension, the scissors, and the brush. None of that seems appropriate in the moment. So... I simple walk to Beauty. She waits for me and as I take the final steps she takes a couple steps towards me. With me kneeling she and I move in familiar patterns, her offering her rump and arching her back as I scratch it. At one point I bend down as she steps towards me. She comes in putting her head right next to mine and after a moment sniffs and licks my head. Somehow we have just agreed one will never be above the other for more than a few moments. Mixed into the play is a time when I am kneeling and she comes in close, reaches her head towards my crotch, and carefully sniffs the end of my belt which had come out of it's belt loop and is extended from my body. Warmth fills me as I accept that we have just become a bit more trusting and intimate. Is that an, *"Oh, you noticed."* I sense from Beauty?

After perhaps 10 minutes of petting and play she moves a couple feet from me and with her body faced away from me she turns her head to look at me. I sense what seems an invite to walk with her, a *"let's move together"* request. I stand and as I come along side her she begins walking. After a few steps I feel a desire to run and have her follow. I break into a run, turning my head back to her. She stops and looks at me with uncertainty. I walk back to her, pet her head and then begin walking. She follows. After a few steps I begin trotting, calling to her. She begins trotting, following me, a few feet back and to my side. After perhaps 20 feet I stop and pet her. Her ears are up, her tail wagging, her mouth open, tongue out. Three steps, she follows, then I begin a slow run and she breaks into a run next to me. It feels incredible, feeling my body move, connecting with her movements. Thirty feet and I stop. She stops next to me leaning her head into me as I pet her. I kneel and begin stroking her and scratching her rump. Her ears are high, her mouth opens further, her tongue comes out further. Then she surprises me, she plops on her side, looking right at me. Still looking at me she rolls towards me onto her back.

With surrender and pleasure I stroke her belly and chest. There is no tension in her body, she is reveling in my attention. After about a minute she rolls onto her side and then gets up. She looks at me and then takes maybe a dozen steps towards the blackberry bushes nearby. Her glance to the bushes and back to me show me where the grass is bent down from her recent time laying there. Another hidy hole shown to me. After I look into her space for several seconds she begins trotting away from me, looking back to see if I am following. I get up and trot to her, then pace myself to be next to her. Soon we are trotting together. Who is leading seems of no importance, we are sharing movement, each adjusting to the other with no thought. Eventually we reach the backyard I had not followed Beauty into. She enters, I do not. She watches me and when I turn away she turns, trotting towards the back corner that is out of sight. A bit discouraged I head back to the car. 2/3rds of the way there she comes out of the backyard, trotting towards me. I wait. She comes within 5 feet and sits. I call her to me, she remains seated. After perhaps 30 seconds I head to the car, my mind confused, something stirring. After 20 feet I stop, turn going back to her and when with her I pet her head. When I start walking towards the car she gets up and trots ahead of me. At the enclosure she waits, jumping into the enclosure when I am a few feet from her. Her turning, standing, facing me, her head at me chest level 10 feet away I have the strangest sense of her whispering, "*I will be with you even as you leave. For now this is my place.*" I continue on to the car, speak to her, and then get in. As I drive away I smile recognizing how the visit had been much more than I expected, how new possibilities now spread before Beauty and I... Oh, and Fawn.

WHERE IS THE BALANCE

May 15th

*A*s I drive out to Beauty I review the day before hoping to understand more how to balance being focused on making specific progress and being relaxed and allowing small changes that shift our possible futures. Focus alone certainly does not work. I know I need to at least know what direction I want she and I to go. Time to review the process the mystic shared with me and helped me understand. "Have a direction you wish to go. Allow the path to show itself. Be centered within the step you are taking. Be aware of the next possible steps. Pay attention, notice which next step becomes easiest." So which step am I taking now. Ah... getting Beauty on leash and into the car. Oops, two steps. Current step? Getting Beauty comfortable, even to enjoying, being on leash. How we go through that process will help me know how to get her into the car. The release of some inner tension, inner pressure, I will never be able to name, lets me know I have further opened the pathways to what Beauty and I desire, to what our souls have long intended.

    As I arrive I notice I am more relaxed and even have a bit of a playful mood. I smile when I see Beauty out in the field laying down, not trying to hide. By the time I park she is standing, ready to either stay or leave. As I swing my legs out of the car I whistle and as I stand Beauty begins walking to me. I sense a warm flow of greetings, my smile deepens. I grin and walk out to her so we can walk to the enclosure together. She stops ten feet from me, I stop five feet from her, bend and reach out my hand. Before my hand stops Beauty has moved forward and begins sniffing and then licking my hand. I grin as I turn sideways, towards the enclosure, pat my thigh, and offer, **"Come on girl."** My grin becomes a smile when she steps in next to me so I can pat her head before we walk to the enclosure together. Fifteen feet from the enclosure Beauty runs ahead, jumps in, and turns around to face me. Her choice to stand back a couple feet from the entry lets me know she expects to go through our formal greeting process. With me on the ground and her up inside the enclosure her head is at my chest level. A little dance with her front paws and soon she has her head pushed against my chest as I pet her head with both hands. Her butt wiggles with her exuberant wagging tail. Ten seconds later she is standing sideways and I am stroking her neck and back. Without thinking I reach to her collar with one hand while the other pets her back. Her ears go back as I pull back and forth gently on her collar. Instinctively I pull her against me with her collar and let her pull away immediately. Two, three, four times and I shift to scratching the base of her tail. When she looks away from me I gently reach over, take hold of her collar and pull her back to facing me. I sense her unsure how to respond. Within a moment I have my hands on both sides of her muzzle, scratching, pushing her head back and forth, and laughing. She looks me in the eyes and jumps back playfully. I lunge in her direction and she jumps again, spins, retreats to under the deck, laying down facing me. The little worry I am carrying disappears as her playful energy washes through me.

Beauty surprises me by waiting there while I return to the car, mix her food, and return to the enclosure. When I return she is laying with her nose six inches from where I place her bowl. As I place her bowl she sniff the food, seems to approve, and heads to the exit. Soon we are out in the field, me kneeling while petting her as she circles around me. On the third circle, while she is behind me my mind and ego slip aside, energies deep, deep within begin guiding me. I draw the rope out of my pocket and toss it on the ground in front of me. Her noticing it causes a moments pause in her circle. As soon as she is standing in front of me enjoying my stroking her neck and back she bends down and sniffs the rope. Sniff, look at me, sniff, look at me, sniff and step forward so I can scratch the base of her tail. As she completes her next circle I am pushing at the rope with a finger. In a moment her nose is with my finger pushing at the rope. Leaving the rope on the ground I slide my hand to her muzzle and then up onto her neck. She is surprised and after a moments pause is enjoying my hands once again petting her. Again I take hold of her collar and gently, playfully push her back and forth with her collar. My other hand pushing and pulling on her hips helps provide distraction. Ten seconds and I move to scratching the base of her tail, as she begins yet another circle around me.

This time when she comes around I am playfully holding the rope at nose level. As my body wiggles in play the rope wiggles. I grin when Beauty brings her nose to the wiggling rope then looks over at me. I drop the rope. She looks at the rope and looks back at me. I begin scratching her head and back carefully moving her collar as I pet her. Beauty sits in front of me with her body easily available to me. I grin begin petting her with one hand while the other hand picks up the rope, wiggles it a bit, rubs it against my arm, then rubs it against her body for a moment before throwing back on the ground. As the rope floats to the ground my mind and ego observe, unable to comprehend the energies guiding my choices, grateful to just observe. Beauty bends and sniffs the rope and looks at me. I have a sense of her whispering, "*Oh, you are learning. Good.*" While petting her head I imagine picking up the rope, rubbing it against her and then looping it around her collar. I seem to hear Beauty whisper, "*Well, okay.*" Surprised and a bit dazed I do what I imagined and soon realize I am sitting there holding both ends of the rope which is linked through her collar. One breath, two breaths, Beauty stands, three breaths, she pulls against the rope, four breaths, I hold her and tell her "**It is okay, girl**." Five breaths and just before I sense her panicking I release one end of the rope as Beauty pulls away.

As Beauty looks back at me from four steps way I sense her confusion. As I hold up the rope and wiggle it she takes a couple more steps away stopping when instinctively I through the rope at her feet and show her both of my hands. I grin when I sense her relief and sorrow and sense a whisper of, "*I would have stayed.*" I knee walk to her pet her a bit, stand and say, "**Come on girl**." as I begin walking. Within three steps Beauty is walking with me. A long loop around the field and we are back at the rope. I grin when Beauty stays close to me as I bend down and pick up the rope. When she does not move away I bend down and quickly loop the rope through her collar. Before she can begin pulling I step forward beginning a walk while gently pulling on the rope. With a second gentle pulling Beauty steps forward with me. I adjust my direction so that we are walking towards the car. Three or four times she pulls against the rope while we walk. Twenty feet from the car I sense she is full. I release one end of the rope, pull it free from her collar and stop. She takes another step and looks back to see me wiggling the rope. Wiggling and telling her she is a good girl I drop to my knees and toss the rope towards the car. She watches the arc of the rope then allows me to take a step to her and then pet her. Before I realize it I am walking to the car. I scoop up the rope as I walk past. At the car I turn and tell Beauty I will see her tomorrow, tell she did really well. I grin when I sense a playful *"Scary good."* from her.

On the way home I have just enough awareness to drive safely. I sense Beauty with me. I sense the connection energies we stirred, energies that open new connections and new possibilities of connection for us. I grin and then laugh when I notice using the rope was equally about 'getting me on leash'. I am momentarily shown new possibilities as I sense Beauty walking with me in our neighborhood.

More Relaxed and Organic

Wednesday, May 16th

This morning I got it right. I arrive at Beauty's area relaxed and eager to be with her as I whistle for her. While I am getting things together she comes out of one of her hiding places, stretches, and sits waiting for me about 150 feet away. After last nights ending I feel a bit of concern which fades when I see her sitting tall, ears up, mouth open, and tongue out. I pick up the dog brush, scissors, treats, and the rope/leash. As soon as I start walking towards her she gets up and begins walking towards me. I have a sense of us being partners beginning a dance. With each step closer my mood improves. When I am within five feet she stops and stands waiting for me. With my last step I do what she expects, what she has let me know is 'polite', I reach my hand down to just in front of her muzzle and wait while she chooses to lick my hand several times. With the third lick her tail comes up and begins wagging. When she chooses to be a bit more intimate she lowers her head slightly and I reach to begin petting her. Soon she is standing sideways in front of me. She does the familiar circle except this time she steps in inches from my back sniffing me from shoulders to rump. I smile as I sense her drawing my desire to be with her deeper within herself, offering a bit more of herself. Already close she steps to my side and when I reached over her back to pet her side she leans into me and we share a flood of warmth. We both enjoy my petting her and grooming her for perhaps five minutes. At one point in the grooming I need a couple seconds to finish clipping a mat out of her hair. I ask her to stay and reach forward lightly taking hold of her hips. To my surprise she responds by stopping and letting me finish. Another step towards her feeling safe with physical restraint by me, just a bit more trust and connection. I am delighted. She ends the grooming session as usual by stepping just out of my reach.

I sense it is time for some leash play/work floating from within. I get out the short rope (leash extension) and show it to her. Her reaction is to shy away from me, pause for a moment, and then turn and head further from me at a fast walk, tail down, slinking away from me. She goes to the hump of dirt 50 feet away and stops looking over her shoulder back at me. Part of me wants to pursue her but I know that will not help. I stand for a few seconds, allowing myself to sense Beauty's fear of being pursued, her need for space. Reluctantly I turn back towards the car walking slowly. When I am 30 feet away Beauty turns towards me, another 15 feet and she sits and her mouth opens. I stop, wait 10-15 seconds and slowly walk back towards her. When I am about 20 feet from her her ears rotate sideways, then back, her mouth closes. I stop. After 30 seconds of talking to her in a relaxed voice, finally she sits, her ears come forward, her mouth opens, her tongue comes out. Whew. I start slowly, cautiously walking towards her. Fifteen feet from her I have to begin dealing with blackberry bushes that partially block me. Beauty watches me carefully. I have the sense that my having to pay attention to my feet, legs, and arms, not Beauty, helps her remain curious about what I am doing rather than focusing on her fears related to the rope. As I take the final couple steps towards her, her tongue disappears and her ears shift. I slowly reached out my hand at muzzle height. She turns her head away then turns back and licks my hand. Her mouth opens, her tongue comes out, she stays seated. After a few minutes of petting her head and her not turning sideways to me I decide it is time to go. Disappointed I say goodbye, turn, and walk towards the car.

When I am almost to the pavement, 30 feet from my car, she gets up and begins walking off the hump. I wait, watching. Once off the hump she stops. I turn to the car and take a few steps. She begins walking towards me. I wait and when she was half way to me I also walk towards her. She stops and sits when 20 feet separated us. I slow, watching her posture, her ears are forward, mouth closed. I carefully remain open, sensing her fear and her hope. With the last step my hand moves in front of her muzzle. She pauses, then sniffs my hand, I begin petting her head. A minute later I shift and kneel close to her shoulders. I take out a treat and offer it to her. She sniffs and accepts one then another, then another. When I am out of treats I head to the car for more. I am pleased that she follows. I get the bag of treats, walk to her, kneel, and begin giving her treats. While giving her treats I fill myself with calm energies, get the rope out and show it to her and toss it on the ground close to her. Her ears go back, she looks away and then glance back to check for another treat. She takes a treat and then sniffs the rope and returns focus to treats. **The** dance of uncertainty within her also dances within me. Soon her ears are forward, her mouth is open, it is time for more. Something in me shifts out of the way, a reservation, a fear, a habit, perhaps all blended together. Our dance of uncertainty shifts, opening new possibilities. Beauty and I seem to slip into a dance together, trusting partners. I reach to her neck and slide my hand down to the clip on her collar. At first she pulls away. A couple more treats and she lets me slip a finger through the clip. I move the rope. She remains focused on the treats. I pick up the rope and ask, "**Can we do this?**" She bends forward to take another treat. I gently reach over her and feed the rope through the clip-on. To my pleasure she turns her head up to me opening her mouth, letting her tongue out. It seems she whispers, "*Oh good. Scary good. I choose more, you too.*" I loop both loops at the ends of the rope over a finger, stand, and we begin walking. An image of Beauty bolting away from me, breaking my finger causes me to shift to simply gripping both ends of the rope. After a couple minutes Beauty's ears shift back and her mouth closes. I sense Beauty is full, unable to handle more. Gently, lovingly I reach down, pet her head, reach over and slip the rope free. She relaxes and as we walk another 20 steps she keeps watching me carefully. I am filled with warmth as I sense that she misses having the rope/leash connecting us. When she stops I get out the rope and threaded it through the clip-on once again. Her mouth opens, her tongue comes out, and as we walk forward her steps have a happy bounce.

After I have guided our movements with the rope leash three or four time Beauty becomes more focused. Each move seems more crisp, more deliberate. She seems more willing to show me what she wants and at the same time accepts when I redirect our movement in a direction other than what she chooses. For the first time I have the sense of us being a team. At one point Beauty heads into thick bushes. I cannot follow. I call to her and pull with firm pressure on the rope. Though it is not easy and is not what she plans she turns around and comes with me while watching me closely. After a half dozen steps she relaxes and her focus returns to sniffing and where we were going.

It seems time for an admission. I have not been trained in working with animals. I have no degrees, no classes, and but a few articles read. From the beginning I sensed that Beauty and I would be guided by energies and understandings beyond what words can express, some label these energies Fate. In truth Beauty lives with those energies moment to moment. I am learning, sometimes grudgingly. I do have sensitivities shown me, opened within me by a mystic, a mental patient, a few friends, several animals, energies barely in the physical, and experiences conspired to by the Universe. As I write this the words of my psychiatrist father to me when I was about eleven float to me, "Son, you are different than others. You are incredibly smart and notice things others ignore. In the grand scheme of things you are neither better nor worse than others. You are simply different. You will be wise, your life will be richer and easier if you accept yourself as different, neither better nor worse." And yes, I will be pleased if the wisdom my father shared supports you having a richer and easier life. Back to Beauty. (grin)

At first I plan to avoid taking Beauty close to the car while on leash. Our walk has taken us back to the pavement and the entrance to the enclosure. We pause there in the shade where I give Beauty more treats. When my supply of treats runs out I need to go to the car for more. Okay, we will see what happens. I get up and lead Beauty towards the car. Her gate is a bit stiff as we approach the car and her ears remain forward. I do my best to flow relaxed playfulness within. She stands as I open the car door and take out the bag of treats. I close the car door, we turn, walking to the field 16 feet away. After a few steps in the grass I stop, kneel, and give Beauty several treats. She relaxes. We get up and walk across the field together. I remove the rope and then get Beauty to do some play chasing. The last "chase" results in her being 20 feet away. It is time to go so I walk up to her pet her, telling her I will see her tomorrow. As I walk back to the car she comes with me. At the pavement she heads into the enclosure. I follow, spend a couple minutes with her and then leave for home. My drive home is filled with energies of satisfaction and opening possibilities dancing within me.

Just Being Us

This evening's visit is fairly short, about 15 minutes. There is a slight chill in the air, early dusk with a few wispy clouds. Beauty is inside the enclosure under the deck when I arrive. As I enter the enclosure to retrieve her food bowl she comes out from under the deck to greet me. She is excited to see me, head high, ears up, mouth open, tail high and wagging so much her hips swing with it, her feet taking small quick steps. Her enthusiastic pleasure fills me. As soon as I move my hand to in front of her muzzle she begins licking and nuzzling it. I am delighted, warmth filling me. The human part of me wants to give her a big hug. After a bit of head scratching she turns sideways and then offers me her rump which I scratch happily. A couple of minutes later I head for her bowl. Beauty ducks under the deck and approaches me. With a little encouragement she comes out from under the deck for treats and attention. She stays in close to me and leans her head into my hand as I scratch her cheek. After a bit I reach under the deck, retrieve her bowl, and return to the car's trunk. I smile as I notice the warm contentment filling me, connecting me with Beauty.

Beauty stays by the entry of the enclosure. With the food mixed and a small baggy of treats I return to the enclosure. Beauty walks onto the fallen fence that forms a platform and waits for me. My body memory heads me towards the spot her food bowl usually is. Something deeper guides me to place the bowl on the platform in front of Beauty. Beauty licks my hand and begins daintily eating. I reach out and pet her head while she eats. With half the food gone she sits back and looks at me. A deep quiet fills me as I sense her offering, "My people now." After an eternity of warm, calm, shared sensations I get up, move her bowl to its usual place and return to the platform. She has ducked under the deck and comes back out to the platform. I sit and begin sharing treats with her mixed with frequent petting. I am pleased when I notice that Beauty is being more direct in letting me know she wants treats. She remains closer to me, moving her head more, sniffing and looking at me. Several times she moves her head a few inches from my body sniffing the baggy of treats. I make note that I will pay attention to boundaries and help Beauty know she is to remain very gentle when close in to me. I am touched and pleased, and feel a bit silly when I notice how gentle she already is as she takes treats from me. Perhaps my thought was more about me noticing what already is.

Several times Beauty glances out at the field. A couple of times she gets up, moves towards the enclosure's entry, towards the field, and then comes back. She seems uncertain, trying to decide what she wants most, to be in the open field or with me enclosed with limited escape routes. When most of the treats are gone I take out a chew stick and give it to Beauty. As soon as she takes it from my hand her head comes up, muzzle raised, showing she now has something special. She pauses, turns, steps a few feet away, then puts the chew stick down, licking and sniffing it. She looks at me and I move to her, touch her muzzle and then pet her head. She mouths the chew stick and then puts it down between her front legs and looks around. Making sure she sees me I reach in and gently pick up the chew stick a couple inches off the ground. I am pleased and relieved that she watches me with mouth open, ears forward, no tensing of her body. Finally she settles into paying attention to her chew stick. As she enjoys her special treat I notice my mind and ego struggling with the dichotomy of having put myself in danger of getting bitten and pride in a successful, ballsy move. I sense Fawn from home wondering where I am and so I lean into Beauty, pet her and say goodbye.

From One Step to the Next

Thursday, May 17th

I arrive at about 1:00 for today's single visit. It is sunny, cool and warming. I am relaxed within gentle flows of energy. I am wearing a light jacket. When I arrive Beauty is at the hedge where she is barely visible and able to see when I arrive. While I mix her food she wanders towards the battery shop, looping closer to me. Before going to put her bowl in the enclosure I walk a few steps towards her and call to her. She wanders towards me. When she gets to me I reach down in front of her muzzle and enjoy being rewarded with more licks than in the past, perhaps a dozen. We interact for a minute or so before I return to the car, pick up her food bowl and wanting to do something different walk to her in the field and put her bowl down. She slowly eats a little more than half while I talk to her, occasionally petting her head.

When Beauty stops eating she stands sideways to me and seems to want something. Unsure of her reaction I take the rope leash out of my pocket and show it to her. She moves her head away about 6 inches and then moves it back towards me. I dangle her rope leash and she sniffs it. She stand still, a slight tension in her stance, while I fed the rope through the clip-on on her collar. As I stand she shifts her head and shoulders so she is looking at me, her mouth open wide, ears up. Within I sense her warm, happy whisper, *"You paid attention and responded."* and sense her opening to me a bit more. Pleased by her response I reach down and pet her head and then back. She steps forward when I do, we are off for a walk. I smile with warmth as I notice Beauty's eagerness. Beauty has never pulled on the leash, she stays with her head close to my knee unless she is sniffing or we are running.

After a few steps she speeds up and soon we are trotting across the field, her gate bouncy and her tail high and wagging. The crib springs that sometimes block access to the forbidden back yard is on the ground giving us access. Somehow it is okay for me to enter with Beauty. As we go in she becomes very intent, her ears forward, her nose sniffing, her head moving back and forth little bits as she scans the back yard. As we get close to some tall grass she spots a cat and becomes even more focused. As the cat comes out of the tall grass towards us Beauty shifts her front feet and then jumps at the cat causing it to run. She shifts her head to follow the cat's movement pulling only slightly on the leash. When she turns and looks at me she somehow lets me know she and the cat are friends, occasionally sharing the tall grass not long after dark.

We leave the back yard and walk to the bushes along the fence behind which are apartments. A fellow I have talked with sees Beauty and I and notices she is on leash. I wave hello, he waves back and says, "Hi". From afar we chat a bit about my progress of having Beauty on leash. Beauty stands next to me, facing him with me, showing no signs of fear. The fellow begins walking towards us and stops about 20 feet away when I ask him to, having noticed Beauty beginning to fidget. We talk a couple more minutes during which Beauty stands next to me watching him. I have a strong sense of Beauty being 'with me', trusting me to protect her. After a walk across the field without thinking I guide Beauty to the car. As I open the back door I grin realizing I am beginning to familiarize Beauty with the car, taking the next steps in 'taking her home'. At first Beauty tries to slide beyond the door and stops with slight leash pressure and looks inside. I turn us back to the field where after a few feet Beauty turns and looks at the enclosure. Together we turn, together we walk to the enclosure and together we jump up through the entry. After a bit of petting her I remove the leash and she goes under the deck. I head to the field to retrieve her food bowl, then return to the enclosure, placing the bowl in it's usual place. As she comes from under the deck I sense she is responding to 'her people'. With each bite of quietly finishing her food while I pet her we slip more deeply into 'being together'. Each time she opens her mouth to take a bite it seems we are both opening more to each other. Taking each bite she 'tastes' more of what I offer. With each swallow she solidifies our expanding bonds.

Once done eating Beauty slips under the deck and lays down. On a sudden urge I go to the car, get my Kindle, and return to the enclosure. I am on autopilot, simply doing what flows from within. I find a bit of shade just out of Beauty's sight. I sit down and call to her making sure she knows where I am. I begin reading. After a couple minutes Beauty comes forward and lays down under the deck where she can see me. I read for about ten minutes at which time Beauty comes out from under the deck, letting me know she wants attention. After a couple of minutes I have a sense within my body that she wants to walk with me. I get out the rope leash and show it to her. She steps closer to me and nudges the rope with her nose. As I put the rope on her I notice deep within myself vague stirrings. Something important has just happened. Moments later we begin a second walk around the field. While trotting with Beauty the vague stirrings take form, for the first time Beauty has come to me, has asked me directly to connect with her, to take control, to take the lead. I am in awe, smiling, close to tears, as the warmth that connect Beauty and I flows through me.

As we loop back towards the car the fellow at the battery shop that is watching my progress notices I have Beauty on leash. Initially he is about 50 feet away. As we chat we test how Beauty will react as he approaches. At 25 feet she is still standing next to me facing him. At 20 feet she turns away. Two more steps and he stops. She only glances at him during the five minutes we talk. As he walks away, returning to his duties, I thank him for his help. A gentle warmth of thanks flows within me.

Beauty and I then return to the enclosure where I remove her rope/leash. She goes under the deck and I say goodbye. Each step towards the car, each mile driven towards home I sense her staying connected with me. As I unlatch the back gate I hear myself saying, "**Yes girl. This is where you will live.**" My mind and ego protest, "Crazy!" and within warmth flows bringing a smile to my face.

Settling More into Us

Friday, May 18th

When I arrive my quiet pleasure is deepened when I see Beauty is in the enclosure. As I get out of the car and walk around the old hot tub towards the enclosure Beauty comes to the entrance. The enclosure is about 30 inches higher than the pavement and field. As I round the hot tub about 12 feet from the entrance Beauty begins doing what I call a 'petty paw dance', shifting her weight from front paw to front paw, moving her paws small distances back and forth. My experience has been that petty paw dances shows anticipation of something enjoyable and sometimes of something possibly unpleasant. Words can only express a small amount of what I feel as Beauty's petty paw dance become more and more exuberant as I approach, her tail wagging, mouth open wide, tongue out. With the final step she begins whimpering with her back side swinging to and fro. As soon as I reach the entrance she moves forward and pushes her head into my hands, then against my chest. I am ecstatic. As I pet her head and shoulders she wiggles with pleasure. For about four minutes she moves in front of me offering herself for petting, sometimes her head, sometimes her side, sometimes her rump, often pushing herself against me. When the movement has settled I step up into the enclosure and Beauty walks with me to her bowl. As I mix Beauty's food at the trunk she sits out from under the deck watching me.

Again Beauty meets me at the entrance, gets some attention, and then slips under deck. As I kneel to place her food bowl she comes forward, sniffs the bowl, and then steps beyond the bowl and out from under the deck, next to me. I offer her a treat which she sniffs, takes in her mouth, and then daintily places on the ground. She sniffs the treat and move her head back to me for petting. After a couple minutes I take out her rope leash and hold it in font of her. The leash gets only enough attention for one sniff, then back to interacting with me. Soon she turns sideways to me making her neck and the clip-on on her collar easily available. I take the hint, pick up the rope, and reach for her collar. I smile when she moves her head away from watching me making it easier to thread the rope through the clip-on loop. I grin as I sense Beauty and I opening new connections, new levels of trust. As I stand she turns and walks with me to exit the enclosure. Stepping down out of the enclosure seems a declaration to the world that we have chosen to be together.

As Beauty and I step down out of the enclosure I notice the car and suddenly find myself turning towards it. Within two steps I realize now is a good time to expose Beauty to being close to the car while on the rope leash. As we walk I am grateful the tools for grooming are in the trunk. It does not feel like time to open a car door with Beauty close to me. As Beauty realizes we are going to the car she holds back a bit. As I sense in my body going to the trunk and opening it just like I do to prepare her food she steps back closer to me and soon we are walking to the car trunk. As we swing behind the car Beauty slows, slightly resisting. A deep breath in, then out while taking the keys out and imagining opening the trunk and Beauty moves with me with no resistance. Beauty watches me carefully as I reach to the trunk with the key and turns to sniff the trunk as soon as it opens. I notice gent warmth in my belly as I hear myself saying, "**Your such a good girl. Here is the brush, and the comb, and the scissors.**" I grin as Beauty reaches her head forward to smell what is in my hand. I am caught for a moment. The leash is too short for reaching up to close the trunk. My other hand is full. I shift the tools and carefully reach up. Beauty steps back uncertain and I offer, "**It's okay girl.**" as the lid comes down and latches.

Beauty moves quickly with me as I swing out into the field only a dozen feet from the drivers door. As I turn back to the car and Beauty she steps in again to sniff the tools in my hand. Her tail comes down, her ears go back when I drop to the ground. I begin worrying when she pulls against the leash. "**It's okay girl.**" and I do a play bow. I grin and relax when she responds with a play bow herself and her tail comes up and begins to wag. Suddenly we are in a space of our own, Beauty, me, and the car. Beauty steps into me offering her back for scratching. A couple of minutes of running my hands on her back, on her chest, on her belly, down her legs, and I get bold. I reach across her and pull her against me. When she pulls away I pull her in tighter for perhaps two seconds and release her. One step away and she leans back into me almost pushing against me.

Ten seconds later I hear myself say, "**Are you ready for grooming?**" and pick up the wire grooming brush. Beauty begins to tense and then relaxes as I move the brush so she can sniff it. For perhaps five minutes Beauty tolerates my attention. Each "**Your going to be so pretty.**" seems to add a few more moments to what she can tolerate. When I am almost finished clipping a mat off her neck she lets me know she is done by stepping one step away and sitting. "**Let me finish this.**" and I lean forward and slowly, carefully finish cutting off the large mat. Just as she begins to tense I am done and sit back. "**Good girl. We can go now.**" In one move I put down the scissors and stand, Beauty stands with me. First step and her ears come forward, second step and her tail comes up, third step and we are moving together, both happy, both relaxed, both looking to see where we want to go. A gong of recognition rings within me, we are together.

I turn towards the hedge across the field and Beauty surrenders to being with me. We walk together, she is my dog, I am her people. She allows me to be in charge provided I let her stop to sniff when she wishes. At the hedge she smells something in the ground, glances at me, and begins to burrow more with her snout than her paws. I am surprised to suddenly find myself kneeling with her, my face inches from hers, muttering, "**What you got girl? Good smells? What is it?**" Beauty blows air out her nose, wiggles, and plunges her nose back into snuffling in the soft ground. Twenty seconds and she is done and turns away from the hole she has created. I can almost hear her say, "*That was fun!*" as she wiggles and then begins walking back out into the field.

The bounce goes out of Beauty's step as I guide us towards the car while sensing myself getting in and driving away. "**I know girl. But I have other things to do.**" Twenty feet from the car I decide to get Beauty as close as possible to the car before taking off the rope. At fifteen feet she slows and so I slow. With each step she resists a bit more. At ten feet the leash becomes tense and I begin taking very small steps. Time slows, each inch is important. With each inch I ask a bit more of Beauty, with each inch Beauty becomes a bit more unsure. Five feet from the car and Beauty digs in unwilling to go further. I finish the step I am taking and turn back to her and kneel down. I choose to smile and hear my soothing voice saying, "**You are such a good girl. Come a bit closer so I can take the rope off.**" While speaking I sense her stepping to me, my hands removing the rope, and her stepping back. One breath, two breaths and she steps forward turning so I can undo the rope. As the rope slips off I find myself leaning forward placing my head inches from her. "**You're such a good girl.**" and I feel her fur brush against my cheek before she draws back and steps away. As I stand I have a sense of her whispering, "*Don't go.*" and hear myself respond, "**I am sorry girl.**" as I turn and step to the car. As I unlock the car Beauty surprises me by walking to the enclosure. As I get in and start the car she jumps into the enclosure, goes under the deck, and lays down. As I drive past the enclosure and out onto the street I feel pulled back towards her. We both seem to want more. I fill with regret as I turn towards Ute's house.

Sudden Terror

Saturday, May 19

More changes, more surprises. When I arrive Beauty is standing about 20 feet outside the gate into the picnic area of the 50s motelish apartments. Several of the people there have barbecues going. When Beauty sees me she seems torn between paying attention to the picnic area and paying attention to me. When I am halfway through mixing her food she decides to walk to within ten feet of me at the back of the car. Grinning I hear myself say, "**Oh, so food gets your attention.**" My grin becomes a smile as I sense her whisper of *"and Us"*. Done with the food I put it on the roof of the car, pet Beauty a bit, and get out the rope leash, comb, and scissors. I pat on Beauty's head and I pick up her bowl. As soon as I head to the entrance of the enclosure Beauty trots there ahead of me, jumps in, and does her petty paw dance of pleasure. Open and filled with warmth I put down the food and we spend a couple minutes with me petting her and enjoying her sometimes responding by rubbing against me. As I walk to place her food bowl she slips under the deck and then slowly comes forward to me at her food and water. After a couple bites she steps even more slowly just beyond her food and out from under the deck offering herself for my attention. 30 seconds is enough and she goes back under the deck staying close to me.

    Wanting more interaction and to have her on leash I move towards the entrance. I grin when as hoped she comes out from under the deck and joins me close to the entry. I pet her for a while as she moves back and forth close to me. When she is close to the swimming pool and just out from under the deck I get out the rope leash and reach to put it through the loop on her collar. Suddenly her body jerks, she lowers her body, her tail goes between her legs, and she rushes away from me out of the enclosure. Surprise, puzzlement, and concern wash through me as I watch her cross the pavement into the field. She keeps going, not looking back, 30 feet, 60 feet, I whistle, she just keeps going. 90 feet, 120 feet, I whistle again and this time she looks back at me but keeps going. If something doesn't change soon she will be gone. 150 feet and as I whistle again and call to her I notice the mournful sound of my voice reflecting the sorrow and uncertainty flowing within me. She looks back and slows her pace. Whew. 180 feet, almost to the mound of dirt that will take her out of the field and out of my sight. I whistle again and finally she stops, turns, and then sit down. Her body is tense, her ears pulled forward, her mouth closed. I speak to her across the distance for about 20 seconds. I know it will take time for her to settle down, that she needs space in which she can let go of her fear and remember her pleasure in being with me.

Okay, I need to wait, I sense Beauty needs space, yet I need to be present for her. I go to the car, get the folding chair and my Kindle. I walk to the field and set up the chair about 10 feet into the field and sit down so I can see Beauty if I turn my head to the left. I call to Beauty and then begin reading. As my mind is busy with reading a part of me notices Beauty and carefully cycles my worry and sorrow within myself allowing quiet space to encircle both Beauty and I. About a minute after I sit down Beauty gets up and began walking away. I feel a surge of panic. I holler, "**Hey Beauty. Where you going?**" She looks back but keeps going. I whistle, she slows and looks at me. I holler, "**Your a good girl.**", the sound carrying my desires to share connection with her. She stops, turns partially back to me, and stands there looking at me then at the mound of dirt, back and forth several times. I look away from her and notice in my peripheral vision she is sitting down. With a bit of relief I begin reading carefully supporting the space we are in, allowing space for her to choose. After a couple minutes Beauty lays down and I relax just a bit. Five long minutes later she walks about 15 feet back towards me and sits facing me, her head up, her ears up, her mouth slightly open. I sense her allowing our connections and allow the slightest bit of desire for connection to float to her, a gentle invitation. I read another minute before turning off my Kindle. For 30 seconds I sit there the question of what to do getting all of my attention. My mind is still, this is not something I can figure out. Subtle sensing and allowing and gently responding open possibilities. I sense I need to approach Beauty slowly, relaxed, with no specific outcome expected. I get up and walk slowly in her direction with relaxed flowing movements. When I have covered 60 of the 140 feet separating us I notice her ears come further forward, I slow my pace and turn a bit more away from her. Her ears relax. About 50 feet from her her ears come forward again and her mouth closes. Without thought I pause and then kneel. She stands up and pauses. I holler, "**Hey girl, come here.**" She begins running towards me, tail high and wagging, mouth open, tongue out. With each step I open more to her, opening a path to me. She comes directly to me, stopping 2 feet from me, licking my extended hand again and again. I allow my relief and pleasure to flow out and enclose us. Finally in surrender to 'us' she stops licking and steps into me. For a couple minutes she moves enjoying my attention, relaxing more, opening more, and then does a play jump away from me. She circles and comes right back in beside me as I lean onto all fours, doing a play bow, down and up. I playfully shift my hips into her and she play jumps again running in a big circle. For three or four minutes we play 'you chase, I chase". Warmth and wonder flow within me as I sense how our actions reflect the deeper "you chase, I chase" game we are playing. In those moments Beauty and I seem to commit to playfully, purposefully connecting deeper and then deeper.

Beauty shifts the space when she walks 30 feet from me and turns her head back, inviting me to come with her, inviting me to move with her. I get up and follow her. She stays 10 to 15 feet from me as we scout the edges of the field. I notice a woman at the entry to the backyard Beauty sometimes invites me to visit. I stroll over and talk with her about Beauty. While we talk Beauty examines the bushes 40 feet from us. Done talking I walk to Beauty. As she waits for me I have the sense she is pleased that we have exposed our connections to another. That sense deepens when she lets me pet her immediately. I walk next to her as 'her person' for about 20 feet as she sniffs the bushes. I feel it is time to express our connection more in the physical so I take the rope out of my pocket and show it to her. She remains relaxed. I wiggle the rope close to her, her mouth closes and she does not move away. Pleased and encouraged I reach over her neck to the clip-on on her collar. I am relieved and pleased when she turns so that I have easier access to her collar. While I feed the rope through the loop her ears are back, her mouth closed, her posture slightly tense. I talk to her in a soft, "happy" voice as I complete threading the rope. I pull the rope through the clip-on so that she sees what is happening. She relaxes, her ears come forward, and as I stand up her head moves so she can look directly at me. In her gaze I sense a whisper of *'we are'* as she fills me with deep, warm, eternal energies of connection. As I stand up her mouth comes open and we begin our walk together. Over the next 5 minutes we walk, sometimes I choose, sometimes she chooses where we will walk, she and I relax more and more into being 'Us'.

Finally I decide to take us back to the car. Beauty moves to take a path around the battery shop to get back to the car, new territory for us. I go with her. As we come out into the parking lot Beauty's body tenses slightly, her mouth closes, she scans the area with repeated head movements side to side. We are in a very exposed position, no bushes for hiding, traffic 25 feet away, a shop with people 20 feet away, several blind corners. Time and space shift as I become hyper aware of our surrounding and Beauty's energies and body. She feels me link in with her, with her worries, her body relaxing slightly, her gate becoming slightly more fluid, her stepping closer to me. I feel pleasure and concern and pride as we cross the 120 feet of exposed, less predictable space together. As our path brings us to the back of the car, Beauty relaxes her body and her mouth opens. I sense her whispering, "T*hat was scary. We did good.*" A plan begins to form in my awareness. I guide Beauty to the space between the car and enclosure fence. As she goes beyond the car's backdoor I use the leash to bring her back towards the rear of the car. Her mouth closes as she circles back. I open the backdoor, she steps just beyond it. I guide her in a tight circle back to the backdoor and pat the seat. Her mouth opens as she looks into the backseat. I pat the seat again, she moves her head slightly, peering into the back of the car. I stand, she steps back and I close the car door. I am pleased that she was relaxed enough to be curious about the backseat. We walk to the enclosure entrance where she jumps in. With the leash still on she immediately turns back to me. I pet her a bit. As I slide the rope from her collar we are only 15 feet from where my starting to put the leash on had startled her and caused her to run from me. Free of the leash she steps into me, a few more warm, gentle pets, and she trots to the deck, going under it.

As I get in my car and drive away I feel the wide spaces between my worry of Beauty running from me, the satisfaction of her recovering, and the pleasure of her trusting me enough to cross an exposed area. As I drive home my mind is quiet and warmth flows within me as I allow myself to notice the many little steps in trust and connection Beauty and I had just taken. As I reflect I sense her with me.

A Bit of Car Exposure

Sunday, May 20

When I arrive Beauty is at the bushes in one of her 'nests'. I whistle and holler "**Hey Beauty.**" Disappointment washes through me when she remains there watching as I get her food bowl, return to the car trunk, and mix her food. As I close the trunk, food in hand, and look up I am startled to see that she is only 15 feet away. As I step from around the back of the car she trots to the enclosure entry waiting there for me. My mind and ego try to ignore the fact that she had just snuck up on me. She is just inside the entry on ground about 30 inches higher than where I stand. Her head is at my chest level and I reach out, over her head to pet her. I am a bit chagrined when she raises her head and takes a step back. I have the sense of her scolding me, *"That is not polite. Show respect."* It takes me a moment to sense what she wants. As I reach out with my hand at her muzzle level she steps forward. As she stops moving I rotate my hand so the back of my hand will stroke her muzzle and pause. She turns her head offering me her muzzle. After I stroke her muzzle a few times she steps into me turning sideways, offering me more of her body. I grin and chatter with her about knowing I need to be polite. Within ten seconds Beauty turns and trots under the deck, lays down to watch me place her now full food bowl. To my surprise she does not come forward to eat. After a few moments, puzzled and curious I stand and head to the entrance. As I step down out of the enclosure I turn and notice she has only a few more steps to reach me. Without thinking I take her rope leash out of my pocket and wave it in front of me. Warmth fills me when I see her respond by wagging her tail. I grin as she steps to me and turns offering me her neck. Soon the rope is through the clip-on and Beauty is jumping down beside me. I grin as my mind plays with how different today and yesterday are. Later I will understand Beauty is insisting that I honor her choice, that I never assume she is 'just my dog'.

    I guide us out into the field where Beauty decides we should go off to the left. And so it begins. During our 20 minute walk sometimes I choose where we go, sometimes she chooses. It is a partnership, the roles of lead and follow flowing back a forth. As I walk us back to the car I am surprised by my mind pointing out that if we were really together I would put Beauty in the backseat and take her home. Grinning I stop about ten feet from the car and pet Beauty a bit. I turn towards the car and ask, "**Do you want to?**" I chuckle softly when Beauty turns and walks with me towards the car. With Beauty next to me I open both a back and a front door. She tenses and pulls back on the leash. I step to her and speak gently as I pet her. I chatter about it being okay, about this being her car, that she can just look. I turn back to the car and pull gently on the leash. Still tense she allows me to guide her to the car where she sniffs the front and back doorways. Twenty five seconds and she is done. Instinctively as she looks up at me I step away from the car. As we walk ten feet from the car her body relaxes and she moves next to me. I hear myself saying "**Okay girl. That is enough.**" as I slip the rope out of the clip-on. Beauty leans against me and seems disappointed with my plan to leave. I stroke her a few moments before a sense of it being time to leave causes me to walk away from her towards the car. I notice different desires stirring within me and simply know it is time to go. I sense Beauty with me as I drive away and wonder if I will ever understand why I needed to leave just then.

Setting Boundaries

Monday, May 21

As I park the car I notice Beauty lying under the deck inside the enclosure. My mood, our mood seems to match today's subdued pause in Spring's dynamic urge for growth. It is a rainy late spring day. I get out of the car and head to retrieve Beauty's food bowl from under the edge of the deck. As I walk I surrender to the rain, a thought of removing my wet clothing at home flits through my mind. Beauty meets me at the enclosure entry, gets a bit of attention and moves back under the deck. She seems a bit aloof and unsure she wants to interact. My mind chatters about possible reasons as I retrieve her bowl and head back to the car. As I step out of the enclosure I choose to relax my mind and focus on preparing Beauty's food as an expression of our connections. When I return to the enclosure Beauty meets me once again staying back a few feet from me. A bit disgruntled I walk around the deck and bend down to place her bowl under the deck. My mood lightens when Beauty comes out from under the deck to me rather than going right to her food. A few polite strokes of the back of my hand on her muzzle and she steps into me leaning against me while I pet her. My disappointment fades replaced by warmth and sharing. Soon Beauty moves to eat her food. Unlike other times she does not go under the deck for protection, she stays out where I can pet her as she eats.

As she eats she often turns her head to look at me. I can almost hear her whisper, *"Thank you for giving me food."* The third time when she turns back and takes a bite of food I am surprised by a sensation of chewing food in my mouth. I am even more surprised when I notice my sensations match the movement of Beauty's mouth. I bit more surprise comes when Beauty turns back to me and seems amused by my surprise and pleased that I have noticed her sharing her sensations. "Crazy" float into my mind and I grin.

When Beauty is done she shows me she wants more by staying out from under the deck and looking at me as if to ask, "*Well?*" Without thinking I pull her rope out of my pocket and wiggle it. I am discouraged when she moves ten feet away towards the entry and looks back at me. I walk to her and wiggle the rope again. She moves ahead of me, out the enclosure, across the parking lot, out to the field. I walk out to her, rope in hand. When I am about ten feet from her I stop, wiggle the rope, and invite, "**Come here, girl**." After a few moments of tension she turns away and begins walking slowly, looking back to invite me along. I wait and repeat, "**Come here.**" She pauses a few seconds, turns and begins walking away. A thousand possibilities float through my mind, through my awareness. And I know it is time to leave, to leave Beauty her freedom, to let her know I require she allow herself to be on leash. Sorrow floats within me mixed with a sense that I am doing as I must. Each movement is a little sorrow, each step, unlocking the car, opening the door, sitting in the car, starting it. Putting the car in gear and taking my foot off the brake brings a blending of doing as I must, abandoning Beauty, and open space filled with uncertainty. A couple blocks and I sense Beauty reaching out with her energy, uncertain, confused. I whisper to myself and her, "I will see you tomorrow, girl."

A Boundary Accepted

Tuesday, May 22

*L*ast night I reviewed whether or not to stay with my decision to not walk with Beauty out beyond the field if she is off leash. Eventually I accept what resonates deep within me, I accept that I will not walk Beauty unless she is on leash. That is the only way I can ensure her safety.

It is rainy once again, with walking Ute's dogs planned after the visit. When I arrive Beauty is in the field a few feet from the pavement. She has placed herself so she can watch me prepare her food at the car trunk. I get out of the car and go to her immediately. She is sitting tall, ears up, mouth open, tongue out, what I have come to view as her telling me, "*I am happy, I want to interact.*" Being the first greeting of the day I walk within 3 feet of her and kneel, extending my hand at muzzle level to her. As I approach her she bows and stretches then remains standing, waiting for me. Warmth flows from my belly throughout my body and to Beauty. With my hand in front of her she immediately begins licking and nuzzling my hand, continuing for 15 seconds. The field fades away as Beauty and I shape a space filled with connection, with acceptance, with desires to share. She steps forward and lowers her head an inch or two stepping a bit sideways to me as I begin petting her. As I begin she starts doing her petty paw movements shuffling closer to me. She continues to move about, giving me different access to pet her, rubbing against me several times. In the space we share there are no barriers only strong flows of desire connecting us. After five full and rich minutes I get up, go to the enclosure, retrieve her food bowl, and return to the car trunk. As I mix her food she crosses onto the pavement and slowly comes closer and closer. When she is within 10 feet I walk to her and pet her head for a few seconds. As I finish mixing her food she comes within 3 feet of the car and stands watching me. I smile sensing she is choosing to be with me at the car. With her food mixed I pick up the bowl, take two steps, pet her a bit, and head to the enclosure saying, "**Come on, girl.**" To my delight she follows me, head high, tail wagging, a bouncy gate, almost prancing. She jumps into the enclosure as I step up into it. My smile deepens when she does not go under the deck as usual but follows me as I walk to place her bowl. As I kneel and place her bowl she ducks under the deck, moving to her bowl. She sniffs and begins eating with me sitting 18 inches away. After six or so bites she looks up at me. I have the sense she is inviting me to pet her as she eats. I reach out and begin petting her head as she eats. Three more bites and she steps sideways, rotating her body, making it easy for me to pet her head and her neck. A few bites later she shifts even closer to me. I smile sensing Beauty offering and then enjoying the same connections Fawn, Mystique and Little Leon enjoy when I pet them as they eat. Beauty eats every bit of food in the bowl, licking it clean.

Once done Beauty retreats under the deck, but unlike other times she comes out as soon as I stand up. Together we walk to the entrance, jump down, and walk to the field. At the field I kneel down, Beauty comes rushing to me immediately and we begin sharing affection. After a couple of minutes Beauty is in front of me, facing me when she steps into me lowering her head to push her forehead against my chest. She wiggles happily as I reach over scratching her shoulders and sides. I am deeply touched by her trust, warmth filling my lower belly and chest. After a bit more play I take the rope out of my pocket, show it to Beauty, and as I kneel ask, "**Do you want to walk?**" To my relief she comes to me, accepts a few pets on the head and then steps sideways in front of me giving me easy access to feeding the rope through the clip-on on her collar. I watch her ears and mouth closely as I reach over her neck and in front of her muzzle connecting the rope. Her stance remains relaxed, her mouth closed, her ears remain forward and relaxed. With the rope/leash in place I stand, somehow I am standing tall as Beauty's person. As I stand Beauty moves her head up, looking at the rope, then at me, opening her mouth, letting her tongue out. Two bouncy steps and she and I begin trotting out into the field. During the walk Beauty pays attention to my movements, keeping her head close to my knee. She responds to gentle pulls of guidance on the leash with relaxed posture, often looking up at me with mouth wide open, tongue out. We are together, our energies and movements easily matching, flowing movements shared.

Twice during the walk I take Beauty to the car, open the back door on the driver's side and pat the seat. On the first pass she steps within three feet of the door opening. On the second pass she stops about four feet from the door opening. After patting the seat I decide to test our connection. I pull forward gently on the leash. Beauty resists. I pull with a bit more force saying, "**Come on, girl**." Beauty's mouth closes. With my stronger pull towards the car door opening her ears go back slightly, she resists a moment and then relaxes and takes a step forward. With continued pressure she takes a second step. I relax the pressure on the leash, say, "**Good girl!**", and reach down gently stroking her back. Her ears immediately come forward and her stance becomes more relaxed. We remain there, her two feet from the door entrance, me petting her, telling her she is a good girl. After 30 seconds I step back and she turns in front of me, we both turn and walk back to the field. I smile, enjoying 'us'. After a small loop I guide her to the enclosure. I remain at the entrance as she jumps in, turning back to me immediately, standing sideways in front of me. A bit of petting and I reach up and withdraw the rope from her collar. She stays in front of me accepting more attention. It is time to go. I say goodbye and Beauty goes under the deck as I walk to my car.

As I start the car I feel a tug to stay and in a moment know it is time to go. As I put the car in gear warmth flows into belly as I sense the connections Beauty and I now share. As the car begins to move the warmth flows into my chest and then fills the car. I feel much better than yesterday, more sure of success.

Rainy Days and Boundaries

Wednesday, May 23rd

It is a wet, gray, rainy day with rain constantly varying from light to heavy. Beauty is in the enclosure when I arrive and comes to meet me at the entrance. We spend 3 or 4 minutes my petting and scratching her, her rubbing against me, licking me, she presenting herself for attention. When I go to pick up her food bowl she comes with me rather than going under the deck. She follows me back to the car and waits 4 feet from me while I mix her food. Part way through mixing her food when I step to her to pet her she remains seated. She is watching her people make food for her. Somehow she lets me know this is how she wants it to always be. She follows me when I return to place her food bowl, once again walking with me rather than going under the deck. With her bowl in place she begins eating, pausing occasionally to look at me, accepting my petting her head. She is a bit more guarded than the day before. The first three times I reach to pet her she lifts her head so that my hand is close to her muzzle before lowering her head and allowing me to pet her.

With her food eaten we go to the enclosure entrance and together jump down to the pavement and cross to the field. As we cross the pavement I take out the rope leash, showing it to her. She does a play jump and runs away as if to start our tour of the field. She looks back twice and when I don't follow she stops, turns to face me and sits. She declines to come closer and when I walk towards her she gets up and runs. It all has the feeling of a game of 'keep away'. Finally I put the rope back in my pocket and call her, offering her a treat. Her behavior is similar to what it had been before she started enjoying my petting her. It takes about 10 treats before she will allow me to pet her, another 6 treats before she will stand sideways to me letting me pet her entire body. She is playing temptress, requiring I show my desire for her. When I draw the rope leash part way out of my pocket she does a play leap and runs several feet away. She pauses and then runs further away, tail wagging, a bouncy gate. I sit, waiting for a couple of minutes and then get up and walk back to the car. With disappointment I sit in the car hoping she will get up and come closer. I wait for about five minutes and then leave.

Much of the drive home I review the last few days wondering whether I have made good choices, worrying I could have done better. Finally, most of the way home a sense of *"you have done as you should"* flows into my belly, up to my heart, and finally to my head. With the sense comes a warm glow as if something deep, deep within me is encouraging me, supporting me.

A Step Barely Noticed

Thursday, May 24th

Today is a day of varied weather. While I am with Beauty we experience both sunshine and fluffy cloud shade in the cool air. Today is a transition day in a couple of ways. Through the last 6 months there have been a few days when I became aware of how much history and conditioning I and Beauty have to release if she is to come to live with me. Yesterday and today I have a glimpses of just how deeply Beauty's fear of being "trapped", how much she wants to know her desires will be respected, and how much I need to earn her trust. The other transition is in the length of visit. Other days I have spent from 20 to 35 minutes with Beauty, ending our time when she walked away, a move I interpret as her "being full", of her having taken in as much change as she can handle. Today I spend close to an hour with her. On three occasions she moves away from me staying energetically connected rather than walking away in a way that feel like an "*I am done.*" indication.

Beauty is under the deck when I arrive. As I turn to park she comes out from under the deck, head and tail high, tail wagging, a prancing gate, mouth wide open and tongue out. I will never be able to express the intricate, stirring delights she opens within me. She meets me at the enclosure entrance, eagerly stepping forward to sniff and lick my hand, pushing her head against my hand as I scratch the side of her head. She shifts and moves offering me every inch of her head, neck, back, and rump. When I lower my head close to her head she quickly licks my cheek and spins away, shifting her side to me. Several times she raises her head to my hand licking it. At one point she shifts her sniffing from my hand to my wrist to my lower arm staying a few seconds at each spot she sniffs. After five minutes or so I step up and walk to her bowl with her prancing along side me, tail wagging energeticly enough to cause her rump to sway back and forth. She stays close as I walk back to the car. Once I open the trunk she lays down about six feet from me watching my work. Part way through I step towards her, offering her a treat. She stands, wags her tail, and takes a couple steps backwards, pauses, and then steps forward taking the treat and dropping it on the pavement. As she looks at me I can almost hear her whisper, "*I am far more complex than a treat.*" I am a bit befuddled as stirrings within alert me that her message will stir within for many hours, bit by bit exposing itself. I am to pay attention.

As soon as I close the trunk and step towards the enclosure she gets up, tail high, mouth open, and follows me. She jumps into the enclosure behind me and quickly slips under the deck. As I place her food she comes forward, sniffs, looks at me, and begins eating with small, careful bites. Every 10 seconds or so she raises her head, turns her ears back, and scans the area outside the enclosure. With 1/3 of the food gone I speak to her and reach out to pet her head. Her head comes up, she sniffs my hand, pauses, and then lowers her head allowing me to pet her head as she eats. Many times when I reach to pet her as she eats she responds with a slight head movement away from me immediately shifting back. Other times she raises her head, intercepting my hand, scanning the area then returning to eat. When she has eaten all the food I am pleased to see her move out from under the deck, stand proud with tail high, mouth open, tongue out and look at me. We spent the next five minutes me stroking and scratching her, her moving with graceful movements around me occasionally leaning against me. I am enchanted as she shares her beauty with me.

I stand and we saunter to the entrance of the enclosure. Beauty let me know she isn't ready to leave the enclosure by trotting past the enclosure entrance and looking back at me. I kneel and she comes to me for more attention. At one point she is standing at my side, looking the same direction I am. I have my hand over her shoulder, scratching. Suddenly I feel myself press my hand against her shoulder, hugging her to me. Immediately she pulls a few inches away and her mouth closes, her ears go back. In that moment I become hyper-alert, raising my head and shoulders as I move my hand to her close shoulder then back to her far shoulder. It takes about 30 seconds for her to little by little relax her body and allow her ears to return to a forward position. She shifts her rump a step away from me as her tail comes back up. A moment later I smile seeing her mouth open and her tail wag. A few moments later I shift and sit with my legs dangling outside the enclosure. Beauty is watching me carefully, staying about five feet away. I realize I am blocking the entrance and increase my focus on Beauty's responses after opening more space within myself. At first she does not come when I beckon her. After perhaps 30 seconds she cautiously steps to me offering only her head. 10 seconds of petting and she steps into me shifting sideways, giving me access to her neck and back. Cool! She seems okay with my sitting blocking the entrance. I notice myself relaxing a bit, sensing that somehow we have moved a bit closer to her being with me at the dome. My mind and body sensations cause my memory to flit back to being outside with my very young children, carefully casting and holding a safe space for them, carefully allowing them to explore the boundaries. I experience a gentle jolt as I realize Beauty and I are doing a boundaries dance. I am learning hers, she is learning mine. We are testing and negotiating new ones for our time together.

A few moments later I get up and we leave the enclosure, heading to the field. I kneel at the edge of the field and she comes closer to me remaining about 8 feet away. A treat tossed 5 feet from me brings her forward. Another brings her within arms reach. The third she takes from my hand. The next three bring her closer. With the next treat I reach to pet her head. Two seconds of contact and she steps back. Expecting a gradual process I shift to a sitting position. It takes 8 or 9 minutes of treats and slow movements before Beauty is standing next to me sideways accepting affection. About three minutes later I withdraw the rope-leash from my pocket. She tenses, pauses, and steps away from me, her ears shifting backwards. She turns, looks at me, does a play jump, and trots 10 feet away, tail high and wagging, and then sits facing me. An offer of a treat creates no response. Two minutes later I know I should go to her and slowly walk towards her. When I am three feet from her she gets up, does a play jump, and with tail high trots away looking over her shoulder at me. Something within me decides to begin our walk with her off leash. We trot across the field together, her staying a couple feet from me. At the blackberry bushes she sniffs and allows me to pet her. Then she leans up against me. As I reach for her collar she holds her body still with slight tension, her mouth closed. Time shifts and I become aware of every detail of my movements and her responses. I hold the collar clip-on and extract the rope from my pocket. Her ears go back and fold down, her body stiffens slightly. Telling her she is a good girl I reach down and thread the leash through the loop. As soon as one hand begins pulling the rope through the loop her body relaxes, her ears remain back as they unfolded. As my hands brings the two ends of the rope together her tail comes up, she looks up at me, there is a slight wag of her tail. I smile as my mind and ego register angst over the slowness of the process and minimal payback for resources. A flow of warmth within my belly and up into my chest tell me that deep within there is contentment, a knowing that things are as they should be.

We begin walking. After a few steps her ears shift part way forward. For the next 2 minutes or so her ears shift from back most of the way to a more normal forward position. Finally her ears come fully forward, her gate loosens, and her mouth opens. She looks up at me, stops, and then steps in closer to me for head and shoulder petting. At the car I had put ShadowMask's retractable leash in my pocket. ShadowMask was a wolf malamute mix that shared life with me for 11 years. Like Beauty at times he could be head strong, wanting things his way. How fitting that his retractable leash is becoming hers. I am excited and worried as my mind and ego paint my next step as 'being huge'. Quietly I slip my hand into my pocket and pull only the clip end of the retractable out, clipping the two loops at the ends of the rope together with it. I do not notice any response from Beauty. I take the handle from my pocket as we continue to walk. A few moments later when we stop for Beauty to sniff and for me to pet her I show her the retractable handle. She sniffs it and returns her nose to the ground. As her nose drops to the ground the tension drops from me. My mind and ego are disgruntled. What they know is a major step is a non-event to Beauty. Deep within I am chuckling with the contrasts. Beauty and I cruise the field for another 10 minutes, at times trotting together, at times my waiting while she enjoys the smells. Then she turns and begins trotting towards the enclosure.

Bringing In Beauty

We swing by the car where once again I open the backdoor and she peers in. We continue to the enclosure where we jump in together.

I undo the retractable and rope leash and toss them aside. Unlike before when Beauty would trot under the deck after 30 seconds of petting she stays with me. Tired of kneeling after 4 minutes I sit against the pool. With me in a new position I have to use a few treats to get Beauty to come to me. After a couple minutes of petting she turns and trots off under the deck. It is sunny and pleasant making it easy to sit there waiting to see if she will come back out. Four minutes later she comes out peaking around the corner at me. She steps into full view and sits there for a couple minutes. She gets up again and disappears under the deck. My wondering whether she will come back or not is answered a minute later when she comes out, walks to within five feet of me and sits. More treats, more petting, enjoying Beauty's choice to be close. Well actually, my mind and ego would only allow themselves to enjoy Beauty's choice. Deep within I experience a resonance that seems to span time and space. The resonance seems to be gently dancing within my belly, expanding to flow warmth into my chest.

With my body beginning to stiffen I get up, telling Beauty it is time for me to go. As I walk to the car she trots over to the field and sits facing me. I sense it is not time for me to leave. Unsure I retrieve more treats out of the trunk and walk to her, kneeling within 5 feet of her. She comes to me with the first treat offered. For the next few treats she allows me to pet her head, not offering her side. After a couple of minutes she is standing sideways next to me. On an impulse I lay down on my side, my head a couple of feet from her feet. After a few treats she lays down and stays there until I reach out and stroke one of her fore feet. Her ears stay forward, her mouth open, she gets up, move fives feet away, and lays down. After a pause I crawl playfully, carefully over towards her and lay down on my belly, her head 30 inches from mine, our bodies forming about a 70 degree angle. After a minute or so of watching me she puts her head down. We lay there for close to 10 minutes, my speaking to her occasionally, her looking at me occasionally. For the first time we are simply being together. In the shared stillness I sense our energies shifting, testing, withdrawing only to return more deeply connected. Beauty seems to understand more than I, a quiet time to simply be together experiencing each other, preparing. With a gentle shock, as if a clapper had finally struck the bell of my awareness, I realize I am simply being with Beauty. A second shock, perhaps for the first time in my life. Beauty seems amused as I lay with the in quiet awe.

With the cold of the ground seeping into me I finally get up and walk to the car. At the car I feel the rawhide chew in my back pocket. Beauty is sitting where I had left her. I show her the chew as I walk to her, she gets up and meets me half way, taking the chew with a single sniff. She walks 10 feet away, lays down, and begins to chew. I am drawn to walk to her where she lays chewing her treat. Her focus remains on the chew as I kneel next to her. Over the next two minutes I talk to her with a light, eager tone, occasionally petting her head, She occasionally glances at me with softness in her eyes, returning to her chew. I am smiling, warmth flowing within me as I share her focus on the task at hand (or paw?). After a couple minutes I get up, walk to the car and leave. As I turn the car my last sight is of her laying there intent on her chew.

A Quick Visit

Friday, May 25th

With today's schedule I only have 25 minutes with Beauty. She is under the deck when I arrive and meets me at the enclosure entrance doing her dance of excitement. Delight and controlled excitement flow within me as I hold my hand before her muzzle, as she sniffs, licks, and nuzzles my hand. With each moment of sharing affection my mood improves as space opens within me. She lowers her head in offer and I begin petting it. Within I sense the dance of testing me, testing to see if I will accept her pace of increasing affection. After perhaps 10 seconds she wants to nuzzle my hand with her muzzle again and for me to scratch her cheek which I do happily. Then it is on to full body stroking and scratching. Several times she comes in close, pushing against me as I stroke her. When she is pushed against me I stroke her far side occasionally putting pressure on her side pulling her tighter against me. Through the whole process she remains relaxed, ears forward, mouth open wide, her movements are free flowing and relaxed. We share a playful, slightly teasing enjoyment.

Beauty prances next to me as I pick up her bowl and return to the enclosure entrance. There I pause and pet her again, clearly blocking her exit with my body. She remains relaxed and jumps out when I move to the car trunk to fix her food. At the trunk she sits on the pavement just three feet behind me to my left. A couple of times during preparing her food I turn and reach out to pet her head as she sits there. The first time she intercepts my hand with her muzzle, licks it, then lowers her head so I can pet her. Other times she simply sits letting her mouth open a bit more when my hand touches her head. With her following me we return to the enclosure, I place her food bowl, and put water in her water bowl. I watch her as she moves to her food, sniffs it, and then comes out from under the deck. We return to the enclosure entrance where we enjoy sharing affection. A warm flow fills my body as I recognize how much more Beauty is choosing to be with me. She has chosen attention over food. Life is good!

Having an appointment I check the time. Though it will make me about 5 minutes late I decide to walk with Beauty. Beauty jumps out of the enclosure right behind me and runs out to field, sitting just beyond the pavement with a look of happy anticipation. Smiling I walk to her, pat her on the head, and kneel. After about a minute I pull the rope out of my pocket and put it on the ground. She steps just out of reach looking at me with ears forward and mouth open. She steps a couple more steps away when I toss the rope on the ground close to her. Her posture stiffens slightly while her ears stay forward and her mouth closes partially. Not having much time I get up with Beauty responding by doing a play jump and trotting, almost prancing, 30 feet away, tail high and wagging, before stopping, looking back at me. It seems as though she is saying, "*Well, you are coming aren't you?*" I begin a fluid, easy trot towards her.

Beauty runs across the field her tail acting as a flag inviting me to follow, to play. On the far side of the field Beauty waits for me, letting me come up to her and pet her head. As soon as I turn sideways to her she shifts her body so that she is pressed against my leg. I am mildly startled by her insistence that we be together. As we walk the next 30 feet her head shifts from sniffing to looking at me. She stops and waits for me to step in beside her, leaning against my leg as I begin to pet her. After 20 seconds of petting I take out the rope leash. She stays leaned against me, her body becomes still and relaxed, her mouth closes a bit, and her ears go back but do not lay down. As the rope slips through the clip-on in her collar her body relaxes a bit. As my hand draws the rope through, her mouth opens and by the time the ends of the rope meet in my hand her ears return forward and as she looks at me her mouth relaxes, opens. I smile when I sense her whisper, "*I trust you now.*" At one point on our walk we come to a cat laying just inside the blackberry bushes, a black cat we had seen once before. Beauty comes up to the bushes and slowly moves her lowered head forward towards the cat. I am heartened as I watch the cat remain laying there as Beauty's nose comes within four inches of the cat's nose. Beauty let out a quiet whimper several times and with a slight pull on the leash she turns away from the cat. In two moments my mind and ego have checked Beauty's behavior with the fact I have two cats at home that she will live with. The next moment my mind and ego express surprise, "She will live with?" Warmth flows within me and I chuckle.

Perhaps I should explain, well, attempt to explain. The mystic I studied with helped us accept that living beings have many different aspects and that in fact our minds and egos are a small, important and small, part of being human. His message, well at least one part I was able to 'grok', is that by opening to notice and honor all aspects of ourselves we expand our fields of choice exponentially. He helped us experience the infinite fields of possibilities open when we but notice, allow, and honor. With a grin he asked, "How many ingredients will you allow in your recipes of life?"

Two more minutes of walking and time is up. We cross the field to the enclosure entry where Beauty jumps up, then turns to face me standing just outside the enclosure. With a slight pull on the leash she turns sideways giving me access to reluctantly remove her rope. As I remove her rope she holds her body still while her ears move only slightly back. As I wrap the rope up, putting it in my pocket, I feel a mild sense of sorrow that the physical connection has been severed. As Beauty turns her head to look at me I have the sense that she is experiencing the same sorrow. As I step away from the entry Beauty turns and disappears under the deck.

Getting Fawn to Accept Beauty

Saturday, May 26

I will visit Beauty twice today. The first time with Fawn, the second time with My friend, Ute.

On my first visit Beauty is under the deck in the enclosure. She meets me at the entry and after a few moments of sharing affection she does a play jump and then bow. I bend over and slap the ground several times with my hands. She jumps in, I move back. She jumps away and I jump towards her. Soon it becomes a dance. I am laughing happily and Beauty playfully growls when she jumps towards me. Suddenly I change things, I do not jump back when Beauty jumps in. I stay where I am and slap the ground several times then leave my hands on the ground inches from Beauty's front feet. To my delight Beauty sits and raises one front paw. In awe and without thought I respond by gently reaching out and placing my hand, palm down, just under Beauty's raised paw. As my mind and ego struggle to understand what is happening Beauty lowers her paw a bit, gently pawing my hand. My mind quiets and I roll my hand over using a finger to stroke her paw and lower leg. A few moments and Beauty lowers her paw. My unplanned response is to turn my hand over a scratch her chest. Beauty show her relaxed surprise by shifting her ears back a bit. As my hand floats a couple inches from her chest she once again raises her paw placing it in my hand. I hear myself saying, "**Your such a good girl.**" as I put both hands on the ground next to her feet. It is my turn to be surprised as she lays down placing her paws on my hands. For almost a minute she plays with my paws as

I play with her paws. A thought of Fawn in the car causes me to turn my head to check on Fawn. Beauty responds by getting up and going under the deck. Soon I am at the car trunk fixing Beauty's food and then placing her food.

With her food placed I call Beauty to me at the enclosure entry. She comes out from under the deck towards me. I pull the rope leash out of my pocket, wiggle it, and with inner images of walking with Beauty and in a playful tone say, "**Are you ready to walk?**" I hold my breath. I can't help but grin as Beauty continues to walk to me, stepping into me and turning to offer me her collar. When Beauty starts to move I hold her back, "**Just a minute girl**." as I reach into my pocket and draw the retractable leash out. Beauty tenses but does not pull away. I pause a couple of moments and then move the retractable so Beauty can sniff it. 20 seconds of moving the retractable in front of her and she relaxes allowing her ears to come forward. She tenses a bit when I move the retractable to my other hand at her side and thankfully remains still as I clip both ends of the rope leash into the clip of the retractable. A warm and mildly excited, "**Your so good, let's go.**", a turn, and we are off on our walk. As we pass the car Fawn barks, a blend of excitement and alarm in her bark. Beauty and I take a loop around the field returning back within 30 feet of the car. Soon after we start she is busy enjoying the smells and affection from me. On the first part of the walk Beauty turns her head back to carefully look at the retractable.

When we stop 30 feet from the car Beauty sits as I undo the retractable and rope. Fawn is barking with a mostly excited tone. My mind and ego carefully ignore a, "This may work." floating from within. I pet Beauty for a few moments and then walk to the car. Fawn wants out of the car! I very carefully open the backdoor blocking her path while I put her on the retractable. Before I stand up I lock the retractable so it has only five feet of play. Fawn leaps out of the car past me immediately lunging in Beauty's direction. Beauty stands, ears back, mouth closed, tail down. I turn away from Beauty and pull Fawn with me trotting out into the field away from Beauty. When I look back Beauty has walked away and is now standing along side the fence of the apartments. I yell, "**Hey Beauty.**" and then continue walking Fawn. The end of our loop around the field bring Fawn and I back close to Beauty. Several times I let Fawn start towards Beauty, yell to Fawn, and then pull her back to me. Beauty watches closely and seems to understand that I am carefully protecting her from Fawn. Back at the car with mild satisfaction I put Fawn into the back seat. Within there are a thousand, thousand sensations that will wait until evening to sort themselves into something my mind can partially comprehend.

When I turn around to Beauty I am surprised to see that she has walked half the distance from the fence to the car. "**Well! Good girl**." brings Beauty forward as I walk towards her. Without thinking I turn so I walk in Beauty's direction and not directly at her. I carefully breath and relax as the gap between Beauty and I close. As Beauty joins me, walking alongside me, I reach into my pocket, get out the rope, and wiggle it in front of her. To my delight when I stop Beauty stops in a position that makes putting the rope on very easy. With the rope in place I assume a 'just doing what is normal' attitude, take out the retractable and clip it into both ends of the rope. Beauty's ears come back for a moment and return forward when we resume walking.

This time I first take Beauty within 15 feet of the car. When I holler to Fawn she is quiet, when I am quiet Fawn barks, then once we are past the car Fawn quiets. At the far side of the field Beauty looks at me and I can almost hear her whisper, *"She can be my friend. With you I feel safe. Is good."* The warmth flowing within me contrasts with my mind and ego busily protesting, "You can't hear her whisper." I grin as we continue our walk. Back at the car I slow when Beauty and I are 50 feet away. Beauty is walking next to me as I lock the retractable. 40 feet from the car and Beauty slows, her ears moving back. I put gentle pressure on the leash while saying. "**It is okay girl**." Beauty allows me to guide her closer to the car. At 30 feet Beauty balks and it takes a bit more pressure to keep her walking with me. At 20 feet we stop and I turn towards her. I sense an inner urge to have Fawn see me petting Beauty. Beauty relaxes as I remove the retractable and rope. I kneel and face her as Fawn barks and then is quiet. Soon Beauty is soaking up my attention, occasionally looking over at the car. With an "**Okay girl**." I stand, pet her head and then walk to the car. Beauty stays where she is as I go through the process of opening the backdoor and getting Fawn on leash. This time I position my body so Fawn's jump out of the car is away from Beauty.

Beauty stands not moving away. I basically drag Fawn directly away from Beauty. Ten steps and Fawn is busy being on a walk with me. She does glance back at Beauty every now and again. As Fawn and I loop back past Beauty, Beauty surprises me by getting up and following us. I hear myself thinking, "This is going far better than I expected." As Fawn and I turn back to the car Fawn notices Beauty, barks in alarm and lunges in Beauty's direction several times. Beauty seems unworried as she simply sits down where she is. A couple of steps and Fawn's interest returns to all the new smells around us. Beauty follows us back to the car and sits about 30 feet away. Suddenly I am on autopilot. I link in with Beauty's energies as I put Fawn into the backseat and imagine I am doing the same with Beauty. I close the door and turn to Beauty. I grin as I sense that Beauty understands that some day I will put her into the backseat and close the door. I smile as Fawn quiets after only a few barks.

As I walk the 30 feet to Beauty who is standing ears forward, mouth open, tongue our, tail wagging I feel a bit feisty and decide to push things a bit more. Ten feet from Beauty I take the retractable out of my pocket holding it so she can see it and saying, "**Hey girl.**" with a playful tone. I walk up to Beauty and without ceremony bend, clip the retractable onto her collar, turn and begin walking. I smile as Beauty's surprised uncertainty become her happily joining me. We make a small loop around the field before heading back to the car. We go directly at the car. 30 feet away I lock the retractable to only 4 feet of leash bringing Beauty in close to me as we walk. I have a plan. Fawn begins barking when we are 20 feet away, excited, get away barks. 15 feet from the car I begin a circle around the car. Beauty seems to catch on right away and beings a prancing gait. I have a sense of Beauty showing off to Fawn. I feel as if Beauty is whispering to Fawn, "*See he is mine too.*" We do two full circles around the car stopping about 12 feet from the driver's door. Fawn has quieted. Beauty leans into me as I reach down and undo the retractable. To my surprise she does not move away as soon as she is free. I pet her for a moment then turn back to the car. Fawn watches me walk back to the car. Beauty heads to the enclosure. After greeting Fawn and giving her reassurance for a few moments I start the car, turn, and begin the drive to the street. As the car swings past the enclosure entry I find myself thinking, "What?" as I see Beauty is jumping down out of the enclosure. My puzzlement increases as Beauty follows my slow moving car towards the street. Soon puzzlement turns to worry, "What if she keeps following me? What will I do?" Relief washes over me as only 20 feet from the street I glance in the rear view mirror and see that Beauty is sitting, watching us leave. The entire drive home my mind chews on the meaning of Beauty following us while within a quiet, loving warmth stirs new possibilities. My inner knowing is celebrating Beauty's choice to open to and support the possibility of coming home with me.

INTRODUCING UTE

The drive for the second visit begins from Ute's house with Ute sitting in the passenger seat. As we begin the drive a storm is raging complete with lightning and hard rain. During my weeks of visiting Beauty I have noticed several stray cats. During the time Chery and Ute were attempting to trap Beauty they also had noticed stray cats. The stray cats had come up in several conversations with Ute. As we drive Ute and I talk about her plans to visit both Beauty and to check on the stray cats. When Beauty first allowed me to put her on leash Ute and I had begun talking about both getting Beauty familiar with Ute and the process of getting Beauty to my home. Both Ute and I are happy that the storm shifts to light rain by the time we turn onto the driveway leading back to the enclosure and field.

We are both surprised to notice Beauty in the enclosure as I drive past the enclosure and park the car. Deep within I sense excitement and pleasure, many energies blending, opportunities being offered. As I park I notice that Beauty has come to the opening into the enclosure, waiting expectantly. Suddenly I sense Beauty noticing Ute in the car with me. Worry, love, concern float within me as time slows, as Beauty seems to scan Ute and then my intent and Ute's intent. My sense of Beauty's concern is reflected in her posture, ears forward and mouth closed. Ute allows me to get out first. As I flow my pleasure in seeing Beauty to her I speak, **"Hey Beauty. I brought a friend to say hello. She is visiting the cats too."** As Beauty backs away from the entry I sense her message of trust. She chooses to go back into the enclosure rather than leave the enclosure for the openness of the field. As Ute and I walk slowly to the entry, Beauty and I agree and claim the enclosure as safe space we will share. Deep within I sense Beauty choosing to trust me, to trust our connections. I subtly sense Beauty choosing to trust Ute, to accept Ute's desire for her well being.

As we reach the entry I sense Ute and Beauty opening to each other, I sense myself becoming a supporting cast member. Time and reason slip away, the three of us are dancing, responding to the vibrant signals guiding us. I move to Beauty while Ute waits. As I approach her the deep connections we share expand and fill the space. I sit next to Beauty, offer her my hand and smile as she offers me her muzzle to stroke. I shift from facing Beauty, expanding our space to include Ute. One breath, a second breath and Ute moves a bit closer to Beauty, tossing a treat to her. Slowly Beauty gets up and moves towards Ute, moves out from behind me, opening her energies to Ute. I hold my energy gently in support. Ute ever so gently moves a bit closer, pauses, tosses another treat. I sense Beauty opening further to me and then stepping towards Ute as she picks up the treat. With gentle warmth Beauty accept my loving, supportive energies and opens further to Ute. In that moment Ute takes another step forward, tosses another treat. As Ute's foot touches the ground connections shift. Now it is about Ute and Beauty offering, testing trust. I am simply holding space for them.

Ute kneels and tosses a treat towards Beauty to a spot just beyond where she would be able to reach out and touch Beauty. Beauty pauses, her ears partially back, her mouth closed. I sense Beauty opening to me for support and as I sense Beauty accepting the love I flow to her I hear myself saying, "**Good girl. It is okay.**" The next moment Beauty's ears come partially forward, her mouth opens slightly, she steps forward and ever so cautiously picks up the treat. As she opens her mouth and takes in the treat I sense her opening more deeply to Ute, drawing and welcoming Ute's love and concern within herself. I am filled with awe as Beauty glances back to me and then sits facing Ute. One breath, two breaths, three breaths, I sense some deep feminine energies I cannot understand being shared by Beauty and Ute. Ute stretches her hand with a treat out to Beauty, a gentle, open offering, an invitation. I smile as I notice Beauty stand and lean forward to accept the treat. With the second and third treat Beauty and Ute seem to sign an agreement of trust. I sense the tension in both relaxing and acceptance opening.

Beauty glances back at me. Before I realize what is happening I accept Beauty's request and move forward, next to her. I reach out to touch Beauty. She follows the movement of my hand, tensing a bit. As I stoke her once and then twice I sense her whispering, *"No. Be close. No touch."* Grinning I draw my hand back. Ute offers another treat. Beauty steps closer taking the treat. A moment or two and it is done, the space shifts and closes. Beauty steps back, sitting next to me, shifting her energies to me. I glance at Ute and shrug my shoulders, smiling when Ute stands and offers, **"I guess I will check on the cats."** Beauty tenses and leans slightly towards me, watching Ute leave the enclosure. In the moment we watch Ute step out of the enclosure the space is filled with only Beauty and I. A warm pleasure, happiness with stepping beyond her fear, floats to me from Beauty. Her mouth is open, her ears forward, tongue out, tail up and wagging slightly, Beauty looks happily at me. As I say **"You did so well!"** Beauty's head raises just a bit, her mouth opens further, her tail wags happily. In that moment we become a team, we agree to face the world together.

Ute spends time checking on the stray cats. One allows her close. Others keep their distance. While Ute is busy with her tasks Beauty and I leave the enclosure and walk. I sense Beauty sensing Ute's intent to help the cats and choosing to open further in trust to Ute. The stray cats have been Beauty's only friends. When Ute walks towards me telling me she is done Beauty walks perhaps 15 feet away and sits. As Ute and I get into the car and drive away Beauty watches us. As I turn onto the street I notice a sense of sorrow from Beauty, a desire to be leaving with us. On the way back to her house Ute and I first talk about the stray cats. I surrender to Ute's pull for my help and the Universe's gentle support. We plan her next steps and my support. In the last bit of the trip we talk about Beauty's progress. As Ute talks about the need to get Beauty away from the area where she is and to my home a deep and gently urgent need to act stirs within me. It is time to plan my taking Beauty home. We speak of it being time to get Beauty used to being in my car.

Maybe My Sister

Sunday, May 27

On my first visit I choose to take Fawn with me. She is delighted to get into the car and pays careful attention once we get beyond the industrial area along Airport Way. As I pull in I scan the field and parking area, disappointed not to see Beauty as I sensed I would. As I drive past the enclosure my disappointment turns to gentle warmth as I spot Beauty already inside the enclosure. Beauty stays in the enclosure as I retrieve her food bowl and mix her food back at the car. I grin while mixing her food as I sense her pleasure, *"My people making for me. Happy."* As I return with her food she meets me at the entry. When I begin to reach over her head to pet her she steps back, her ears go back, and as she looks at me I sense her whisper of, *"Not that way. Be respectful. Offer me choice."* As an emotion of 'oh, oops' moves through me she steps forward. With a grin I reach forward, hand low, and stroke her muzzle with the back of my fingers and hand. As I sense a, *"That is better."* Beauty steps forward and turns offering me her body. As the soft fur on her shoulders yield to my touch I sense her yielding, opening to accept the pleasure I offer. In a moment I notice how I open in response to her, how her energy and mine are blending as we share the pleasures of touch induced closeness. Perhaps a minute and it is enough. As Beauty steps away opening the path for me I sense her, *"Hungry now."* and sense within my mouth her chewing and enjoying the taste of the food I am giving her. She seems to giggle in response to my noticing her message.

After eating perhaps half her food Beauty goes under the deck and reappears at the entry to the enclosure. There she stands, waiting for me. As I round the deck and take the retractable out of my pocket sensing clipping it onto her collar her tail begins to wag. My mind tries to ignore when I sense her anticipating jumping down out of the enclosure with the the slight pull of her collar being attached to the retractable. My ego scoffs as I sense Beauty's pleasure as she enjoys how the physical connection of the leash will reflect the inner connections that are becoming stronger, more real in the world she and I share. I grin and enjoy the warmth of 'being with my dog'.

Beauty and I's walk begins with a loop past the car. Fawn begins her insistent barking. Without thinking I open up to Fawn and as I call out, "**Hey Fawn I am walking your sister.**" In that moment Fawn's barking seems to shift from alarm to eagerness blended with uncertainty. My mind wonders if I am not a fool as I sense Fawn's energy shifting from 'get away' to 'get over here'. Another question asked, never to be answered. Soon we are past the car walking along the bushes and then along the blackberries. As we walk Beauty and I are moving together, sometimes I follow, sometimes she follows. I sense Fawn's energy with us, curious and uncertain at the same time. We walk back towards the car. When we are 40 feet away Fawn begins to bark and bark. At 20 feet I stop, pet Beauty a bit, and remove the retractable. As I pet her I sense myself putting Fawn on the retractable and holding her back from Beauty. My mind carefully ignores my sense that Beauty understands and agrees with my plan. My mind flinches a bit when Beauty sits, seeming to whisper "*Okay*".

At the car Fawn is eager to get out. I have to be very careful to get her on the retractable before I allow her room to jump out of the car. By the time her back feet hit the ground she is focused on getting to Beauty. Two steps and I am pulling her away from Beauty who is sitting, surprisingly relaxed. I hear myself yelling "**Good girl Beauty.**" as I link energies with Fawn, moving both my body and energy towards the hedge, away from Beauty. Fawn's attention moves to the unfamiliar smells. As we turn the corner from hedge to blackberry bushes both I and Fawn glance back towards the car. I deal with happy surprise that Beauty is moving with us about 30 feet away and Fawn's reaction to noticing Beauty is close. As Fawn barks and pulls Beauty seems amused. I talk with Fawn, "**It is okay, girl. Be with me.**" and allow myself to sense Fawn accepting Beauty as part of our family. Within a moment Fawn quiets, barks once more, moves her nose to the ground, and turns to walk with me. As we walk the quarter mile of blackberry bushes Fawns occasionally turns her attention to Beauty, barks and lunges towards Beauty, then quickly returns to experiencing the smells. As we turn at the far end of the field Fawn's response to Beauty turns to curiosity mixed with uncertainty. As we turn back to the car Fawn seems to accept Beauty moving with us. It seems as though Fawn is whispering, *"Well, maybe it's good she moves with us."* Half way back to the car I glance back and smile as I notice Beauty is walking with us, only 15 feet behind. As I turn my attention back towards the car I sense, *"Yes, moving with you and Fawn."*

At the car Fawn notices Beauty is close and turns barking in protest. Beauty walks five feet away and sits. With effort I turn Fawn back to the car, open the back door, and insist she jump in. As I close the door and turn back towards Beauty I have a sense of Beauty's sorrow and uncertainty, *"I want to come too and I am scared."* Confusion washes over me, through me, Beauty is with Fawn and I and yet she is staying separate, left out in the field by herself. I surrender to the contrast of knowing Beauty is with us and not knowing how that will come to be. Each of my moves suddenly is a dance of conflicts, getting in the car, putting the key in, starting the car, putting it in gear, turning towards the street, and finally turning onto the street. As I drive towards home I sense a path opening for Beauty to come home with me. Early in the trip home Fawn and I stop at the walking trail along the Columbia Slough. Somehow it is important I walk with Fawn in nature allowing Beauty's energies to blend with ours. A ritual before returning home without Beauty.

Family

On my second visit I am pleased to see Beauty in the enclosure when I get there. My pleasure deepens when Beauty comes out from under the deck to meet me at the entry. Her wagging tail seems to fan the warmth within me. After perhaps two minutes of saying hello Beauty turns away from me and offering me her butt to scratch. As Beauty wiggles her butt enjoying my scratching with both hands I hear myself saying, **"Oh Beauty, you trust me more."** In response her hips wiggle even more and I sense warmth and *"trust now."* A couple more moments and Beauty steps away, heading under the deck. I get her bowl and return to the trunk of the car. While I mix her food Beauty stands at the entry waiting for me and then walks with me to place her food. As I stand up I notice Ute driving up and parking her car. As Ute gets out of her car and yells hello to us Beauty's attention shifts from her food to Ute. It seems Beauty whispers to me, *"Safe if you close."*

There are two reasons for Ute to meet me. First she wants to check again on the stray cats, secondly we want Beauty to become comfortable with her. Ute and I have been talking about how to get Beauty to my house. The first step is to get Beauty okay with being in the backseat of the car. The second step is to get both doors closed and then drive her to my house. The problem is that I cannot sense Beauty being okay with being in the backseat when I get out and then get back into the driver's seat. As I sense myself doing that I have a strong sense of Beauty panicking. When Ute suggests that she drive us home while I stay in the backseat with Beauty my tension and worry dissipate. Today I will help Beauty open trust and acceptance with Ute.

As I walk to the entry to meet Ute, Beauty goes under the deck and then comes out from under the deck close to the entry. I sense Beauty's curiosity when Ute and I hug. Without thinking, as I turn back to Beauty I open and blend the energies that connect me with Beauty with the energies that connect me to Ute. In that moment Beauty's head tilts sideways and I sense a whisper of "*What?*" from her. I grin. Ute waits while I walk the few steps to Beauty carefully putting out a 'let's play' energy as I imagine both Ute and I touching Beauty. Beauty takes a step back, seems to shrug her shoulders, and steps forward to meet me. As I pet Beauty her attention moves to Ute and I sense her whisper to Ute, "*You can come too.*" In that same moment Ute steps forward, treat in hand. Beauty waits, hanging on the edge of trusting or leaving. As I pet Beauty and energetically welcome Ute I hear myself saying, "**Your a good girl**." As Ute's energy opens into the space Beauty and I share Beauty relaxes and I sense her whisper, "*Maybe family.*" I am in awe as the space the three of us share deepens. At first Beauty is uninterested in the treats Ute offers. As I go down onto my knees Beauty looks at me and then relaxes a bit more. As she turns back to Ute I sense more openness, more trust. Ute drops a treat for Beauty. For one moment, two moments, three moments Beauty sniffs the treat, seeming to wonder whether to accept the bond Ute offers with the treat. Instinctively I pet Beauty and hear myself saying, "**Your a good girl. It's okay.**" A fourth moment and Beauty picks up the treat, raises her head, and while looking at Ute chews and swallows. I notice a warm smile form on Ute's face. The next treat Beauty carefully takes from Ute's hand as I pet Beauty. With each treat Beauty opens to my protection a bit more and opens more in connection with Ute.

After several treats Beauty steps back seeming to whisper, "*Too much closeness, need open space.*" As I stand Ute is already turning towards the entry. As Beauty moves behind us I sense her worry of our blocking her exit. In the last steps to the entry I share with Beauty a sense of Ute and I stepping aside, giving her freedom as soon as we exit the enclosure. As we step down Ute stepping to the side, making room for me to follow her surprises me. I have no words to describe the incredible pleasures I sense from Beauty as she claims her freedom by jumping down out of the entry, glancing at Ute and I, and then trotting across the pavement to the field. As Ute and I begin to walk towards her I hear myself saying, "**She is a happy girl.**" Beauty's wagging tail and wiggling body echo our pleasure. I grin as I sense Ute and I being is sync. Words are not needed. Ute waits at the edge of the field while I walk out to Beauty. Beauty sits, waits for me. Soon I am kneeling next to her petting her. When I think of clipping the retractable on Beauty's collar she gets up and looks at Ute who is walking towards us. I grin as I sense Beauty whispering, "*I want to show her my territory, our territory.*" I put the retractable back in my pocket. As Ute gets close Beauty turns and heads towards the hedge glancing over her shoulder to make sure I am walking with her and that Ute is close but not too close. Beauty begins showing us both her area with me 5 feet from her and Ute 10 to 15 feet behind us. Beauty shows Ute one of her three hidy holes in the hedge as we walk along the hedge. As we walk along the blackberries Beauty suddenly disappears into the blackberries and a couple moments later sticks just her head back out. As Beauty's playful energy washes over me I hear myself saying, "**Oh! Is that so?**" Beauty disappears back into the blackberries. I stand and wait somehow knowing Beauty wants Ute's attention. Ute steps up to the opening and bends down, talking with Beauty. I smile as I sense Beauty opening further, allowing herself to trust Ute, to play with Ute. Ute steps back, opening space for Beauty, and Beauty comes out of the blackberry bushes. Deep within I sense the flow of rich, open, accepting energies enveloping us as many energies are happily filling the space we share.

As Beauty continues leading our tour the natural flow puts Ute to Beauty's left, me to Beauty's right. Ute and I are about 20 feet apart. Sometimes Beauty is closer to me, sometime she is closer to Ute. As we get to the far end of the field Beauty's movements become less fluid, she seems unsure, a bit confused, unfocused. In a moment I too am uncertain, unsure. First I try walking towards Beauty. No change. Then I begin walking back towards the car with Beauty following. No change. I accept a vague urge and walk towards Ute. I am rewarded by Beauty's body posture relaxing and the uncertainty draining from my body. I turn back to Beauty and kneel as Beauty steps in close, turning sideways, letting me know I should begin petting her. Beauty steps in closer to me and looks at Ute. I am between Ute and Beauty as Ute slowly walks toward us. When Ute is two steps away, with my attention still with

Beauty and a bit of confusion I hear myself saying to Ute, "**Pet me.**" I can almost hear Ute saying, "What? Oh! Okay." with her energy. Beauty watches as Ute pets my right shoulder and upper arm while my left hand strokes Beauty's back. With a step forward Beauty moves close enough for Ute to reach her hand down close to Beauty's head. Beauty glances at Ute's left hand on my shoulder and then carefully reach her head forward to sniff Ute's outstretched right hand. In the few moments of her sniffing I sense the three of us linking as trusted friends, maybe family. Deep warmth flows through me and out, blending with Beauty's and Ute's energies forming 'our space'.

Another breath and Beauty turns to walk back towards the car and enclosure. After a couple steps Beauty turns and waits for Ute and I to join her. Together we walk towards the car, Ute about 10 feet from Beauty and I. About half way to the car Beauty leads me towards Ute. Ute stops and turns towards us. My mind and ego carefully ignore a sense that Beauty is guiding all of us. I walk to Ute with Beauty following me. As I get to Ute I turn back to Beauty and standing next to Ute I kneel. Beauty steps in front of me, offering the side of her body to me, letting me know she wants to be petted, her head a little more than a foot from Ute's hand. As Beauty enjoys on my attention she accepts Ute reaching down and lightly touching her shoulders. Two breathes, three breaths of us 'being together' and I lighten my touch while Ute increases her touch. I feel Ute touching my shoulder, gently allowing her energies flowing to Beauty to link with her energies flowing to me. Immediately Beauty's head comes up and she looks directly at Ute. An uncomfortable moment later Beauty steps away from us, loops out ten feet and sits. I am washed over by a sense of Beauty declaring, *"I am done."* As I stand quietly Ute draws a chew stick from her pocket and shows it to Beauty. I walk a bit closer to Beauty and turn back to Ute. In that moment, without words, we agree that Ute will leave soon. Beauty relaxes a bit, looks at Ute seeming to say, *"I will take your treat then you can leave."* I watch in awe, a bystander, as Ute steps forward within 2 feet of Beauty and reaches out offering the chew stick and much more. Beauty, alert yet relaxed, reaches out and takes the chew stick and more. I have the sense of a private bargain being struck between Ute and Beauty. My ego's protest is quieted by warm pleasures flowing through my body and an unspoken whisper of "*It is as it should be.*"

As my attention returns to the physical world I notice Ute is almost to her car, Beauty is laying close to me chewing on Ute's gift, softening it, making it her own. I glance up to see Ute's car turning out onto the street and disappear. Time and space have vanished, all that exist are Beauty and I and perhaps 20 feet of the world surrounding us. Grinning I lay down close to Beauty, petting her as she enjoys her treat, allowing myself to notice deep energies play within her, within me.

TRUST AND THE CAR

Monday, May 28

During today's single visit I plan to do more with Beauty and the car. I sense Beauty waiting for me as I drive. I do not sense her in the enclosure as I wait for the final turn onto the pavement surrounding the hottub shop. As I drive past the enclosure I do not see her. Curious and concerned I whistle as I get out of the car. As my eyes scan the hedge and then the blackberry bushes I sense her and then see her step out of the blackberry bushes over 200 feet away. Bubbling energies enliven me as I watch her bounding towards me. **"Hey girl! Your such a good girl."** seems to quicken her pace which in turn causes me to trot towards her. At 20 feet apart we both seem unsure of how to proceed. Without thinking I shift my direction so I am trotting just off to her side. She leaps to the side and we begin a big circle that quickly begins shrinking. When we are about 15 feet apart I plop down on the ground and roll over, growling playfully. Half a circle and Beauty is close to me. I roll away from her and lay on my belly and wait, wondering where on my body she will engage me. Beauty comes in from my right side, close to my shoulders then bends down to sniff my neck and head. A few sniffs and I raise up to my hands and knees carefully exposing my neck to her. She playfully lunges in then immediately bounds away from me. As I sit back on my hunches she spins around to face me and does petty paw movements when I bow and wiggle.

    I get a sense of *"What?"* from her when I take off trotting towards the enclosure. A moment later she is bounding after me. To my surprise she veers off towards the car waiting there while I get her bowl. Back at the car she is sitting close to the trunk seeming content and pleased as she watches me fix her food. Grinning I say, "**Well girl, so I am supposed to give you food?**" I smile as I sense her response of, "*Yes, from my people, my food.*" She stands when I pick up her bowl and close the trunk. By the time I turn she has started walking towards the enclosure. I whistle and wait while she returns. She watches as I open first one and then the other backdoors of the car. I sense her puzzlement when I reach in and place her food bowl on the backseat just inside the door and then go sit about ten feet from the car. She walks over to me, and moves away when I reach out to pet her. I laugh lightly and ask, "**Well girl, what are you going to do?**" while imagining her standing on the door sill sniffing her food. I am a bit startled when she turns and walks back to the car, sniffs the door sill then puts her front paws up to sniff her food. "**Hey girl. What you doing?**" comes out of my mouth as I stand up. With my movement she backs away from the car opening space for me to get her bowl. As I walk towards the enclosure she follows, her bouncy steps reinforcing my sense that she is pleased to have done something new, something a little bit scary.

I have plans so I simply place her bowl and exit the enclosure waiting at the entry for her. When she joins me at the entry I already have the retractable out. When I reach down and take hold of her collar she tries to back away. "**Come on girl. I have plans today.**" said with a playful tone results in her standing, waiting for me to clip the retractable to her collar. The next moment she is jumping down out of the enclosure and heads off towards the field. I head towards the car. Four steps and I lock the retractable, pulling lightly, "**Come on girl.**" One step pulling against me and she turns, joining me in walking to the car. As we approach the car she goes ahead and to my pleasure goes to the backdoor, sniffing the sill and backseat. I wait 10 seconds and then move in closer to her, blocking her exit away from the car. She tenses and I talk softly, "**It is okay girl. Not yet.**" A moment or two later she relaxes and looks up at me with a questioning look. "**Good girl.**" and I turn and step to the back of the car. Beauty pauses, seeming a bit surprised, even a bit disappointed I had not pressured her more. Soon we are at the other backdoor. I get there first and stand my body is an extension of the open door. Beauty stops six feet away looking unsure. I can almost hear her whisper, "*I don't know about this.*" I pull gently on the leash and say, "**Come here girl.**" She takes one step and stops. I pull just a bit harder. She takes one more step. I turn just a bit and bend so my head is inside the car. Beauty pulls back and then relaxes, curious about what I am doing. I pat the seat several times and hear myself saying, "**Hey girl. This is your car too.**" while imagining Beauty on the backseat. With that Beauty pulls hard stopping and sitting after I let her take two steps away. In the same moment Beauty and I accept that we are testing how much she is willing to surrender to my insistence. With a playful, "**Good girl.**" I turn take a step and sit down onto the backseat, my feet still on the ground. Beauty looks at me and I sense her confusion. I chatter to her quietly and when she relaxes a bit I pull on the leash and say, "**Come here girl.**" She balks pulling back. At the same moment I say, "**Come here girl.**" and sense her coming to me for a couple moments before we begin our walk. A moment later her head is at my knees and I am petting her. Before I could have counted to three I sense she is full and as she backs away I stand and we are beginning our walk.

    I grin as I sense Beauty's desire and intent that she lead me on our walk. In the same moment I begin to move with her and sense us back at the car, me petting her as I sit on the backseat and she stands just outside the car. I sense her, "*I lead first.*" and continue to follow her. With both backdoors of the car open I am uncomfortable going to the far end of the field. Beauty takes me to the hidy-hole she had shown Ute and disappears into the blackberry bushes. I shrug my shoulders and hope the retractable does not get tangled in the vines. My mind plays with how I will deal with that happening. To my relief Beauty only goes in about 10 feet before turning and coming back out. As she steps out of the bushes and next to me she gives the lead back to me and we walk back to the car. It is a sunny day and warm. The grass in the field has been cut filling the air with fresh cut grass smells. I am happy, a beautiful day with my Beauty. As we approach the car Beauty drops back just a bit behind my left knee.

    I notice I have no idea where my choices are coming from, they seem to flow easily from deep within. As we approach the car I guide us around the back of the car to the passenger side. I walk past the open back door pausing to allow Beauty to stay back and sniff the sill.

I grin as I notice Beauty step in closer and put her head into the car to sniff the floor. I make note of putting treats on the floor for her to find. We loop back around to the drivers side where Beauty spends almost a minute sniffing the sill, the floor and the backseat without stepping up onto the sill. I speak to Beauty and when she looks around at me I take a couple steps closer to her so I am blocking her leaving. A couple more sniffs and she is needs space. I back up two steps and relax. She seem uncertain and simply stands there looking at me. I pull slightly on the retractable and she steps past me, her ears coming forward as she passes. I go to her and kneel in front of her. Less than 10 feet from the car she lowers her head into me, licking my hands as I stroke her muzzle. She raises her head and looks me in the eyes, a deep, soft, loving gaze. As she lowers her head she steps into me and turning sideways offers me her body. For reasons I will never know I wait, one breath, two breathes, three breaths. Beauty shifts her body even closer to me almost bumping against me. As my hands float to her time slows, our world is she, I, and the car, transportation to our home. A minute, five minutes, ten minutes, I do not know. Eventually I sense a transition, the car seems to be beckoning Beauty and I. As my mind and ego protest I stand and with Beauty next to me walk to the car. While Beauty waits I lower myself to sit in the car on the backseat and swing my legs into the car. With my free hand I pat my lap and hear myself saying, "**Come here girl.**" Beauty takes one step and stops. Just as she begins to sit I pull on the retractable. One pull backwards and then Beauty steps to me, her head where I can easily pet it. I do just that. Beauty shifts herself so she can lean her head against my thigh as I pet her. There is a gentle warmth that fills the car, fills Beauty, fills me. Within three minutes we are done. I unclip the retractable from Beauty's collar and toss it on the seat. Beauty seems surprised to be given her freedom, accepts a little more attention and then walks a few feet from the car.

    I grin and get out of the car calling Beauty to follow me to the other side. My sense of being guided is still with me. Once there I take out a treat and offer it to her. Without pause she comes in and accepts my offering. She is at the open backdoor, I am behind her blocking her exit. I slowly reach down and pet her as she sniffs the sill of the door, noticing the retractable on the seat. I consider pushing Beauty into the car with my knees and notice her ears coming back and her body tensing. "**Not yet girl?.**" and I step back. I sense her surprise and smile when she chooses to sniff the sill a few more times before turning and walking away from the car. Three steps from the car and she begins to prance a bit. I sense her pride in her own bravery, her pleasure in trusting me more. With "**You did well girl.**" her head comes up a bit higher and her tail wags. I challenge her with a "**Come here girl.**" in a commanding tone and bending down for her. She pauses then comes to me as I kneel at the open backdoor. I sense her whispering, *"See, I am brave."* A few moments and I stand, take hold of her collar and shift so I am behind her. She pushes against me trying to turn away from the car. As I say, "**Good girl. Your car.**" I imagine myself behind her pushing against her butt with both knees and imagine her jumping up onto the seat. She tenses and to my pleasure does not try to force past me to get away. I smile, bringing warm playful energy into my belly and flowing it to Beauty as I shift her so her head is almost inside the car and in the same fluid movement bend my knees putting first gentle and then more forceful pressure on her butt. I relax and laugh gently as I press just a bit harder imagining her giving into the pressure and putting her front paws up on the car seat. Before it can register with me her front feet are up on the seat and I am struggling to position myself to move with her. My knees press harder, more for my balance than to urge her further. I feel as though I am the klutz in a comedy routine caught in a turmoil of movement and laugh. My laugh deepens as I notice Beauty has shifted forward, further into the car, her chest now resting on the seat, her back feet on the ground. Before my mind notices what is happening I sense that Beauty is more curious than scared, worry blended with playfulness. As I regain my balance I reach down with both hands and rub Beauty's shoulders. She tenses and then seems to notice I am not trying to get her further into the car. Her body relaxes and before I begin a second breath she is pushing gently back against my legs. With three small steps backwards for her and I bring her out of the car giving her room to escape. It is my turn to be curious, she turns to her escape route and then continues turning until she is looking at me. She waits until I have reached down and scratch her shoulders and then bounds away, tail high.

Soon she and I are jumping and running in play. Out of the corner of my eye I notice the Arab woman with two children I had talked with watching me. I have a sense that my play with Beauty confuses her, "*Why would a person play like a dog?*" floats into my mind. As I kneel and call Beauty to me I notice Beauty's lack of certainty. I crawl the few feet to her and turn my body sideways to her. Beauty steps in pushing her side against my side. A few moments of celebration she gets up, turns and trots to the enclosure to rest a bit and then eat. "**Okay girl. I will see you tomorrow**." floats out as I stand up and go to close the car doors. A few moment later Beauty is laying under the deck and I am pulling onto the street en-route home. As the trip begins I am grinning with satisfaction. Within a few blocks my mind and ego are assessing what we have accomplished and what more is to be done. I am careful to keep a playful tone to their ponderings.

Declaring 'Us' to Others

Tuesday, May 29

*A*s is often the case now, Beauty is under the deck when I arrive. She meets me at the entrance with much affection, hand licking, wide open mouth, and petty paw movement. A couple of times she buries her head against my chest as my shoulders and head bend over her neck and back. I marvel at her trust, her enjoying me enclosing her in my affection. A stark contrast with her first tentative allowing of my touch. Her joy, and pleasure, and openness wash away my concerns from the day before. After three or four minutes of celebration I step up into the enclosure and recover her food bowl returning to the car trunk to mix her food. My steps are light and easy, warmth filling my belly, flowing up to fill my chest. She follows me to get the bowl and back to the car. At the car she comes in close standing on my right side just behind me. I grin noting how she is beginning to act like 'my dog'. In response to sensing her waiting for a bit attention I step back and turn to her. While I am petting her head she gets up and walks to the back passenger door looking at the door and then sniffing the crack where the door meets the door frame as the door shuts. I am fascinated by her interest given that she has gone to is the door where I had forced her to partially enter the day before. Not sure what she would do I step forward and open the door. Once the door comes open she loses interest and returns to her position for watching me prepare her food. Several times as I mix her food I turn to talk with her or pet her.

Once the food is mixed I spend time getting the retractable leash, some water, and her brush. We then go into the enclosure and she happily watches as I place her food bowl. As I pour water into her water bowl she drink from the falling water, drinking more from the bowl once the flow stops. I smile sensing her enjoyment at being 'my dog'. Within I mark off one more step towards her coming home with me. She sniffs her food and takes a couple bites. When I go to the enclosure entrance she stays under the deck. I have a sense of her 'being independent' and decide to sit with my legs dangling out of the enclosure. After a couple minutes I grin as she joins me and we walk out to the field. At the field I kneel and she comes to me immediately. The warmth within me deepens as she and I open to being 'with and within' each other. After a bit of petting I take out the brush and brush her for about three minutes before she begins to fidget. When I say 'walk' and reach for her collar she slowly pulls away and then bounds out into the field, her wide wagging tail signaling her pleasure. At the blackberry bushes she waits for me and after she disappears into the blackberry bushes where I cannot follow a few times she comes to me standing with her shoulders by my knees. Responding to her invitation I reach down, moving my hand to her collar. She waits, ears mostly forward, mouth open, body relaxed while I attach the retractable.

Off we go, sometimes her leading, sometimes me leading. Twice I stop and spend a couple minutes brushing her. Each session lasts three to four minutes, a bit better than the previous one to two minutes. At one point I guide her to the fence by the 50s style motel now apartments. At the fence I purposely kneel with her between me and the fence. I am pleased that she stays there. After a couple of minutes of brushing she sits. I am surprised and find myself smiling. She is sitting in a "trapped" position allowing me to groom her. As I groom her I have the sense of her acknowledging that she is choosing to trust me. There is a playful, alluring tone to her mood. After about three minutes two women from the apartments come around the corner only 20 feet from us. I am pleased that Beauty stands as I do (rather than bolting) and walks in a large half circle away from the women and back to my side. The women stop as soon as they see us. Beauty and I slip into a space where we dance together, Beauty showing the women I am her partner. As Beauty's half circle ends at my side she continues a couple steps towards the women her tail up, not wagging. I and the women are surprised and delighted. In a declaration of partnership I move forward to Beauty and stop along side her. I am filled with pleasure as I sense Beauty and I shaping a deeper bond of trust and declaring our bond to the women. Beauty stands and watches the women walk only 12 feet away from us as they pass. Only a few days before Beauty had come at closest within 30 feet of them and then her tail was down.

Each day I try to do things that give Beauty and I new shared experiences. Today, after the women have walked by I walk Beauty to the far side of the apartments, then to the front of the apartments and along the sidewalk by the busy street. This route exposes us to a person walking on the sidewalk in an area where escape is limited. Beauty does wonderfully as two people pass, walking close to me, tail up, ears slightly back, a slightly tense walk. Rounding the apartments we turn back towards the field. After about 10 steps I stop and pet Beauty telling her, "**Your a good girl. You did wonderfully.**" Her head comes up, her tail begins to wag slowly, her ears come mostly forward, and her body relaxes. I am smiling and find I have a bounce in my step as we walk towards the field. My smile deepens when I notice a matching bounce in Beauty's step.

At the pavement Beauty walks towards the enclosure. At the enclosure entrance I undo the retractable leash and she heads under the deck. After getting a drink she lays down where she can see me. Responding to a quiet urge I enter and lay down next to the deck. After about four minutes she gets up, retreats further under the deck, and lays down facing partially away from me. With Beauty's request for space it seems time to go. I get up, go to the car, and pick up the baggy with cat food. I then go to the Quonset hut where I put some cat food in a bowl. Ute wants to retrieve a stray cat and I am putting the cat food out to help my friend. As I tuck the food bowl back out of sight Beauty joins me by stepping in next to me. With the bowl in place she trots out to the field and waits for me. I am smiling as I walk to her, pleased that she is choosing more time with me. I reach down and connect the retractable. Her body is relaxed, ears mostly forward, tail up. As soon as the leash is attached she turns and we head off to explore blackberry bushes. There is a new sweetness to our being together that I can neither describe nor name. Ten minutes later our time together is somehow over. We loop back to the enclosure, I remove the retractable and say goodbye to Beauty. As I drive home I sense Beauty with me. Warmth and gentle sorrow stir within me, contentment and desire. I want Beauty with me at home. As I sense her being with me warmth flows, tempered by the sorrow of knowing it is not yet time. Deep within I sense stirrings, inner guidance moving into my belly, beginning to reshape so it can guide my choices in the next few weeks. As I drive home a pleasant jolt notifies me, *"Beauty trusts us enough to be with us in exposed situations."*

Time for Focus

Wednesday, May 30

As I drive to be with Beauty the stirrings within my lower belly insist I pay attention. I have a vague sense that the time for transition, the time for Beauty to be safe in my home, safe in our home, her new home, is approaching. Dangers are gathering for her. It is clear I must get her into the backseat of the car soon. I sense that the freedom to take a relaxed easy pace with Beauty is being pinched off by gathering dangers. I need to push myself and to ask more of Beauty. I sense that soon I will need to insist Beauty do what I guide her to do. I also sense that being insistent in the wrong moments will destroy the trust we have built. I am jolted by the recognition that the process has been just as much about me growing to trust Beauty as it has been about Beauty growing to trust me. As I pull behind the shop I have the sense of being on a narrowing path with only a narrow board over a ravine Beauty and I must cross soon.

Beauty is out in the field when I arrive. She sits up as I approach her and stands when I am a few steps from her. She seems relaxed and slightly amused as I reach down to pet her. A few moments and she leads the way to the enclosure. With her food mixed and placed I jump out of the enclosure, turning to her as she steps to the entry. As I click the retractable onto her collar I hear myself saying, "**We have some work to do today girl.**" My mood lightens a bit when I sense Beauty whispering, "*Oh good. You boss.*" and notice the free flow of her movements reflecting her eagerness and trust. She is a bit surprised when I head straight for the car, pulling me towards the field a bit before changing directions to come with me. At the car I open both backdoors and stand back while she sniffs the door sills. I override a pull to walk with her in the field, go to the driver's side and sit on the backseat leaving my feet on the ground. Beauty is sitting about ten feet away watching me carefully. I call to her. As she sits there not responding I feel myself tensing a bit. In an unplanned clipped tone I voice a command, "**Come here girl**." Beauty stands and with a slight pull on the retractable she takes one then two then three steps to me. With her head at my knees I lean forward and pet her relaxing a bit when she steps in closer. I bend over her and stroke her neck and shoulders several times taking hold of her collar. My pleasure barely slips past my focus into my awareness. Breath in, breath out, relax. I take hold of Beauty's collar and then swing my feet into the car. She pulls back once gently, harder a second time. "**It is okay Beauty. Stay with me**." and she quiets allowing me to pet her shoulders and back. A wondering of 'what next' brings forth a sense of my sliding further into the car and asking Beauty to get in next to me.

As I follow my sense Beauty steps back pulling slightly on the retractable. I wait doing my best to be calm and gentle yet commanding. With movements that seems to say "*Oh well.*" Beauty begins sniffing the door sill. I grin as she reaches her head inside the car to sniff the floor. When she raises her head to look at me I pull gently on the retractable, "**Come on girl**." Beauty braces herself, not budging. "**Okay girl**." and I lighten the tension on the retractable. Beauty backs a couple steps away. Without planning it I pat the seat next to me and call Beauty again. Her ears come forward and she steps closer smelling the seat where I patted it then backing away. I call her again and when she reaches her head up to sniff I pull hard enough on the retractable that she in a stumbling movement puts her front paws on the seat. She is startled and as I sense her deciding whether to panic or not I bring playful energy into myself and flow it out to her with a "**Your such a brave girl**." I am relieved when her body relaxes a bit and her ears come forward. "**I know girl. It is scary. Good girl**." and I reach out to stroke her muzzle. Beauty allows me to touch her remaining very still. Keeping the retractable tight I sit back giving Beauty space to deal with her conflicting needs. Three or four moments later Beauty pulls hard on the retractable. I want to let her back away and feel a need to ask more of her. Over three seconds I tighten the pressure on her retractable while imagining her jumping into the car. Beauty will have none of it. She rolls her chest right then left her determination and the edges of terror flowing to me. I ease the pressure on the retractable, no longer pulling her towards me. She pauses and looks at me pleading for her freedom. "**Okay girl.**" and I let her slowly back out of the car and move 10 feet away. Part of me wants to go to her to give her loving. I can't yet. Two, three, four breaths while Beauty calms down and then sits. She stands when I slide over and off the backseat. Together we walk about 30 feet from the car where I turn towards the car and call her to me. I am relieved when she comes to me.

    I kneel and we begin to relax into being with each other. Finally Beauty looks at me and playfully bounds sideways. In the next moment we are trotting out into the field. For the next half hour we walk together her often leading, my occasionally insisting she follow me. Suddenly I have a sense that Beauty is ready to be separate, to process what we have done. "**Okay girl. Let's go back to the car.**" I have the distinct impression that going back to the car is not what Beauty plans. I tighten my resolve and step to her, set the retractable to only four feet, and pulling on her, begin walking to the car. One pull against the retractable and Beauty begins walking next to me keeping varying degrees of pressure on the retractable. Her resistance increases when we are 30 feet from the car. Uncomfortable I energetically grit my teeth and say, "**Come with me girl.**" Beauty balks several times as we walk to the car. Ten feet from the car and I increase the retractable length to six feet so Beauty can walk just behind me. At five feet from the car Beauty is pulling back hard on the retractable. I drag her with me to the backdoor and at the backdoor reach over and swing the door closed. With the sound of the door closing Beauty's head comes up and she looks at me in surprise. Much of the tension flows out of her body. With only a slight pull she follows me around to the other backdoor and watches as I close the door. While she is still standing wondering what is going on I step over and undo the retractable from her collar and walk towards the Quonset hut to feed the stray cat. When I glance back I see Beauty sniffing the sill of the backdoor. I grin as I sense Beauty's curiosity and surprise that I did not force her into the car. Soon she is watching me tuck the bowl of cat food out of sight just inside the Quonset hut. A moment later Beauty is pressing against me as I pet her. All is well.

On the way home I stop and buy beef that I can cut up and fry. It is time for some extra tasty treats to entice Beauty into the backseat.

LITTLE PROGRESS

Thursday, May 31

A cloudy day, cool with no rain make it easy to spend more time with Beauty. I visit twice, once at about 2 PM and a second time at about 8 PM.

When I park at the enclosure Beauty comes out from under the deck and we meet at the entrance for a celebration, her licking my hand, doing her petty paw dance, rubbing against me, offering me every part of her head, neck, back, and rump. After three minutes of exuberance and with happy ease I step into the enclosure, retrieve her bowl, and return to the car trunk. She follows me and sits a couple of feet behind me to my right. Preparing her food is mixed with occasional attention. She follows me into the enclosure with a gate I would characterize as "strutting her stuff". She sniffs her food and then looks at me and seems to whisper, *"Okay, now what?"*. I get up and we head to the field. I stop at the car and get the retractable, her comb, and the baggy of bits of steak. As I reach for the steak I sense the narrowness of the path now before Beauty and I. Warmth and pleasure of being with Beauty mixes with responsibility and careful attention. Beauty follows, watching me. We walk to the field and as I kneel Beauty turns and sits in front of me. I pet her for a while then get out the comb. After a couple minutes of grooming beauty stands up, walks a couple steps, turns to look over her back at me. I easily get up and follow her as she runs off in a prancing gate, tail high and wagging, I smile noticing my worries slip behind the pleasures of being with Beauty. At the blackberry bushes she waits for me, then goes in to explore one spot. When she comes out she moves to me and stands by me so I can attach the retractable leash. As we move around the field I stop several times to groom her. Each time her ears are fully forward, her mouth open and tongue out. She remains calm and receptive when I begin combing the back of her back legs an area previously off limits. Part way through our tour of the field I take her back to the car and around to the backdoor on the passenger side. I place several pieces of steak inside the back at varying distance from the door. Beauty steps into the car with her front feet, moving further and further in. She stretches her neck and body to reach the last two pieces which are just out of reach. She pauses, I hold my breath. Finally she lifts one of her back legs a little but does not step into the car with her back feet. She stays there fully extended for several seconds, backing out partially when I reach in and pet her, telling her she is a good dog. Her ears remain forward, her mouth open, her posture slightly tense. After 10 seconds or so of petting she backs out of the car. I repeat placing treats for her twice more with one back paw coming closer to the sill each time.

I sense Beauty being unsure and in response we go out into the field again. After a few minutes Beauty lays down ears forward, mouth closed. As I turn and walk to her her mouth opens and her tongue comes out. As I kneel close to her she raises her head in greeting. We both surrender into enjoying being together. After a minute or so she shifts to lay partially on one hip, her back feet extending away from me. With slight pressure from my hand on her side she rolls over partly giving me access to her chest and belly. A minute or so of attention and she rolls onto her back raising her front legs, relaxing her paws so that her paws frame her face with its wide open mouth, tongue hanging to the side, a look of happy surrender. In that moment I sense myself deep, deep within surrendering more to being with Beauty. She remains on her back allowing me to examine the coat on her belly and chest. There are many mats to be removed! I sense a loving whisper from Beauty, *"Yes, I surrender my belly and chest for you to groom. I trust 'us'"* In quiet reverence I groom her. A couple minutes later Beauty rolls to her side and gets up. Though deep currents of desire to simply be with Beauty flow within me, my awareness of the gathering darkness cause me to take us back to the car for more backseat exposure.

The results at the car are much the same as before. Beauty extends her body into the back but will not step up onto the back seat with her back feet. A couple of ventures into the back seat and we head back to the field where we lay close to each other, her often on her side enjoying my petting her chest and belly. Then it is time to go. I place food for the stray cat, get in my car, say goodbye to Beauty, and drive off, disappointed that Beauty is not in the backseat.

As I drive home I come to understand that I need once again to surrender to the timing of the process with Beauty. I grin as I think, "Beauty cannot be hurried." I can feel expectation, desires, control, and doubt all pulling at me, reflected in tension within my body. As I drive I will myself to relax, to open, to enjoy the pleasures I have shared with Beauty. Warmth and wonder fill me as I compare the last half hour with Beauty to earlier times.

A Step in the Right Direction

In the evening when I park the car and remain in the drivers seat with the door open to gather items Beauty comes out of the enclosure, circles the scrap hot tub, and walks up to me. I am surprised at how relaxed she is as she steps up to me sitting in the car. I smile realizing how she is beginning to trust being close to the car. I gather a few things and eagerly get out of the car to a dog with wagging tail and wide opened mouth. I immediately kneel enjoying Beauty doing her petty paw dance and pushing her head in against my chest. After a couple of minutes of petting we cross the pavement to the field. At the field Beauty turns to face me rather than running off to begin our walk. After a moment of puzzlement I notice Beauty holding her body with some tension, that her ears are fully forward and raised. As playful energies fill my body I know it is play time. Two steps from Beauty I jump up, coming down with my feet wide apart, bending over towards Beauty. She pauses a second before doing a play jump and scampering in a large circle and then a second circle when I jump towards her again. I chase her for about ten steps, her running away with a bouncy gate, tail wagging wildly. I turn and run, looking back at her. She turns towards me, mouth closed, ears forward for a moment until suddenly her mouth opens wide, her tongue comes out and for the first time she begins to chase me. We go back a forth, her chasing then me chasing until my body lets me know it is time to slow down. When I stop Beauty lays down facing me and waits for me to join her. The next three or four minutes are spent with me petting her, sometimes on her belly and chest. Warmth and pleasure flow through me, shared with Beauty, expanded by Beauty, shared with me.

With a sudden bit of heaviness I know it is time to give Beauty more exposure to the car, to see if she will get further into the back. I get up and lead the way to the car. We circle around the trunk and I open the back passenger side door. With the first round of treats Beauty enters only as far as she can without stepping in with her back feet. Okay. I place even more bits of steak making sure every inch further in from the door will provide Beauty a treat. I had slid the passenger seat all the way forward leaving enough space on the floor for Beauty to sit. She enters with her front feet gathering each bit of steak. Fully stretched out she pauses stretching her neck a bit more. She pauses, then lifts one back foot missing the door sill edge. She tries again, raising her foot, misses, then raises it further catching the sill. A seconds pause and she shifts her weight onto the back foot just inside the door. Another momentary pause and she stands, lifting her other foot in, immediately taking the steak bits now within reach. She pauses and shifts to take the steak bits on the seat. To my surprise she turns a bit further and sits on the floor looking at me. Stunned I have the sense she is showing off for me. In a trance I lean into the car and pet her delighted to see her ears forward, her body relaxed, her mouth open and her tongue out. For perhaps 20 seconds I pet her and wonder whether I should close the backdoor. My answer comes when Beauty moves her head towards the open door, looks at me, turns her body a bit more towards the door. I am fascinated that she remains seated while once again pointed towards the door with her head, somehow letting me know, *"You are going to have to move so I can get out."* In that moment I know it is not time to test her further, that building trust is more important. As I back up clearing a path for her, I notice her mouth has closed, her body has tensed slightly. She moves slowly, letting me clear a space for her rather than pushing against me. I clear the door and step back further, she follows. As we loop back to the freedom of the field I feel a degree of disappointment at the same time I celebrate how Beauty had been relaxed enough to sit down in the back of the car.

We lay down in the field, spending a good 15 minutes being close to each other. Some of the time I pet Beauty, some of the time we simply lay close to each other enjoying the surroundings. As we lay there a cat that my friend wants to rescue comes out of the Quonset hut. Part of me is tempted to begin writing of that newly beginning journey. Then again. At this point I will only say that in response to my meowing the cat eventually comes to me and allowing me to pet it. Beauty is interested in the cat and somehow knows to leave me space to interact with the cat. Before leaving I spend another minute focused with Beauty.

CROSSING OVER

Friday, June 1

I am in a funky mood as I drive to feed Beauty. Relationship challenges and money concerns have most of my attention. Sitting at the traffic signal, waiting to turn left into the paved area my mood lightens when I sense Beauty waiting for me. I am a bit surprised that she is out in the field perhaps 25 feet from where I normally park. She stands when she sees the car seeming unsure it is me. As I park the car I bring the pleasure of seeing her forward allowing my funk to dissipate. I grin as Beauty's ears come up, her mouth opens, her tongue comes out and her tail begins to wag. My mind and ego try to ignore my sense of her whispering to me, "*Oh, there you are. Bye bye funkiness.*" I walk to her and in the warm early summer sun I kneel down opening my energy to the earth, the grass in the field, and to Beauty. Beauty rewards me by snuggling in against me.

Soon we are walking to the enclosure where I pick up her food bowl and return to the car trunk. As I prepare her food Beauty goes to a backdoor and sniffs. I sense her request, noticing the feel and taste of steak in my mouth. When I look up at her she seems to smile at me as she licks her lips. Beauty surprises me by waiting at the car while I place her food. As I jump down out of the enclosure I once again sense the feel and taste of steak in my mouth. Back at the car Beauty seems amused and happy that I have noticed. Her energy whispers of, "*You learn too.*" slip past my mind and ego defenses for a flitting moment. Grinning I slip into a relaxed energy with just a touch of business. I open both backdoors of the car and begin placing bits of steak so that from the beginning Beauty must step into the car with her front feet. Four pieces on the floor, two on the seat where Beauty can get them with only her front feet in the car. Two pieces on the seat where she will have to get all four feet into the back of the car. With the pieces of steak in place I step back from the car. Beauty walks to the car and takes the first bit of steak by stretching her neck as far as possible. She turns around and looks at me with her mouth partially closed. Without thinking I step back allowing her more space. I grin when her mouth opens and she turns back to the car. Perceptions shift, it seems both hers and mine, as my intent and her desires and energies with no names shape a small area beyond time and space, where physical surfaces sheen with the deep flowing playful energies. My mind and ego only touch those surfaces doing their best not to glance deeper.

She steps forward placing her front feet on the floor of the car, picks up a piece of steak from the floor, inches forward, picks up another, inches forward, lifts and turns her head to look at me and then takes a piece of steak from the backseat. I grin happily as she gathers a second and third piece from the backseat. I realize I am holding my breath as I wait, hoping she will lift her back feet into the car. Twice she lifts a back foot but does not step in. It is too much, she backs out. **"Come here girl."** and she comes over to take a couple pieces from my hand.

I pet her and wait until she nuzzles the pocket where I have the steak. **"Oh, you want more. Okay."** I draw out the bag and step to the car. I place three pieces of steak on the floor and step so that I am standing just back of the door opening. Beauty looks at me, looks at the door opening, seeming to measure how easily I could grab her and searching my energy for any intent to grab her. I sense within her, within me an ache to trust. A few seconds and she steps forward, steps into the car onto the floor with her front feet and enjoys each of the pieces of steak. I grin when she steps out, staying close in giving me just enough room to place more steak. Two on the floor, three on the seat, two more on the seat further into the car. As soon as I stand Beauty steps her front feet into the car, taking first the pieces on the floor and then the three closer in on the seat. Again she pauses gazing at the remain pieces just out of reach. I grin noticing I am enjoying Beauty and I's game. While Beauty still has her front feet in the car I reach down and pat her shoulders, imagining her backing out so I can place more steak. She backs out and I place two pieces on the seat, my left knee pushing against her as I lean into the car.

As I stand Beauty looks at me seeming to protest the lack of pieces on the floor. A couple moments later she steps into the car with her front feet and stretches to take the steak pieces on the seat. "**Good girl.**" and she steps in with her back feet moving forward to take the pieces further in. I grin and instinctively step to block Beauty from backing out. She is startled, turning to look at me. I reach past her and toss a piece of steak on the far side of the backseat, close to the open backdoor at the other end of the seat. I can almost hear Beauty happily whisper, "*Oh, out that way.*" as she steps over picks up the piece of steak and exists through the far door. I am relieved and pleased when she loops out from the car coming back to the door she had just existed looking across the backseat at me. In the blink of her eyes we are enveloped in playful energies, we are testing how far we can go, how much we can trust. As she watches I take out a couple of pieces of steak and wave them. For a moment she considers getting into the car shifting her weight forward and then balking. I hear myself saying "**Its okay girl I will come to you.**" as I imagine crawling across the seat and her stepping onto the floor with her front feet to get her treats. Before I realize it I am kneeling on the back seat crawling towards Beauty. Beauty leans forward and looks surprised when instead of reaching directly to her I reach my hand out over the floor board. Wag, wag of the steak and she gives in, stepping onto the floor with her front feet and stretching to take the steak from my hand. In the pause of a couple of breaths before offering her the second piece, grinning as she considers whether to wait or retreat I notice energies doing a little happy dance within me. The moment my hand moves forward her head comes forward. She pauses, unsure, when I don't release the steak to her immediately. She looks me in the eyes, I smile, and open my hand. Her warm, trusting energy flows to me, opens me, as she takes the steak. Munch, munch and she backs out of the car. Somehow I know we are done so I crawl to her, clumsily get out of the car and tell her she is a good dog. Three minutes of petting and I am in the car heading home. As I drive images of possible ways to build further trust with Beauty float from deep within. I feel more and more confident as more and more possibilities present themselves. I notice my mind and ego are not sure having more possibilities is good, so many choices, too many possibilities. From somewhere within me comes a laughing, "*Watch and learn.*"

Day of Chase

Saturday, June 2

*A*s I drive out to feed Beauty I do not sense her energies in the area. I shrug and continue driving. As I park at the location I neither sense her nor see her. Worry washes through me and I sense the edges of panic. I get out of the car, plant my feet on the ground, one breath, two breathes, let go of tension, let it drain into the earth. Notice my belly, sense my belly opening to the energies of the earth, another breath and then another. I sense deep energies flowing out, searching for Beauty's energies. I sense her, only the faintest traces. Fear, being chased, several young males, young hunters, Beauty being the hunted. I sense Beauty hiding, far from the field, on the edges of her territories, energies withdrawn, sorrow, a desire to be with me, to be connected and protected. Too much fear, too much sorrow. *"I will stay here, hiding, encapsulated in my egg of terror. Perhaps tonight in the darkness I will creep in to accept the food that connects us."*

Sorrow and rage play within me as I walk to the enclosure. As I return to the car with Beauty's bowl from deep within there is a whisper, *"Rage will destroy your connections. Open to the sorrow, open beyond your worldly rage. Flow love, flow concern, flow senses of tomorrow's meeting. Experience each of those and share each with her."*

At the trunk as I surrender to the whispers and begin preparing Beauty's food deep knowings open. Beauty's food must be prepared with no poisoning rage. I am to provide nourishing food filled with the love we share, the love that connects she and I, shaping 'us'. Two and then three breathes as I connect with the earth, open spaces deep, deep within my belly, allow dark, dense, rich energies to shape as love flowing within my belly, flowing into Beauty's food, flowing to Beauty. I sense a quiet, complex, rich thank you from Beauty and know I am doing as I must. As if in a trance, carefully fostering deep knowings, I mix her food and walk to where I will place it. When there I pause allowing dark, rich love to fill me, the food, the space in which I stand. As I place her food upon the earth I draw dark richness from the earth, from deep within myself, from within Beauty and fill the enclosure with those energies. I stand, anchor the energies deeper in the earth, open the flow further, smile as I sense Beauty linking with me, with my intent for us. There is no time, only the flow of deep, rich energies. The honk of a car horn brings the physical world back to me. Within a breath the deep knowing within me whispers *"Anchor it!"* In total confusion my mind and ego notice as I jump up in the air, spread my feet, come down driving my feet onto the earth. I sense my energies, Beauty's energies, penetrate the Earth, blending with the Earth, anchoring our intent, anchoring and filling the enclosure with dark, primal, loving energies. Three, then four breaths and I step back. It is done. I am just real enough in the physical world to walk back to my car. A few moments more and I sense it is safe to drive. Keeping awareness of Beauty's presence I drive out onto the street and head back home. As I drive my mind and ego accept I have done something they will never understand.

Help from the Neighbors

Sunday, June 3

Today will be a day of two visits. As I drive out I sense Beauty's presence, her waiting for me. As I drive past the business and to the edge of the field I am drawn to look over at the hedge and to me relief and delight she is there. By the time I am getting out of the car she begins walking to me and as soon as I turn towards her she begins to trot. I take two steps towards her, kneel, and then bend forward so I am on all four. As my hands meet the ground Beauty jumps forward into a run. I growl and shake my head sitting back up just as she reaches me. Within her pleasure and mine floats remnants of yesterday's fears making our greetings that much sweeter. Within moments Beauty is pushing herself against me as I pet her. Her insistence draws the deep, rich energies that she and I share into my awareness.

A minute, five minutes later I am walking with her to the enclosure. As we walk I hear the sounds of people from the apartments enjoying a barbecue behind the fence separating their courtyard from the field. Beauty stays within three feet of me as we retrieve her bowl, return to the car, mix her food, and then return to place her bowl. When I step down out of the enclosure she stays just inside, stepping forward so I can pet her and attach the retractable to her collar. For the first time I have a sense that she wants the physical connection, being on the retractable has become a physical reflection of deeper, expanding connections we share. Marvel and warmth flow through me as I accept Beauty surrendering to my being her people, her guide, her protector in the world. "Expressions of the sacred masculine" flits through my mind and I grin noticing tickling energies in my belly.

I am surprised when Beauty jumps down out of the enclosure and walks towards the sounds of people enjoying themselves. I shrug and follow her wondering what she has planned. As we approach the 6 foot high fence I hear the voice of the fellow I have talked with several times. He is a salt of the earth type fellow, earthy, relaxed, open, hoping for the same from others. A former chef he enjoys doing barbecues for those living in the apartments, carefully preparing the meat, marinades, and then cooking while others enjoy the gathering he has shaped. Raised in a family where I learned to focus on 'doing what needs to be done' I find the group's relaxed acceptance of life fascinating, puzzling, and refreshing. I had talked with the fellow several time, once while Beauty was on leash with me. As my attention returns to Beauty I am gently startled to notice she is drawn to the man's voice and the open, accepting, happy energies of the group. Her movements make it clear she does not want to go around the fence and join the group. As the next breath flows out I am again gently startled by the sense that Beauty wants to introduce 'us' to the group. I holler "**Hello**" to the fellow and after a moments pause hear the group become quiet and the fellow respond. "**Oh hey! Just doing a barbecue for us. Is Beauty with you?**" "**Yes, she is. I think the smell of your cooking captured her nose.**" A laugh and several surprised voices float back to me. "**I have to stay here with the meat.**" comes over the fence as two women and one of their kids peak around the fence and then quietly step into view. As the young boy begins to step forward his mother catches his arm, "**She is scared of people, stay back.**" One more step and the boy stops, unsure what to do. He smiles and relaxes when I catch his eyes and offer, "**Thank you. She is just learning to trust people. Walk very gently towards us and notice if she steps back. That will be the signal for you to stop**." The boy glances at his Mom and with the nod of her head he steps forward slowly. His Mom is smiling and follows a couple steps behind him. As the boy comes within twelve feet of us Beauty fidgets and steps back. The boy frowns and stops. "**Cool. Now let me see if Beauty will step towards you with me.**" One short step, Beauty remains still, a second step and she tucks herself behind me, moving with me. Two more steps and she stops, behind me now only three feet from the boy. In a moment Beauty moves her head next to my knee, her body carefully tucked behind me. Smiling I say to the boy, "**This is really good. This is the closest she has been to anyone other than me. Thank you for helping her learn to trust people.**" Suddenly the boy is standing a little taller, his Mom smiling as she watches. "**Okay, now turn a little so you are looking out into the field and not directly at Beauty.**" Puzzled the boy does as I ask. "**Good! See how she is a little less tense? See her ears are now up and forward as she looks at you.**" I reach down and touch Beauty's head then allow my hand to slip back to her shoulders. "**Good girl!**" The Mom looks at me with an unasked question. I hear myself saying, "**Sure. Take two or three steps and watch her ears. Look more at me than at her.**" The Mom steps forward stopping when she is next to her son, hugging his shoulders. In that moment I sense Beauty accepting, declaring that she and I are a bonded pair just like the Mom and son are a bounded pair. I struggle to keep tears from filling my eyes. As I look at the boy and then his Mom I sense her honoring Beauty's declaration as Beauty honors the bond she and her son share. I hear her, "**Thank you.**" as she steps back three steps, drawing her son with her. A smile from her, a nod from the boy and they turn, returning to their gathering. As they disappear around the fence Beauty takes two steps in their direction and then turns leading us out into the field. I notice deep stirrings within myself, understandings, connections being shaped. I grin and begin trotting out into the field along side Beauty.

With Me Inside

By the time we are part way across the field I sense us walking along the street nearby and allow my body to turn towards the street. Beauty seems to understand my plan and agree. Four steps, five steps and my mind catches up, time for me to take her into a situation where I will be her guide and protector, time to deepen our trust. Soon we are walking along the busy street. Beauty stays close to me, no sniffing, her attention and mine tightly connected. I am paying careful attention to the world around us, she is carefully paying attention to my movements. We walk past three people. Each time she glances at the person and then swings her attention to me and doing what I imagine, us walking past the person. We walk about a block before turning back towards the car. As we approach the field Beauty moves out in front of me letting me know she is happy our work is done. At the field, just beyond the car I call Beauty to me and once she is near I reach down and unclip the retractable. Her look asks me what I plan. A glance at the car and my imagining the feel and taste of the meat treats answer her question and before I can say any words she turns to the car with me. I am pleased that she stays with me watching as I open one backdoor and then the other. With both doors open I call Beauty to me, take hold of her collar and lead her to the door opening. She comes with me balking when we are three feet from the door. I bend and pet her and imagine her stepping to the door opening with me. As I pull on her collar and step towards the car I say, "**We are going to do this**." Reluctantly she lets me half guide, half pull her to the car door opening. As she looks inside I connect with her and imagine her getting into the car, walking across the backseat and jumping out the other side. Her body relaxes as she notices the open door and the freedom beyond it. She freezes when I let go of her collar and take three steps back. She looks at me, looks at the far door opening, looks at me, looks at the far door opening, turns and comes to me burying her head against my legs. Soon she is stretching her neck so her nose is just brushing the bottom of the jacket pocket with her steak treats. "**Okay girl.**"

Beauty watches as I go to the front passenger door, open it, slide the seat all the way forward, and close the door. When I take the baggy of steak treats out of my pocket and step to the passenger side backdoor Beauty comes with me. Beauty follows my hand movements and as I hope, sniffs the large floor space as I pat it with my hand. Okay. As before I place treats both on the floor and on the seat, the final treats requiring Beauty step fully into the car. "**Okay girl.**" and I step back from the car, pat Beauty, and walk around to the other backdoor, bending to put my hands on the seat, imagining Beauty picking up the treats. I grin as Beauty steps onto the larger floor space takes her treats and with only the slightest pause steps in with her hind feet to get the treats on the seat, looks at me and backs out.

I am grinning as I sit down on the backseat and slide towards the open backdoor where Beauty is waiting for more treats. Beauty's ears go back and she steps back. Sitting behind the driver's seat I reach over and place treats on the floor and seat tossing the last treat out the open passenger side backdoor. As hoped the treat lands at Beauty's feet. She picks it up and immediately begins following the trail of treats leading to me. With little hesitation she gathers the second treat from the car floor. A glance at me and she steps onto the car floor with her front feet to gather another and another. She looks at me and seems to be measuring the distance each treat is from me. Cautiously she lifts one and then another back foot up into the car, gathers a treat from the seat, looks at me and stretches her head to take the treat laying next to my leg. When she looks back at me I am holding a treat in my hand. She stays where she is as I reach out and give her the treat. I hear myself saying "**Good girl. Do you want more?**" as I imagine her taking another treat from my hand. To my surprise and delight Beauty sits. Two more treats from my hand and I ask, "**Can I pet you?**" I reach forward slowly, carefully, rolling my hand over so the back of my fingers stroke her muzzle. Beauty tenses and stays seated. "**You are such a good girl**." and Beauty leans her head forward allowing me to slip my hand to pet her head. I sense one more challenge for she and I. I lean further forward, Beauty tenses a bit while remaining still. My hand slides down onto her neck, brushing her collar as it slides to her shoulders. A few strokes and my hand slides back up to her neck stroking her neck and her collar. Beauty is still. I ever so gently move her collar with my hand. She remains still. My hand arches along her collar and soon I am scratching the under side of her neck, moving her collar in the process. Beauty looks at me when my hand movements stop. As she gazes in my eyes I curl my fingers taking hold of her collar. Beauty pulls back slightly. I coo, "**Good girl. You are okay**." Beauty relaxes as holding her collar I bend down to nuzzle her muzzle with the side of my face, hearing myself say, "**I love you so much**." Four breaths of pleasure and we are done. I sit up and release Beauty's collar. To my delight she remains seated, looking at me. A couple more treats and she declares her freedom by turning and jumping out of the car. I get out my side and we both circle to meet behind the car. A couple pieces of steak and some loving and I am driving away.

On the way home some part of me deep within insists we have a label for the state I was in while working with Beauty. Descriptions that might point towards an effective label cause possible labels to begin floating into my awareness. Oh, I guess I should share a bit more. When studying with a mystic he helped us learn to use words and phrases as touchstones for deeper understandings and encouraged us to discover the labels waiting for us. "It is a bit like a lover's name. A single word that brings common traits, events, and emotions forth and that allows you to touch, to access, uncountable and indescribable energies that connect the two of you." And so my mind, my body, my energies began tossing thousands of little perception from Beauty and I's time together into (dare I say) a caldera. (grin) As I turn into my driveway I let go of the process knowing that within the next few hours or days a word or phrase will pop into my awareness and be woven into what is already there.

Beauty and the Cat

It is about 9 PM that evening when I turn to drive behind the spa shop, hoping I will find Beauty there. That afternoon I had taken care of Ute's dogs at the dome. I had returned them to her house and spent time with her before heading to see Beauty and to visit the stray cat Ute hopes to rescue. When I arrive the field is being touch by the beginnings of night. As I park I see Beauty trotting to greet me. With each of her steps more warmth stirs within me. With her last steps I go down on my knees and soon we are pushing against each other, tussling, playing. Crawling on my hands and knees I notice a woman at the apartments watching and chuckle as I wonder what she is thinking as she watches us. A few moments later and Beauty is leading me on a trip around the field. As we swing back to the car I see the stray cat watching us. Beauty sees the cat too, tenses, looks at me, and then relaxes as I meow. I am rewarded by the cat getting up a walking towards us. I kneel and pet Beauty as the cat walks from the Quonset hut to us. Beauty's attention goes to the cat and I hear myself saying **"Be gentle girl."** imagining Beauty sniffing the cat with quiet energy. The cat walks to me without hesitation, Beauty waits while I greet the cat and pet it while it circles my hand and swishes it's tail seeming intent on catching up on attention it has not had. As the cat's enthusiasm cools I sense Beauty and notice out of the corner of my eye that she has moved next to me. With my other hand I reach over and pet Beauty. The cat notices, tenses, then relaxes, stepping towards Beauty and touching noses with her. Beauty whines gently and does a short petty paw dance with her front feet. At first the cat is startled then within a moment the cat is once again circling my hand insisting I pay attention to her too. Perhaps a minute passes before I sit down on the ground and relax into being in the field with two creatures intent upon enjoying life with each other, with me. As I glance out I notice the cloak of night is descending, The distant blackberry bushes are a blur of unclear shapes, the grass nearby holds deep shadows. I am surprised to notice my body opening to the quiet of night. I lay back and soon Beauty is at my head, the cat is by my side, each is enjoying the movements of one of my hands. Two minutes or twenty I do not know. Eventually I sit up, the cat runs away. I stand up, Beauty standing with me. I walk to the car and open the front door. As I turn back to the field I am surprised and pleased to find Beauty standing with her head next to my knee. I wonder if it is time to bring Beauty home and accept her answer of stepping away from me. As I drive out onto the street I smile, happy to know that Beauty will enjoy being with my cats, Mystique and Little Leon. On the way home I sense Beauty wanting to be with me, I sense her being in our home, I sense dark energies threatening to separate Beauty from me. I will need to force my will upon Beauty soon, trusting her awareness and my awareness. Failure to act will allow others to separate Beauty from me.

More Socializing

Monday, June 4 – My Birthday

I arrive in Beauty's area at about 1:45 on this cloudy and cool day. There is light rain a couple of times during my visit, not enough to end it. When I arrive Beauty is laying on the pavement close to where I park my car. As I park the car her head comes up and her ears come forward. I sit in the car with my feet swung out onto the ground and wait for her to come to me. Over the last week Beauty has become more comfortable approaching the car even with doors open. After a couple minutes of greeting Beauty steps away and waits. When I get out of the car she immediately goes to the field and sits, looking at me, ears up, mouth wide open, tongue out. It seems she wants more attention. I join her and we play. Sometimes my moving towards her, sometimes her moving towards me. Her movement during the play are exuberant covering a lot of space. Also when she charges in towards me her movements are quicker and she almost always comes in physical contact with me. Most of the way through our play I stand up sometimes chasing her, sometimes running from her with her chasing. It does not take much chasing back and forth to wind me. As I stand catching my breath Beauty comes to me and looks up expectantly, open, and trusting. I move to show her we will begin our walk and she immediately runs out 20 feet from me with a bounding gate. I am a bit surprised when she turns and trots back to me. I pet her expecting her to take off, beginning our walk off leash as usual. After 20 seconds of her staying close to me, looking up at me I catch on. She wants the connection of being on leash, the safety of letting me lead. I reach down, find the clip on of her collar and attach the retractable. As she looks more directly at me I sense her gratitude that I finally understand. She turns, and begins trotting in a prancing gate. I happily jog to catch up and trot along side her. We do a tour of the field with her checking smells and looking for any of the stray cats, her friends, that live on the edges of the field.

As we loop back towards the car Beauty lays down just short of the pavement. I kneel next to her and begin to pet her. She sits up and begins licking my hand. At first I think she is licking because of taste left from the treats. After a minute of licking it becomes clear she was licking my hand for another reason. As she continues, I become quiet. The sense she is simply showing her pleasure of being with me washes through me, warming me, lightening my mood. A moment later I realize her licking is also an offer, a request I open to deeper connections with her. Quiet, expansive spaces that we share open, our deep energies blend. For about 3 minutes her licking holds us beyond time and space.

When she stops we head to the enclosure where I take her off the retractable and enter to retrieve her food bowl which I take back to the car. While I prepare her food she sits just behind me. With the food mixed I pick up the bowl and the baggy of cat food. Beauty follows me as I place her food, showing no interest in eating immediately. I leave the enclosure and turn to feed the stray cat. Beauty watches me as I reach in for the bowl then slips around the corner to wait until I fill the bowl and place it. The stray cat who had answered my meow when I first reach for the bowl begins eating as soon as the bowl is in place. With the bowl in place Beauty and I head to the car for some back seat familiarization. Beauty's posture is more relaxed and with treats she enters the floor space of the back seat more quickly. She also stays inside when I lean in to place additional treats. However she never lifts her back feet into the car. Today does not seem to be a day to push Beauty for more. With the meat soon gone we leave the car.

I walk over to the cat's entrance into the Quonset hut, bend and meow. I smile when after my third meow I hear the cat's answering meow and sense her cautious '*Oh, good*'. Within a minute the cat is at the entrance looking to see if the coast is clear for her to come out. Beauty is near and watching perhaps 12 feet away. Slowly the cat comes out and enjoys me petting her head and occasionally her back. After a couple of minutes Beauty comes up and sits right behind me, letting me know it is time to pay attention to her too. With my attention on the cat feeling safe I barely notice Beauty extending the circle of energy we share to include the cat. I do notice the cat accepting Beauty's offer by stepping in closer to me, closer to Beauty. Beauty's glance out into the field and a sense of she and I together walking causes me to stand.

Within a moment we are heading out into the field. At the far side of the field when I turn to head back towards the car I notice that the cat in an uncharacteristic move has followed Beauty and I out into the field. Once Beauty, I, and the cat are back closer to the Quonset hut I meow to the cat, inviting her to come to me. Even with Beauty next to me she comes, slow and cautious in her approach. While I am petting her two mothers from the apartments come around the corner. One has already come close to Beauty and wants to try again. With my smile of approval I sense our energies linking in deepening Beauty's trust of people. Beauty stays seated by me until the woman is about 12 feet away. Beauty stands and with a gesture I suggest the woman kneel which she does. Beauty in response sits. During the whole approach Beauty's ears are up and forward. Little by little over a couple of minutes the woman knee walks forward, one step and a pause. When she is about three feet from Beauty she reaches out offering the back of her hand for Beauty to sniff. To her delight and my surprise Beauty stretches her neck forward and sniffs her hand. That is enough. Beauty gets up and slowly moves about 8 feet away where she lays down.

About that time the cat who was outside the hut meows letting us know she is there. I meow in return. The women watch both curious and surprised as the cat slowly comes to me, coming a bit closer each time I meow. I am too busy to discern whether they are most surprised by my meowing or the cat's response to my meows. A couple of minutes of my petting the cat and the cat swings her head to look at the women. Each extends a hand. The cat visits first one and then the other, spending about a minute with each. As the women get up to leave the cat wanders back to the hut. I go over to Beauty who is laying close by and happily pet her, enjoying her pleasure with my telling her both in words and energy that she is a brave girl and I am delighted with her. I realize it is about time for me to go so I get up and go to the car where I take Beauty's leash off. To my surprise when I open the back door Beauty moves to the back door and sniffs the entry. Encouraged I get in the back seat and offer her treats. She cautiously takes treats from me occasionally stepping her front feet into the car. Each time Beauty steps her front feet into the car I imagine her getting all the way in. After several treats as Beauty steps into the car I imagine closing the doors on us. Beauty takes the treat and retreats, moving off and laying down. I have a clear sense of Beauty whispering, '*Not yet*'. I get out of the car with the rawhide chew I have brought for her. Grinning I give her the chew and as expected she trots out into the field to enjoy it. It is time to go.

As I get back into the car and start it I have a sense of Beauty being with me. While my mind and ego protest I relax and welcome her presence. The whole trip home and as I get out of the car and go into the backyard I sense Beauty being with me. I feels as though Beauty is traveling with me, checking to see what coming home with me will be like. I allow myself to respond to my sense that Beauty wants a tour of the backyard, slowly walking through the yard, enjoying a sense of Beauty and I sharing the space.

Unleashing Fear

Tuesday, June 5

*B*eauty is laying on the pavement when I drive up and park. As soon as I open the door she comes to me, tail wagging, a bounce in her step, and spends a couple minutes sharing affection with me while I sit in the car. Her warmth and pleasure whisper to me, "*You are my people now.*" I hear myself whispering, "**And you are my girl.**" as she snuggles against me. Beauty backs up as I lean forward and get out of the car. She walks with me, her head inches from my left knee, staying close as we get her bowl and fill it. I notice the leash laying in the trunk and sense it is time to get Beauty to accept being on the leash rather than the retractable. "**Hey girl, look at this**." and I pick up the leash showing it to her. She immediately steps back, mouth closing, ears going back. With her just four feet from me, I fling the leash out to the side, away from her. She is startled and looks from me to the leash and back several times. I pick up her bowl, begin walking to the enclosure and gently shout, "**Come on, girl.**" Beauty is puzzled. A few tense steps to the leash and she sniffs it, looks up and bounds after me.

We place her bowl. My schedule is tight so I feed the cat and head back to the car. Beauty seems uncertain, following me. I go to the leash and kneel. Beauty stops a few feet away. I do a couple of play bows, fill myself with playful energy, and then pick up the leash and wave it. Two more play bows and I toss the leash almost to Beauty. She bravely watches it sail through the air and land only a step from her. I crawl to her and begin petting her, telling her she is a good girl. The third time she looks at the leash I reach over and move it, leaving it on the ground. During the next minute of petting I take hold of her collar several times.

Malcolm Pullen

Beauty leans forward and ever so carefully sniffs the leash. While she is sniffing it I nudge it with my hand. She pulls her head back just a bit. Encouraged I pick up the leash and hold it for her to sniff. With the leash in one hand I pet her with the other hand. Quietly I reach up and drape the leash over Beauty's back. A breath, two breaths and I pet Beauty with the hand holding the leash, imagining her being on leash while we walk. Beauty tenses and then relaxes as I move both hands to pet her head. She is curious and worried twisting her head to get a glimpse of the leash. The next thing I know I have grabbed the leash and thrown it on the ground in front of us. Beauty relaxes and sits, soon enjoying me happily petting her and telling her she is a good girl. A minute later I stand, turn towards the car, bending to grab the leash as I step away from Beauty. Beauty follows two steps back watching as I toss the leash into the trunk. A bit more snuggling and petting and I am in the car headed to my appointment.

WHAT PAINS HER

Wednesday, June 6

Today I have Fawn with me. Beauty is in the enclosure when I arrive and waits for me at the entrance. As I take the last four steps to her I hear Beauty doing her "*I am excited and can hardly wait.*" whimpering. It is incredibly rewarding to have her so pleased to see me. I exuberantly surrender into us spend a good four minutes loving each other. I mix her food and place it before putting the retractable on her at the enclosure entry. Fawn does her usual barking at Beauty. After a loop around the field Beauty goes into the enclosure and I feed the stray cat who now has the name of Missy. As I place the cat's food Beauty comes out of the enclosure to watch me, sitting five feet behind me. I feel the pull to return to my primary task for the day, getting Fawn and Beauty more acquainted with each other. It is time to walk Fawn. Beauty follows me to the car and sits about 8 feet away while I get Fawn out. Fawn's reaction is to snarl and bark at Beauty which results in me pulling Fawn to me, telling her "**NO!**", and tapping the side of her muzzle with one finger. She quiets immediately and focuses on me. I am delighted in her change of behavior and sense new possibilities opening up. I am a bit disappointed when Beauty moves out onto the field and certainly understand her choice. At the edge of the field I spend a couple minutes getting Fawn's attention with treats. We then start our tour of the field with Beauty following about 40 feet behind us. About half way through the walk Fawn begins to focus on the walk and me rather than Beauty. Back close to the car I have Fawn sit for treats. I smile when Beauty comes within 15 feet, sits watching and after about a minute lay down to watch. Fawn settles down, keeping an eye on Beauty while getting treats and attention from me. For the first time I have a sense of Fawn accepting Beauty's connection with me. With treats gone Beauty watches as I put Fawn in the car.

Beauty is shedding more and really needs more brushing so I walk to the field, put the retractable on her, kneel beside her, and begin brushing her. It feels important to check her collar so I reach for her collar and rotated it so the buckle is where I can see it. Beauty's ears move back some while her mouth remain open, her tail up. I want to see if I can loosen her collar, to see how much she accepts me handling her collar. With a bit of uncertainty I take hold of her collar her body tightens and then 5 seconds later relaxes. I undo the buckle moving it one hole looser. I notice I am tense, yet open to every possible signal from Beauty. Beauty remains quiet. With a slow breath in and then out I relax my body, opening to notice more. When I slide the collar up on her neck to her head I discover she will be able to slip her head out with the collar as loose as it now is. I am pleased that Beauty remains relaxed as I test the collar. I re-buckle the collar one hole tighter, back where it had been. Paying attention to Beauty's signals I reach under her neck, just below her collar and check for mats. One mat comes loose immediately offering itself to be cut off. I get out the scissors and show them to Beauty. After a moment of blocking my hand with her head she moves to allow me to cut the mat off which I do. I show it too her. I smile as Beauty relaxes a bit, leaning towards me, offering herself to me. Warmth fills me as I sense her pleasure, her expanding trust. I reach under her neck again to see what else I will find. I soon find a large mat. With concentration I am able to shift the fur around it so I can cut it off. Beauty is both curious about what I am doing and a bit nervous with my focus. Her ears move from mostly back to partially back. With some gentle maneuvering and a couple of "Good girl."s I am able to cut most of the mat free. I show the mat to Beauty who takes it in her mouth playfully and with intent. The mat is moist with a brown fluid, something I find puzzling. Then Beauty begins licking my hand, and licking my hand, and licking my hand. My body senses Beauty's message, my mind is puzzled, unable to generate words. When her licking slows I return to checking the underside of her neck near her collar. I find a second mat and with some gentle adjusting of position with Beauty I am able to cut it off. Once again the mat is moist with a brown fluid.

I pet Beauty for a couple of minutes waiting for her to relax and for her ears to come forward. With her ears forward I reach under her neck again. I find a large mat that arcs allowing my finger to slide between the mat and her skin. It takes two minutes, three tries, encouragement, and carefully timed pauses to get my finger all the way under the mat. Beauty is doing well, her body tenses for a few seconds and then relaxes as I back off a bit. I gently move Beauty so I can cut the large mat by sliding one blade of the scissors between the mat and her skin. I smile as she allows me to move the scissors into place and find myself saying **"Oh cool!"** as I cut the mat in half. When I withdraw my fingers Beauty carefully licks them as I use the other hand to check on the mat. It turns out one of the 'halves' has most of the mass. I move my hand from Beauty's licking, gently position my hands and Beauty, and then reach up with the scissors and ever so carefully cut the mat free. As soon as the mat is free I show it to Beauty. She takes it, lays down, and begins licking it intently. She is so intent that I shift to brushing the mats at the base of her tail. For five minutes it feels Beauty and I are focused on taking care of her coat. Finally Beauty stops licking and looks back at me. When I reached up to pet her head she surprises me by rolling on her side and then back and wiggling with pleasure. A bit of happy belly and chest rubbing and I move my hands to her neck for a visual check of the matting. Beauty tenses when my hands first move to her neck. A bit of gentle fingering of her coat and she relaxes, lowering her head to the ground, giving me access to her neck. "Sweet surrender." floats through my mind, warmth floats through my body. As I part her fur I find a sore, bright red, the width of her collar and at least four inches long. Ten seconds of checking the sore, wondering what to do and Beauty announces she is done by rolling to her side and then to her belly. I praise her while waiting for her body to relax and her ears to come at least part way forward. A minute later with her relaxed I reach under her neck to get an idea of how much more matting exists. Beauty allows me about 20 seconds of access, moves her ears back and then stands up. As soon as a hand is close to her muzzle Beauty begins licking it intently. As she licks what my body senses takes shape in my mind. With her licking she is asking me, encouraging me to tend to the sores she cannot reach. In those moments I sense within my body how Beauty now trusts me enough to want me to "tend to her sores". Deepening warmth within my body signal that the bond between us has deepened. I sense a rich warmth flowing from my belly to my heart and out into my body as Beauty's energy and her leaning into me verify more openness between us. In those moments I sense Beauty at home with me, trust and warmth and acceptance filling the space we share.

The grooming session over we walk to the pavement where I remove Beauty's retractable. A bit of snuggling and Beauty enters the enclosure, watching as I drive off.

As I turn onto the street I sense Beauty traveling with me, I sense our bond, our agreement to be together, and I wonder how the transition will occur. I sense Beauty in the backseat, on her leash, not the retractable. I am in the backseat with her, Ute is driving. As I travel the sweeping turn onto Airport Way I sense Beauty's awareness with me noticing how I experience the drive, the surroundings we will travel together some day soon. I grin as my mind and ego uncomfortably insist I never admit what I am experiencing to another human being. As I acknowledge their message they quiet and I return to sensing the flow of my surroundings, sharing what I sense with Beauty.

Inner Weavings

Thursday, June 7th

I arrive at Beauty's area about 1:45 on this cool, cloudy day. There has been rain for much of the night leaving the ground wet. I don't see Beauty as I park and as I get out of my car I worry that something has happened to her. After scanning the field I turn to the enclosure and see her standing there tail high but not wagging. We meet at the enclosure entrance for about a minute of enthusiastic greetings. At that point she jumps down and walks to the field. I get the retractable, brush, and scissors. She walks to me and waits for me to put on her retractable. It is very clear that she has decided we will walk. We are off. This time Beauty wants to take me beyond the field into a different area she wanders in. As we 'explore' sometimes she leads, sometimes I lead. I enjoy how easily we move together, how easily she responds to a slight pull on her retractable. Beauty's prancing gate, her frequent glances back at me, her insistence I follow at times wrap me in a sense that she now wants me to know more of her territory, more of her. Her moving to my side, allowing me to guide when tense situations appear fills me with a warm understanding of her trust, her pleasure that I provide protection and guidance.

After 20 minutes we return to the field where I sit with her and cut away mats in the area of her neck. She relaxes and allows me to reach into the fur on her neck with little protest. A couple times after smelling a mat I cut out she licks my hand intently, filling me, filling the space we share with warmth and acceptance. After about eight minutes Beauty rolls onto her side and then onto her back allowing me to see more easily under her chin. There are three or four times when Beauty's ears rotated back, a signal she is unsure of what is happening. Each time I stop grooming her, pet her, gently wait for her ears to come forward again. After a couple more minutes of mat removal she rolls over, gets up, and steps a couple steps from me. The message is clear, *"I am done for now."* Three minutes later she comes back to me for more attention, allowing me to cut a couple more mats free. Within a deep urge stirs. I so much want to remove her collar, to give the skin around her neck, especially the sore, time to recover. Regrettably that will have to wait until she is at my house. As the thought of her sore comes to mind Beauty magically moves, giving me easy access to check on the sore. Gingerly I reach to her neck slipping fingers under her collar on either side of the sore. Beauty stands very still as I move her collar away from the sore. I am relieved as I notice the sore seems a bit less inflamed. Beauty remains still as I gently move the fur around the sore, checking for any signs of infection. I grin as Beauty and I seem to agree that the best course is for me to simply check each day. As I move her collar back in place Beauty steps away and I wonder whether she would permit me to put suave on her sore. Beauty seems to agree that hopefully that will not be needed.

While I am grooming Beauty, Missy, the stray cat, comes about halfway to us, watching us and at times rolling on her back.

It is time for me to feed Beauty and Missy. Beauty follows me to retrieve her bowl but unlike other times she stays by the car as I place her bowl back in the enclosure. When I walk to feed the cat Beauty follows me then turns away, going into the enclosure. The cat fed I call Beauty who comes out to me and then walks with me to the car. I have the strange sense that Beauty is choosing to work with me, that she understands car familiarization is us getting ready for her trip home. My mind and ego struggle with an understanding that Beauty is intent on preparing with me. My mind offers, "She is just a dog." while my ego insists, "We will never share such crazy talk." I join Beauty, open both back doors, get in, and spend the next ten minutes enticing her to get further and further into the car. It is the first session where I am in the car the whole time. Twice Beauty gets to the point where she walks away from the car and sits down. After a couple of minutes she returns for more treats. My mind and ego carefully avoid noticing that deep within Beauty and I have begun working together to get her home.

My grin reflects my awareness that my mind and ego are unready to acknowledge what my inner knowing has long whispered, *"You will be together, a reflection of an eternal bond."*

    The treats gone I get out, close both doors and join Beauty in the field. I am tempted to do more grooming and sense that the time would be better spent being quiet with Beauty. After a minute of petting Beauty rolls on her side and with a bit of encouragement onto her back. For about three minutes she stays there body relaxed as I pet her. She rolls over, gets up, moves 5 feet away, and sits facing away from me. I wait a minute or so and without thinking knee walk to her, and lay down close to her. She lays down, her head a foot from mine. The next 5 minutes we spend in simply being close to each other, together noticing what is going on in the field. My mind and ego carefully ignore the weaving Beauty and I's energies are doing deep, deep within shaping the spaces we will share. At the end of the five minutes I sense it is time for me to go. I give Beauty the rawhide chew I have for her and say goodbye. There is both satisfaction and sorrow flowing within me as I leave. Satisfaction that the visit has gone well and sorrow that Beauty is not coming home with me yet. Once again as I drive home I notice Beauty's energy with me. I sense Beauty carefully noticing what she will experience on our first drive home.

Transition to Leash

Friday, June 8

Driving out I review getting Beauty home hoping to notice what further steps need to be completed that can be considered for today and tomorrow. Certainly getting Beauty to be comfortable being in the backseat with me is a major key. As I think the process through an image takes shape within my body. Well, actually, a short movie plays within me. Ute is there, off away from the car. I have Beauty on the leash. Ah, the leash will give me better control, the retractable will not work as well. The leash will allow me more control both at the car and at home getting Beauty into the backyard and then into the house. By the time I turn off the street at the field I know today will be a leash familiarization day.

Beauty is in the enclosure when I arrive. She waits for me to get her bowl and then follows me as I make her food and return to place her bowl in the enclosure. I smile enjoying her choosing to be 'with' me. I leave the car with her food bowl, her leash, and her brush. With the bowl placed we go out into the field. I casually toss the leash on the ground and kneel next to it. At the sight of the leash lying on the ground Beauty balks, standing about five feet from me. As I pick up the leash and playfully toss it to her feet time slows becoming a flow of thousands of little changes. Her ears creep back and a sense of her uncertainty washes through me. I purposely imagine her sniffing the leash and then myself clipping the leash on her collar. One breath, two breaths and she leans forward to sniff the leash. A breath, then another and I knee walk to her while imagining her staying still while I pickup the leash and clip it to her collar. Her ears go back, her stance stiffens, *and* she stays where she is. I feel and hear myself saying, "**Your such a good girl.**" as I pick up the leash and take hold of her collar. I pause, let the tension out of my body, and sense myself lovingly attaching the leash to Beauty's collar. A moment, then two moments and I am doing exactly that. Beauty looks at me and I feel myself washed with her love, concern, and acceptance. Instinctively I release the leash allowing it to drape onto the ground, moving my hands to my side. A moment of curiosity and Beauty relaxes. In molasses like movements my hands float to each side of her muzzle and she leans into me. I sense her energies, my energies quietly celebrating our surrender into trusting each other.

    I reach for her brush, show it to her, and reach taking hold of her leash. After a few strokes brushing her chest I use tension on the leash to guide her to stand so I can groom her back. I am pleased that she accepts my guidance. As she stands time slips back to a more normal flow. A few strokes of the brush on her back and with her watching I put down the brush and pick up the portion of the leash beyond my gripping hand. Beauty tenses a bit as I lift the slack part of the leash and begin petting her back with it. With each stroke Beauty relaxes a bit more. Finally I bring the leash up to her shoulders and pet her with the slack of the leash flopping at her side. I then with focused intent let the free end of the leash drop to the ground. I feel as though Beauty whispers to me, *"Oh, okay. With you leash is love."* as she snuggle against me. The warmth we share seems to flow out shaping a sphere of trust and acceptance.

    A moment later I am standing, holding Beauty's leash, guiding her to come with me. I purposely take us out to the busy street. Through our half hour walk Beauty more and more accepts that the leash, like the retractable, allows me to protect and guide her. By the time we turn back towards the field Beauty is relaxed and responsive to signals given via the leash.

    We go to the car. I carefully use the leash to keep Beauty right next to me as I open first one backdoor and then the other. I sense myself using the leash to unyieldingly guide Beauty to the car on the day she comes home with me. Back in the current time I set a mood of Beauty and I working together. We become separate from the rest of the world. I close the backdoors. Then a dozen time I begin 20 feet from the car. With the leash I guide Beauty to stand next to me. With a **"let's go"**

I guide her to the car keeping her inches from my leg with pressure on the leash. At the car I keep her close, opening driver side backdoor, then guiding her to step so her head is at the door opening and I am in position to push her in with my knees. I carefully relax and feel playful as I pet her and tell her she is a good girl. The first time I hold her there only a couple seconds. By the twelfth time I am holding her there 30 or 40 seconds. After the 12th time I walk her back out into the field, pet her, remove the leash and release the energy of focus. I grin, tell her "**Good girl!**", and jump away from her in play. She responds immediately and we begin chasing each other round and round. I am soon winded and pause, considering whether I should leave or not. I sense that am not done, we are not done.

Beauty is 20 feet from me when I call her, holding the leash up, I float to her the sensations of my clipping the leash on her collar. The first time, the second time Beauty just looks at me. Finally on the third time she surrenders, walking over to me and turning, offering me her collar. "**Good girl. You are such a good girl.**" is spoken and bubbles within me as I clip the leash on her collar. A few strokes on her head and I turn taking her to the car, using the leash to guide her into a position where I could force her into the car. This time I bend down putting gentle pressure on her butt with my knees. Beauty pushes back, staying where she is while I keep the pressure on her. Three seconds, "**Good girl.**", another second, and I am backing up, allowing Beauty to move back from the car. I keep Beauty close to the car, step in front of her, pull up on the leash and repeat "**Sit**." To my pleasure Beauty does just that looking up at me with both disapproval and pleasure. I reach down and undo her leash, letting it drop to the ground, holding Beauty where she is by her collar. "**Your such a good girl. You are so brave.**" and Beauty relaxes then seems to fill with pleasure at passing my challenge. Beauty stays there while I pick up her leash. She seems disappointed when I toss the leash into the backseat. Grinning I tell her, "**Enough for today**." In a moment I have dropped onto my knees and I am petting her with both hands. My mind registers we are only 5 feet from the backdoor. After a few moments of celebration, in the same moment Beauty and I get up. She turns and sits to face me as I offer "**See you tomorrow.**", and slip into the driver's seat. To my surprise Beauty sits there while I start the car, put it in gear, and drive towards the street. As I drive onto the street I smile knowing Beauty and I have just made important steps. As I head home I hear myself telling Fawn that Beauty will soon be with us. As I drive home I allow myself to experience the thousands of tiny emotions I held within, out of the way, while Beauty and I did necessary work. Some of those emotions have names, most are far more subtle than language can express. If you are still in this moment you may sense a few of them.

Sorrow and Separation

Saturday, June 9

As I make the sweeping turn from Airport Way, up towards Beauty's area, I cannot sense her energy. My mind and ego begin their worries. What if she is injured? With her becoming more trusting did some rescue take her? What if the 'young hunters' had gotten to her? Each block my worry deepens. Yet when I check deep within my belly there is quiet. My mind and ego's worries become less intense, shifting to worry and curiosity.

As I turn into the field I do not see Beauty. I park, get out of the car, and whistle once, then twice, and many more times. With a heavy heart I turn to the enclosure and head to retrieve Beauty's food bowl. The short walk seems much longer than usual. As I step up into the enclosure I open my energy further, scanning the area. No sign of her. At the deck I bend to pick up her bowl. At the moment I touch her food bowl I sense her. She is hiding somewhere out just beyond the edges of her territory, driven there by the young hunters. Relief, pain, anger, worry are stirred within me by each step back to the car. As I mix her food I sense Beauty with me, gentle gratitude flowing to me through a cloak of pain, confusion, sorrow. The walk back to place her bowl is less difficult, the grief far easier to move through than the unknowing of a few moments before.

The bend to place her bowl just under the deck shifts into my sitting and placing her food bowl. As I cross my legs I allow my inner knowing to guide me into a meditative state. The enclosure is 'safe territory'. The food bowl filled with just made food somehow connect she and I. My mind and ego slip into a quiet observer mode. I sense Beauty's sorrow, desires, her gratitude fills me. I am within her, she is within me. Our energies blend, stirred by the love, trust, and intimacies we share. Her sorrow, my sorrow ease shifting into a deep yearning and gratitude. A slight smile forms as I sense her intent, my intent that tomorrow we will touch each other. For now she will remain hidden. In the early morning as light touches the eastern sky she will creep out of hiding and slink back to the protection of the enclosure.

    I have no idea how long I sit there encapsulated in the energies Beauty and I share. The arrival of a delivery truck brings me back to the physical world. As I hear the truck door close I unravel my legs and stand. The drivers seems startled by my sudden appearance. A few sentences about Beauty and I am in the car, heading home. Beauty is with me. I sense her curiosity, her whispers, *"I yearn to be with you more than I fear the changes."*

Speaking with the Police

Sunday, June 10

While I am driving on Airport Way, three miles from Beauty's area I sense Beauty waiting for me. I grin as she responds to my energy. There is a quiet warmth and confidence as she whispers, "*Yes, you are my people coming to be with me as you should.*" I grin as a playful warmth fills me. With edged playful tones my ego quips, "Funny Farm For Sure".

Beauty is waiting for me away from the enclosure, in the bushes off to the West. By the time my car stops she is trotting to me and seems a bit perturbed that I am out of the car before she gets to me. A few moments of affection and all is well. Beauty walks with me as I retrieve her bowl, watches me mix her food, and returns with me to place it in the enclosure. When we jump out of the enclosure together she goes right to the car. Somehow today does not seem to be a day for car familiarization so I simply grab her leash and her brush. I am careful that she sees me take out her leash and relax a bit when she seems unworried by it.

Beauty runs out into the field and waits for me. When I get close she does a play bow, I jump towards her, and she happily jumps sideways and runs a big loop. As she comes back towards me I charge at her. She weaves sideways and begins a second loop. Tired and a bit out of sorts I simply drop to my knees and call her to me. She dodges back and forth several times before walking to me and sitting. As soon as she sits I show her the leash and then attach it to her collar. She is surprised and allows me to begin grooming her. When I first guide her to move for me using the leash she balks. I keep the tension on the leash and gently whisper, "**It is okay, girl. I need you to be okay with the leash.**" One breath, two breaths, three breaths and she relaxes allowing herself to respond to my guidance via her leash. Perhaps five minutes of business like grooming and she is ready to be moving.

As she gets up she lets me know she has a plan. Grinning I follow her. She leads me southwest, off into areas with more businesses, people, and cars. We loop towards the Goodwill store and then head further south. Unfamiliar with the area I carefully note landmarks as we go. After about a half hour Beauty turns back towards the spa business and field. As we pass in front of the Gresham Police Rockwood Station I am a bit uncomfortable knowing I am walking an unlicensed stray dog. Yes, there is a part of me that prefers to follow the rules. Down the street a bit we turn back and walk across the street from the police station. I am surprised when Beauty seems intent upon crossing in the middle of the street to walk through the police parking lot. The worry of my mind and ego are overridden by Beauty's determination and something stirring deep within me. As we step onto the sidewalk behind the police station a police SUV pulls in and parks 50 feet away. The officer gets out glances at us takes a step, stops and looks at us. I feel drawn towards the officer by his curiosity. With a shake of his head the officer turns and heads towards the building entrance. Three steps and the officer stops turns and looks at us. A sense of "*I have got to ask.*" washes through me, followed by a "*Oh, he and the dog are walking towards me.*" When I am 20 feet from the officer I hear, "**Is that dog the one...**" and hear myself answering, "**Yes, she is.**" before his question is completed. "**Oh, she? I almost didn't recognize... you said she? She looks so much better.**" "**Yes, she has been letting me groom her.**" "**Oh, then she is your dog.**" "**Well, no. Not yet.**" A moment later, as the officer's head tilts a bit I am washed over by his sense of cognitive dissonance. "**Uh??? How does work?**" "**She isn't ready to get into my car yet. I feed her and walk her. I am hoping that soon she will get in my car and come home.**" "**Oh, okay... but where?**" Before I answer my mind and ego warn me about 'keeping things secret'. "**The spa shop manager lets me feed her behind his shop. When we are done walking I will let her off leash and she will stay here when I go home.**" Wrinkled brows and silence. Finally a, "**Well you are doing a good job with her. I**

will let the other officers know what is happening." "That would be great. Thank you." A smile, a nod and the officer turns back to his duties. As Beauty and I turn towards the spa shop I sense that somehow this encounter is important to Beauty's safety and feel a sense of gratitude towards the officer.

Back at the field I let Beauty off her leash, snuggle with her a bit, and head off to an appointment. Somehow things are different. As I drive I realize that for the first time I have made an official declaration of my plan for Beauty to share my home.

Announcing 'Us'

Monday, June 11

A pleasant early summer day, not quite as warm as yesterday and with those high hazy clouds that lessen the intensity of the sunshine. As I drive into Beauty's area she comes out from under the deck and by the time I am parking she is nearing the enclosure entrance. The bounce in her gate, her posture with head and tail high, the swing of her head to look at me, mouth fully open, tongue hanging out, all of these things show me her name is well chosen. As she jumps out of the enclosure I open my car door and feeling no urge to get out, I simply undo my seat belt and turn my upper body to her. With ears high and fully forward she comes right to me, stepping her front feet onto the door sill so that she can bring her head to my chest, making it easy to scratch her head with both hands. She remains there wiggling and wagging her tail as I tell her I am happy to see her. After a little more than a minute she gets down, backs up a step, and waits for me to get out. We go to the field where Beauty stands waiting for me to put on her leash. Somehow it does not feel like time for the leash so I simple kneel in front of her and begin affectionately petting her. I am amused as I realize that no matter what my mood as I drive to see Beauty I am always happy within a minute or two of greeting her. A sharp, "Not repeatable to others" from my ego fuels the transition of a grin into a smile.

After several minutes of attention I get up and Beauty begins running playfully out into the field. It is clear she wants to be off leash to begin our tour of the field. I am pleased and grateful when a few minutes into the tour Beauty stands so I can attach the leash. My mind and ego seem almost ready to accept the whispered *'she is my dog'* deep within. At the end of the tour we loop back to the car where I take Beauty off leash and go through the feeding ritual. As I place her food bowl Beauty stands watching and then sniffs and takes a couple of polite bites. Time for work.

We exit the enclosure moving back to the car where I open both back doors and get my baggy of steak treats. We start on the passenger side, my placing several treats and then Beauty stepping in with her front feet to retrieve what she can. When she has taken the bits easily available she waits inside the car for me to place more treats. With considerable uncertainty I do just that, carefully leaning in over Beauty. After retrieving those bits she leaves the car moving several feet away letting me know she is done for the moment. On impulse I move to the other side of the car and place a couple pieces. She steps in with her front feet, remaining there while I lean in over her and place a few more. She takes the added treats, eyes the treats just out of reach, and to my delight begins lifting her right back leg to the door sill. Three tries and she has traction, lifting herself, stepping to the door sill with her back left leg. My sense of time shifts and suddenly she is surprising me again, in slow motion she steps both hind legs up onto the backseat. I am in awe seeing what I had hoped for over several weeks is now happening. Beauty is standing in the middle of the back seat eating treats. Enthralled I gently lean in over her and toss additional treats onto the seat. As each treat arcs through the air and lands, as Beauty reaches down and takes each treat I sense our many weeks of sharing blending to shape these moments of transition, of change. Down to three treats I wait. Beauty is facing away from me, enjoying my petting her. When no more treats come she turns and faces me, her ears are forward, her mouth open. I give each of the remaining treats, one, a pause, two, a pause, three, and I reach in to scratch her head with both hands. I notice every detail, I notice the flow of time within me. I notice how Beauty standing in the middle of the backseat taking treats is shifting our future, opening the path for Beauty to travel to what in this moment is becoming our home. After perhaps 15 seconds of petting Beauty's ears go back and she takes a step towards me, letting me know she is ready to get out. I pet her another five seconds, praising her, and then step back giving her a clear path to exit the car. Beauty jumps out of the car stopping next to me, ears forward, mouth open, accepting my attention, showing she is enjoying my attention by leaning her head into my hand. She seems to lovingly whisper to me, "*Yes, I will be with you.*" I could have easily done a jig at that point.

On instinct I reach down and attach Beauty's leash. Suddenly her posture changes showing me she has decided to do something. What I can offer is that she seems to stand a bit taller, maybe an inch. Her posture and movements become more specific as her head and body turn in the direction she plans to go. As she steps forward her head is perhaps an inch or two more extended from her body. She exudes a sense of purpose. Beauty turns towards the gate entry into the enclosure and begins walking with "I am going here" posture and movements. I follow wondering what she plans. As we pass the gate into the enclosure Beauty in an unusual move heads toward the back entry of the shop. As we approach the entry I have a clear sense that she wants to see the fellow who manages the shop.

The back entry door is open and I am intrigued as Beauty becomes very alert and walks into the shop. She scans what she can see of the shop from just inside the back entry. Unable to see anyone she steps in further, scanning around corners. While she is scanning the manager comes out from the storage area. Beauty is not startled and seems pleased that he is there. As the manager and I begin to talk we are standing perhaps 3 feet apart inside the building while Beauty has placed herself eight feet away, just inside the entry. Then to my surprise Beauty steps closer to the manager and sits. I ask the manager if he wants to offer her a treat which he agrees to with a smile. I watch curiously as he takes a step forward, lowers his hand, offering Beauty the treat. With ears forward Beauty steps forward and gently takes the treat. The manager's expression displays both surprise and being touched by Beauty's trust. Warmth fills me. Beauty steps forward for a second, a third, and a fourth treat, each time remaining a bit longer before stepping back. Not having more treats the manager and I chat about Beauty. When I glance back at Beauty she is laying down about six feet from us, her head resting on her front paws, facing away from us. I have the sense that she is simply waiting for "her person and a friend" to finish talking. Soon our chat ends and Beauty and I head out of the enclosure. Each step seems to carry me further into knowing Beauty has just declared to the world that she has accepted me as her people, that we are now a bonded pair. I gently set aside most of what is stirring within me. On the drive home I will afford myself the luxury of experiencing the beginning edges. At home, in quiet reflection far more will float forward filling me with wonder and beauty.

We take a long walk up the street to the Salvation Army building and lot. On our walk two young girls comment to me that my dog is really pretty. Both smile when I tell them I have named her Beauty. Beauty seems to whisper, *"Yes, I am your Beauty."* When Beauty and I return to the field I groom her for a while before she heads back into the enclosure to eat and then lays down in the shade. It is time for me to head home. As I drive out of the lot and along the way home I enjoy remembering Beauty in the backseat, Beauty greeting me, and Beauty seeking out the manager of store connected to the enclosure where I feed her. What a life!

QUICK VISIT

Tuesday, June 12

Today will be a short visit, I am stopping by on my way to walk Ute's dogs. Beauty is in the enclosure, comes out from under the deck as I park, and comes running out to meet me as soon as she hears my voice. She rounds the hot tub and comes right to me sitting in the car. Many snuggles and much petting later I float out of the car and walk to the field where we spend about 5 uninhibited minutes enjoying being with each other. I put her leash on and we go for a long walk at the end of which I fix her food. On our walks Beauty is less tense with more tail wagging. She also is more willing to walk close to people, always on the far side of me and often with her ears partially back. While at the car Beauty stands at the back door looking in. Unfortunately I do not have time to do any backseat familiarization. With the food placed I have to get going so I say goodbye. As I drive away I realize how focused I was on 'getting it done'. The moments had been full of rich possibilities most of which I did not notice. With a shake of my head I tell myself, "I will choose differently tomorrow."

Jumping In

Wednesday, June 13

Today is a gray cool day with clouds and very little sun. When I reach Beauty's area she is laying on the pavement. She stands and watches me park, ears partially back, tail down, I sense her uncertainty. As soon as I roll down the window and speak to her her tail comes up wagging, her ears come forward, her mouth opens, the corners of her mouth move back, and her tongue comes out. As I open the door she comes bounding to me stepping up on the door sill to put her face in front of my chest. She licks my hands and at one point reaches up and licks my face. Finally I surrender to the pleasure of her acceptance and affection. Thirty seconds of greeting and she backs off 5 feet and sits. Now full of energy I get out, pat her head and trot to the field where we play, jumping, running, dodging. Soon she let me know she has decided it is time to begin our walk by running from me with her tail high, often looking back over her shoulder to see if I am following. As we move to the far right corner of the field she stays well ahead of me and then heads out the driveway past the motel. I call her, she turns around, looks at me, and then keeps going. She seems intent on being off leash. Worry washes through me as she goes out of sight. I consider following her and with a moment, from deep within know I should not. After about three minutes she comes running back to me. I am grinning, worry gone as she slows six feet from me with her ears moving back as she takes the last few steps to me. As I pet her and tell her she is a good dog her ears come forward. Somehow I have passed one of her tests of me. I reach towards her collar, she holds still, her ears go partially back. As I touch her collar, feeling for the leash clip, her body relaxes and I attach the leash. Off we go on a long walk which includes crossing the busy street I had avoided before. For about 45 minutes Beauty and I walk. As we tour the new territory across the busy street I watch how relaxed Beauty is and how her tail remains high, often wagging. My sense is she is enjoying openly visiting areas where she had always been cautious. Several times when she looks at me intently warmth flows within me as I sense her energies whispering, "*It is better with you.*" As we cross the street back to the field I am flooded with contentment and a sense that I am walking 'my dog'. My mind and ego carefully ignore a deep sense that Beauty and I's bond is timeless.

Back at the car we go through the feeding routine then I go to Beauty where she is waiting, stroke her head and we head to the car. On the second time of placing treats in the back seat Beauty starts to reach a back foot onto the door sill. I am pleased when she accepts my reaching behind her and helping her step her back feet onto the sill. Beauty stays standing on the seat while I playfully drop additional treats on the seat. After about two minutes she turns around to face me. I happily scratch both sides of her head while she "grins" at me. Ten seconds of petting and Beauty shows me she is ready to get out by taking a step towards me. I purposely pet her for another ten seconds before stepping back and allowing her to jump out. I smile as I watch her wait, her body remaining relaxed, her ears mostly forward, as I block her departure. When she jumps down she immediately turns, sits, and offers her head for my attention. I am smiling as I recognize we are moving closer to her trusting me when I close the doors 'trapping' us both inside the car. With the meat treats gone I go to the field with Beauty where we play, chasing each other, lunging, dodging. Soon tired I call her to me and begin grooming her. At times she seems to enjoy being groomed and at times she tolerates it. Today she is tolerating my efforts seeming to whisper, "*Well okay, I will let you.*" As I groom her she begins to relax a bit more, then a bit more. A few moments before grooming ends I sense her allowing our energies to blend, her shaping our energies into us becoming a team. Something new is stirring within me, I grin knowing in an hour, a day, the stirrings will become understanding.

I have been with Beauty for almost an hour and a half and it seems time to head home. I get up and go to the car. Before I reach the car

Beauty gets up and runs to me stopping near the back door. I feel myself deciding, "*Okay, a chance to do more backseat familiarization.*" I pop the trunk and get several treats. Beauty shows little interest in getting treats while I am standing at the backdoor so I decide to try something different. With uncertainty I get into the back seat. I am pleased when Beauty immediately comes to the door. A few treats and I scoot further into the car forcing Beauty to get in further for treats. After I scoot in a second time, when Beauty needs to put her back feet on the sill to get treats she backs out and disappears to the back of the car. I wonder and wait and notice the playfulness surrounding me. With a grin I choose to open to it. It seems like a long wait (about 90 seconds). Finally Beauty shows up at the backdoor again. I hold out a treat. To my surprise Beauty jumps onto the back seat, and with all four feet on the seat stretches her neck out to take the treat I offer. I am stunned and fumble to offer her another treat, then another. Time shifts, the world shrinks to Beauty and I inside the car. I reach up and pet her head before getting another treat for her. To my utter delight Beauty shifts herself a bit and sits down facing me, ears forward, mouth open wide, tongue out. Filled with awe I switch back and forth between giving her treats and scratching her head as I tell her she is a good girl. At one point I reach up with both hands scratching both sides of her head and her shoulders. To my utter delight and amazement she sits there completely relaxed. When I pause she looks left and then right several times. As she stops, raising her chin a bit higher than usual and looking towards me, I have the sense of her claiming the backseat as part of her territory. It is as if she is whispering, "*I am here, I am safe, I am with you, this is mine.*" A sense of being with my dog in our car washes through me. A few more treats and pets, perhaps 30 seconds worth, and she stands, turns, and jumps out of the backseat. As I get out of the car I notice my mind and ego trying to understand what has happened, what it all means, what labels to apply. I grin, sensing that it will take a few hours for it all to shift and a small part of it to filter into a form my mind can "hold".

Out of the car I reach into my back pocket, take out the rawhide chew and walk to Beauty who is waiting in the field. She happily takes the treat, walks five feet away, and lays down. I pause, then knee walk over to her. As she looks at me I can almost hear, "*Well?*" I pick up the rawhide and toss it for her. She runs to it, grabs it, and then lays down waiting for me to do it again. I do it again, and again, and again, and ... On the last toss she runs to the chew, picks it up, drops it, runs back to me and plops herself down next to me, partially on her side, leaning against me. With a broad smile on my face I reach out to pet her, two strokes and she rolls onto her side then back, letting most of the tension out of her body. As I pet her belly, warmth fills the space we share. We are sealing the deal, I am her people, she is my dog, we are a bonded pair. With each stroke of my hand on her belly our agreement goes deeper within each of us, somehow our connections are expanding beyond time and space. Thankfully my mind is puzzled and quiet. After three or so minutes she rolls back onto her belly gently sealing our new connections within. With reluctance I get up and walk to the car. I seem to be moving through molasses as I open the car door, get in, start the car, and then drive away. Beauty is with me as I drive home. As I sit at home I sense Beauty with me. I feels as though she is examining her new home through my eyes, through my energies. As warmth flows through me I notice my mind and ego are not ready to accept what I sense.

THANKS AND GOODBYES

Thursday, June 14

Today is a bright sunny day, a pleasant 75 degrees. As I park Beauty comes from under the deck. She moves to the entrance of the enclosure and waits until she hears my voice to bound out of the enclosure and run to me. With each of her steps the warmth within me deepens and expands. At first she does not step up on the door sill, waiting on the ground for my attention. I sense her whisper, *"Show me you want me."* Grinning I pat my chest, motion with my hands, and sense myself drawing her to me. She steps up, raises her head to mine, and for the first time licks my face as part of our greeting. As we enjoy each others touch I am washed by amazement of how much she and I have opened to each other. I get out of the car as she dances back and forth, her tail swinging vigorously enough to wag her butt. As I walk to the field she prances close by. We move together on many levels. At the field we spend about five minutes saying hello, my scratching her, her rubbing against me, in close for full contact, a loop out and back to me, a burst of speed, a quick dodge, her facing me and moving her head and shoulder back and forth in a series of faints. A celebration of 'us'. Tuckered out I get up and go to the car to retrieve the leash and her brush. She walks with me then sits and waits until I turn and attach the leash to her collar. Then it is off to the races. We run across the field to the blackberries where she searches for one of her stray cat friends. To her delight we find one that after a few faints from five feet away runs back into the berry bushes. Beauty pushes little by little into the bushes looking for the cat. After several whimpers the cat rewards Beauty by moving further away. Beauty follows the cat, moving slowly, a bit forward, a pause, forward again. When Beauty realizes the cat had moved too deeply into the bushes for her to follow she whimpers several times, turns and returns to me, sharing her disappointment with me. We loop around the motel and then Beauty takes me on a tour of a part of her territory we had not visited before. At one point she wants to cross the light rail tracks. Funny... she seems unconcerned by the "Unsafe to Cross" and "No Trespassing" signs. I am pleased that she follows my lead, waiting until we reach an intersection to cross the tracks. I can almost hear her chuckling whisper, "*Okay, your safe.*" As we walk Beauty's stride has a bounce to it, her ears vary from forward to partially back, her tail is high, sometimes wagging.

Back at the field we begin a backseat familiarization session. She goes partway into the backseat when I stand outside. The steak treats are soon gone and she has not gotten all the way in. A bit disappointed I sense an urge to feed her and so move through the process of fixing her food with her watching. Once her food is placed I feed the stray cat my friend hopes to place in a good home. As I finish placing the food Beauty comes out of the enclosure and moves to the field, a respectable distance from me and the cat. Done with the feeding I go to Beauty, take out the brush, and begin grooming her. She shows she is not really interested by getting up and wandering to the car. I follow her, open both back doors, and roll down the front windows. She immediately peers into the backseat. When I get in the backseat on the drivers side she goes around to the passenger side and peers in at me. I put one and then another treat on the seat. Soon she has crawled up onto the seat to join me and receive treats. Less than a minute later she sits down. Then about three minutes later, to my delight, she lays down, her front legs touching the side of my leg. With deep satisfaction I begin interchanging treats and attention. After a couple minutes she sits up and carefully scans the area outside the car. After a minute of scanning she lays back down. We spend the next 10 minutes together, enjoying the shade of the car and being with each other. Then she decides it is time for to get up which she does. Once out of the car she goes back into the enclosure.

I find myself following her rather than leaving right away. While in the enclosure I notice the spa shop manager by the back entry to the shop. I walk over to him and share that Beauty had just laid down in the backseat with me. When I begin speaking Beauty comes out from under the deck and wanders over to join us. To my and the manager's surprise she moves into the shop, carefully sniffing and looking. We hold ourselves still and watch. Three minutes and she is done, walks just outside the back entry and lays down. There is a sense of comradery and pleasure with Beauty's changes as the manager and I chat. Our sharing ends when a customer comes into the shop. As I walk away I am surprised that Beauty remains laying just outside the shop entry. She stays there, letting me see how brave she now is. When I call her, she trots to me. While I am saying goodbye to her energies shift, somehow she is now a bit more my dog. With gentle warmth flowing within me I head home.

As I turn onto the street a gentle stirring in my belly lets me know to be quiet and pay attention. Surprise mixed with disbelief appear as I sense Beauty's message within her behavior. *"I have made peace with the shopkeeper. I have thanked him for his kindness and said goodbye. I am almost ready to leave this place, to be with you in our territory."* In those moments I am filled with yearning, sorrow, and joy.

Subtle Changes

Friday, June 15

Not much to report. It is a hot day so our early afternoon meeting is not very long. Basically we go for a walk around the field, spent some time being together, and I feed Beauty. It is far too hot to do any car familiarization. When I leave I tell Beauty I will be back that evening.

When I arrive back at the field it is cooler, about 9 PM. Beauty comes out from under the deck to greet me with a slower gate than during the day. She is more nervous than during the day, looking around two or three times a minute rather than every two or three minutes. We go for a walk in the field and play a bit. I then take her to the car for some familiarization. She is never comfortable enough to put more than the upper part of her body in the car. She also withdraws often to look around. The visit and day end with my feeling empty and uncertain. Most of the way home I connect Beauty's nervousness with the young hunters chasing her as part of their evening fun. Things need to change soon.

Quiet Day Getting Ready

Saturday, June 16

Today is cooler with high clouds and a gentle breeze. Beauty comes to me as soon as I pull in and call her name. She comes to me slowly while I sit in the car and pauses before stepping up onto the door sill. I am relieved that when we step out into the field she is eager and rambunctious as we play. She waits for me to put her leash on before we walk the field.

There is something going on for her. What I sense is a reluctance to leave the field, the area, a reluctance to make the final move to my home, to our home. While other days she had readily come to the car for treats and was willing to take chances last night and today she has been cautious around the car, less willing to take risks, and quick to steps away from the car. Right now I am at a bit of a loss. When I am quiet all I sense is *"wait"*.

There have been a couple of times during today's visit when Beauty and I both relax and are able to simply enjoy being together. Several times she rolls over on her side or back so I can stroke her chest and belly.

After today's visit, without thought, I stop by the local pet shop where I purchase a collar and tag for Beauty. I smile as I read the tag, Beauty's name and my phone number, before attaching it to her collar. It will be interesting to see how she responds when I put her new collar on her. With a subtle smile I sense how the actions I have just completed and how putting on her collar place her and I being together into our near future.

Time to Plan

Sunday, June 17

When I arrive I do not see Beauty. As I get out of the car a whistle, a single long whistle beginning low and raising in volume and pitch. On the fourth whistle I see her looping towards me, out from under the shade of a few small trees at the far side of the field. I relax and call to her, "**Hey Beauty. Good girl. Such a Beauty.**" On impulse I duck inside the car and grab her leash then take a few steps towards her as she loops towards me. She slows with her last three steps and turns so she bumps her shoulders into my legs. Her bump stirs deep, playful energies within me. Without thinking I clip her leash on and we begin to walk. As we get closer to the motelish apartments a fellow I had talked briefly with a couple of times suddenly appears. He is short and slight and is dressed simply with a broad brimmed hat. He has the appearance someone who has grown up on the land. Earlier I had guessed he learned English south of the boarder.

What impressed me each time I met him was his energy, calm, deep, contained, observing without interacting. The first time I said Hi to him I sensed him scanning my energy. In a moment his light 'silly gringo' attitude shifted to 'interesting' and then a recognition of the energetic links between Beauty and I. In the meetings before few words were spoken.

This time he walks towards me and after a hello he half states, half asks, "**She is your Beauty.**" I nod and offer, "**Yes, I hope to take her home soon**." Energies shift. We are encapsulated. He, I, Beauty, and the small patch of grass we stand on are all that exist. I hear and deep inside myself feel him state, "**There are people around here**

who want her dead." My mind seems to have stepped away and I hear myself saying, "**Thank you. Very soon!**" A nod and the fellow steps away leaving me suspended in time sensing flows of energy. With my mind quiet I am able to sense, to understand the energies that are holding space for Beauty to be in this field are collapsing. Soon she will be with me or she will be dead.

As my awareness comes back to the 'real world' I notice Beauty gazing at me, gazing deep into my eyes. The fellow is nowhere to be seen. During the next breath we agree that she is to be with me. The energies of death seem to retreat, they do not leave. From within I hear a whisper, "*Less than a week.*"

I remember very little of Beauty and I's walk. After I place her food she and I focus on backseat familiarization. After getting her to come into the car using treats I feel an urge to be more aggressive. I get out of the car and call her to me about 15 feet from the car. I clip her leash on and holding her close to me turn to the car. Without words she and I agree, it is time to work. I walk to the open backdoor positioning her so she is between me and the open door. "**Good girl.**" and I slip behind her. She tenses but stays at the backdoor opening. I bend down, thrusting my knees forward, pushing against her butt. I use her leash to keep her from veering away from the door. I imagine her jumping into the backseat. To my relief she does just that and turns around to look at me. She seems both annoyed with my pressure and pleased with her new show of bravery. As I lean into the car she pushes her head against my chest allowing me to wrap my arms around her. One breath and she begins to pull away. I hold her a second and then a third breath. I release her and stay where I am, blocking her exit from the car. She sits and enjoys me stroking her face with both hands. Ten seconds and I back out of the car, stepping aside to let her jump past me to freedom.

I want to do more. And as I look at Beauty and relax I know pushing now will collapse her trust. A quick movie of walking her the many miles home plays before me. My body lets me know that possibility should be held as a last resort. Unhooking Beauty's leash is an unpleasant necessity. So is getting in the car and heading home without her. As I drive home I sense myself instinctively setting the intent of Beauty being with me on the drive home soon. Very soon.

Bringing In Beauty

That evening I call Ute. Somehow it does not seem right to talk about the fellow's warning. I simply tell Ute it is time to bring Beauty in and ask her how soon we can arrange it. We agree that on the 20th she will come over to my house. She will drive us out to the field in my car and then take a walk while I coax Beauty into the backseat and close both doors. She will then get into the front and drive us home while I calm Beauty. We agree that we can talk specifics on the drive out. The rest of the evening I experience a strange blend of anticipation, worry, and awareness of Beauty. Several times I sense an urgency and decide to keep walking Beauty the 11 miles home as a possibility.

Through the evening and next morning deep energies are stirring within me, around me. They seem to be allowing some possibilities to collapse, to hold space for other possibilities, to be forcing open space for other possibilities. Change is afoot.

More Willingness to Trust

Monday, June 18

*D*riving out I sense Beauty waiting for me. I am very aware that this is one of the last few times I will make the drive. My mind and ego very effectively present me with the many things that could go wrong, things that would interfere with our plan. Noticing my breath and sensing the knowing deep in my belly allow me to at least appear sane.

When I arrive Beauty is in the shade of the blackberry bushes and comes running as soon as I whistle. My mind and ego push to do car familiarization immediately. A whisper from within suggests, *"As normal as possible."* After greetings Beauty and I walk. As has become the pattern sometimes she leads, sometime I lead. Back at the car I mix then place her food before beginning backseat familiarization. We do the usual steak treat enticing. I am pleased that on the first try Beauty gets all the way into the backseat and sits with me enjoying treats and being stroked. On an impulse I take hold of her collar and lean over to close the door closest to me. Beauty is not happy, ears back, mouth closed, tension in her body. Even so she allows me to hold her there. Bit by bit over the next three minutes she relaxes and even stays with me when I let go of her collar. A minute later I imagine her getting out of the car and she does just that. She goes a few feet away and turns to look at me. I grin. Her ears are up, her tail is wagging, she is proud of herself. I am proud of us.

A few minutes later she comes to the open backdoor. I scoot over next to the closed door and call her, **"Come to me girl, come on, I want to pet you, come be with me."** While I chatter to her I imagine her jumping into the car. Twice she pauses at the open door, not jumping in, then backing away. The third time she comes to the door and without a pause jumps into the backseat. I am stunned and excited at the same time. Soon she is laying on the seat next to me as I pet her and give her treats. The sound of a car driving past us catches all of Beauty's attention. I hear myself saying, "**Be with me girl. It is leaving**." Beauty waits and as soon as the car is 20 feet past us she is out the backdoor. I scoot to the edge of the seat putting my feet out on the ground. Beauty is 15 feet from the car watching me. Instinctively I stretch my arms towards her, opening and closing my hands I call, "**Come here girl. Come get some love**." I grin when she immediately walks to me, pushing against me as I pet her. The moment I wonder what else we can do I know it is time to let Beauty rest. With an, "**Okay girl.**" I stand up, close the door, pet her a bit, open the driver's door, and get in. Beauty sits and watches as I close the door, start the car, and then drive off. I sense Beauty with me as I drive home. It feels as though we are rehearsing her trip home with me over the route along Airport Way.

EASY DAY

Tuesday, June 19

*D*riving out I sense that today is a day for enjoying the connections Beauty and I have opened, a day to enjoy and celebrate. As I drive behind the spa shop I see Beauty laying in the field a few feet from where I will park. Her long reddish hair is a wonderful contrast with the lush green of early summer grass. As her head comes up I am washed over by her regal presence and I sense her celebration of her people arriving. To my surprise she remains still while I drive close to her and park. By the time I have my door open she is there waiting for me to swing my legs out. As my feet touch the ground she steps onto the door sill and pushes her head into my chest. As I pet her she whimpers, gentle sounds that penetrate to the core of who I am. Two minutes, five minutes, ten, I do not know. We are immersed in sharing with each other. Eventually she steps back, looking at me with a 'Well?' energy. I stand, open the backdoor, and gather her leash along with the baggy of treats. Beauty nudges the bag of treats with her nose and gazes into the backseat of the car. In that instant my plans change.

    I crawl into the backseat and reach over and open the far door. As I turn back I am surprised to see that Beauty is already partially in the car. I hear myself saying, "**Okay, come on in.**" and reach my hands towards her. In the next moment she jumps onto the backseat stretching her nose towards the baggy of treats. "**Oh, so that is what you want. Well I guess that is what we do.**" I sense a playful, '*Oh, you understand.*' energy from her as I open the bag of treats. After several treats and much petting without thinking I reach over and close the far door. Beauty turns and looks out the door she is standing near.

As I imagine her turning back to me she does just that. "**Your such a Beauty**." floats out of my mouth as I get out more treats. Soon the treats are gone. I show Beauty the empty bag and reach both hands to pet her. She turns, looks out the door, and turns back to me. A few moments of petting and she is out the door.

I crawl out of the backseat, leaving the door open. Beauty looks puzzled when I don't move to her, rather I go to the enclosure. Ten steps and she catches on, bounding after me. We playfully run together. At the enclosure she jumps in first and goes to her bowl. We return to the car and soon are back at the enclosure placing her food. Beauty takes two careful bites and then follows me out towards the field. She sits just beyond the pavement edge and offers me her neck as soon as I am close. Grinning I connect her leash. With the car door open I am not willing to go beyond the field. We make a large loop and soon have returned to the car.

Twenty feet from the car I tell Beauty "**Be with me**." and guide her to walking with her head next to me knee. I shift my grip on the leash and with a slight pull let Beauty know I am taking control of our path. I grin as I notice an, *'Oh, okay'* energy from her. We walk right to the open backseat door. Our movement makes it easiest for Beauty to simply jump in. At the door Beauty balks a moment and then with a bit of pressure on her leash she does jump in. As soon as her front feet leave the ground I release the leash and watch as Beauty goes in a little ways, immediately turning to look at me. As she considers trying to leave I bend down and kneel on the door sill, filling the space with my body. My body and energies are alert to the slightest of movement. As Beauty relaxes and sits, I relax. As I watch Beauty looks around connecting with being 'trapped' and measuring the possibility of forcing her way past me. To my delight I sense her choosing to surrender into trust of me, of herself, of us. As she settles I reach out and stroke her muzzle. One breath, two breaths and she surrenders into enjoying my attention. I keep her in the car for several minutes. Twice she considers forcing her way out only to relax into more lovings from me.

Without thinking I lean, back out of the car, and stand. I wait while Beauty comes forward and begin petting her head with both hands as soon as she is at the door opening. When she leans to go around me

I lean to block her. With a grin I bend down, hold her head, and ask, **"Do you want out?"** with a playful tone. I unclip her leash and when I wiggle my butt Beauty begins wagging her tail while pushing her head against my belly. Once, twice, and on the third push I step aside, turn and run out into the field. In a moment Beauty is with me playing. She charges at me and veers away, I charge at her and veer away. Soon I am tired and collapse onto my knees. Beauty moves in letting me know she wants to snuggle by pushing her head against my chest.

My mind wonders when it notices me carefully calming my breath and opening to Beauty. Beauty notices and calms. **"I love you so much. Tomorrow you come home with me."** Beauty's response is to push closer into me, staying there for 30 seconds. Feeling clumsy and a little uncertain I sit for a few breaths. Suddenly I am standing and walking towards the car. I am half way there before Beauty follows. As I close the backdoor and open the driver's door Beauty comes to me. I sense her whispering, *"You can stay."* and feel her yearnings stir within me. I swing my butt onto the seat leaving my feet out on the ground and reach for Beauty. I smile as she steps to me. **"I know girl. Tomorrow will end our yearnings, tomorrow you will be in your new home."** As I speak I imagine I am sitting on the couch with Beauty before me. Beauty looks in my eyes and I sense us making the final choice. Warmth, connection, deep bonds flow within us, between us. From somewhere I sense a whisper, *"She is your Beauty."*

I cannot tell you how it happened. The next thing I notice is making the sweeping turn onto Airport Way. The drive home is quiet.

Wednesday, June 20

I will do two visits today, the first at about noon. It is a pleasant 70 degrees with bright sunshine. When I arrive and whistle Beauty comes out of the bushes across the field to the left. She trots across the field to me by the edge of the field where we spend about 5 minutes saying hello with much jumping and circling and rubbing against. I marvel at how much she has changed, how much I have changed.

Once the greetings quiets down I retrieve her leash, brush, and comb from the car, walk to her, and put her on leash. It is off at a jog to tour the field and walk to the east. At times I let Beauty chose our direction, at times I choose. I grin in contentment as I accept that I am walking 'my dog'.

When we return to the field we sit in the shade and I begin to groom her. After five minutes she gets up to move. Since she is still on leash I can easily keep her from leaving and do just that. Over the last five days I have had a growing sense that I need to gradually get her more used to me choosing what we do. When I pull back on the leash Beauty simply sits down, looks at me over her shoulder, and looks away. After a few seconds she relaxes her body, shifting to lay on her side. A bit of praise and scratching of her head and cheeks and I return to grooming her. There is a sense of *'oh, if you must'* and a deeper whisper of *"I really like you caring for me."*

Once we return to the car I open the back doors then get in and entice her in with bits of bacon. Like yesterday she still has her leash on. She enters only as far as she can with her front feet, allowing me to pet her head between bacon bits. When I consider pulling her in to me with her leash I sense an immediate, *"No!"* in my belly. A bit longer and she decides it is time to eat. I remove her leash, she jumps out, and I watch as she walks away and then jumps into the enclosure. As I drive away I holler **"See you later Beauty."**

The Future Arrives

*A*s we had arranged Ute shows up at my house about 6:30. After she shows up and we chat a bit she drives us out to Beauty's area in my car, her first time driving it. Ute wants to check for stray cats other than the two she had already rescued and found new homes for. Our hope is that I will be able to get Beauty into the backseat with me at which point Ute will drive us home while I calm Beauty. As we drive out we chat about the possibility of having to try several evenings before we succeed and about how Ute will provide support for the few days I will be house bound providing calming support for Beauty and Fawn. On Airport Way, once we get past the busy sections Ute comments on how peaceful it is. I agree and tell her the peacefulness will make the trip home easier for Beauty. I readily agree when she quips, "**And you**."

When we arrive Beauty is in the field. Ute parks differently than I usually do so Beauty waits in the field, watching. The drivers side is closest to Beauty so Beauty sees Ute get out first. Her ears go partially back as she sits there. Her ears come forward and her mouth opens as soon as I speak to her over the roof of the car. Wagging her tail she comes to the edge of the pavement, sits, and waits. Once I am with Beauty Ute walks slowly toward us. Beauty begins to back away. I tell Ute I feel having Beauty on leash will help and walk to the car, returning with the leash. Beauty waits where she is seated as I walk up and put her leash on. She looks up at me with her ears forward, her mouth open. I sense warm energies opening within me, within Beauty, blending, preparing us. I turn towards Ute, Beauty stands, and we walk to within 8 feet of Ute at which point Beauty sits down. As I kneel by Beauty I release my building tension into the ground. Ute approaches slowly offering a lamb treat.

Beauty stands and extends her head to the treat, sniffs it, and draws her head back. On the second try Beauty takes the treat and immediately drops it. In answer to Ute's unspoken query I tell her where the bacon treats are in the car. A few moments later she returns with the bag of cooked bacon strips and the bag of steak treats in her hand. This time Beauty takes a bacon treat and eats it. She takes a second bacon treat and retreats. I suggest Ute try the steak treats. When Ute kneels on one knee and offers it Beauty takes the first treat carefully and then steps closer to take the second treat. With the third treat Beauty steps so that she is closer to Ute than to me. I smile and nod to Ute. Ute puts a steak treat on her the bent knee of her forward leg. With little pause Beauty steps forward and takes the treat from Ute's knee, eats it and then steps back one step. With the second treat Beauty stays in close for a third, fourth, and fifth treat each taken off Ute's leg. When Beauty steps back Ute senses the shift in flow and stands. As I stand Ute suggests I show her where I had seen stray cats and bring Beauty along. Together the three of us tour the blackberry bushes across the field.

With a bag of cat food in hand Ute begins leaving food hoping to draw out any strays close by. As she does that I return to the car. With Beauty on leash I get into the back seat of the car and offer her bacon treats. At first I sit at the door by Beauty. A little at a time I withdraw into the car having Beauty stretch a bit further in. With the leash on I keep Beauty close to the door entry, not allowing her to walk away when she becomes a little uncomfortable. Beauty does well but does not step into the car with her back feet. After six or seven minutes Beauty loses interest. At the same time Ute returns from her stray cat hunt. Ute has an idea. She suggests that I take Beauty to the other side of the car and open that back door too. Meanwhile Ute will lean into the backseat from the drivers side offering treats. In agreement I walk to the other side and open the door. Staying out of the car I lean in to place bacon treats on the seat. After taking two bacon treats from the seat Beauty notices Ute across the back seat. Her response is to show both curiosity and surprise. Rather than drawing back Beauty looks at Ute, pauses with ears back, then still looking at Ute her ears come forward and she leans towards Ute. I notice I am holding my breath, one deep breath in and out to relax and I notice time shifting. Beauty glances back at me and then at Ute. I am startled by a sense of Beauty and I sitting in the back seat with Ute driving. My mind offers, "I guess it is going to happen." I sense Beauty, Ute, and myself surrendering into the flow of many little choices before us, each of us playing our own central role. I am a puppet watching myself do what has already been decided.

While Ute kneels with her head and shoulders in the car I place bacon treats for Beauty to retrieve, some on the floor, some on the seat. After perhaps ten treats being placed and retrieved Beauty has most of her body in the car. I feel a quiet knowing that it is time. Staying relaxed with a "We will see." attitude I place three more treats. As Beauty stretches to retrieve the second one I scoop my hands onto the upper part of her back legs from behind and lift her. Time slows to a string of infinitesimally small movements shaping each moment. Beauty pushes back, I apply a bit more pressure. Beauty surrenders and steps, floats into the car. As she starts to turn around I move in behind her gently pushing her further into the car. She goes in and as my butt settles on the seat she turns, ears mostly back, mouth closed, looking at me. I am washed over with hers energies of worry, the edge of panic, a desire for reassurance, and a sense of *"I trust you"*. I allow Beauty's worry to flow within me, mixing with my worry, my love, my deep need to protect her. As Beauty begins to turn her body to me I tell Ute to close the door on her side. With Beauty fully turned to me, Ute's door still open, and on the edge of panic myself, I repeat my instruction in what seems slow motion. My attention is so fully with Beauty that it is the sound of the door closing that let me know Ute heard me and has closed the door.

The world collapses to Beauty, me, the backseat, and a blaring awareness of myself being between Beauty and the open door. Beauty turns to see what the sound was. In the few moments it takes her to understand that the door close to her is closed I shift my body so that I can both block her getting past me and so that I can reach the door handle behind me. As Beauty turns back to me I sense her need to find a way out and at the same time a connection with me that is stronger than her desire to flee. As she turns fully to me, facing the open door just beyond me, my attention turns to reassuring her while carefully containing the storm of fears within me. Once, twice, three times she tries to push past me. With each try I sense my energy saying, *"I know you want out... stay with me, be with me now."* As she settles back from the third attempt Beauty sits, settles her energies and posture looking right at me, looking into me. I smile, set aside my fears and worry, connect deeply within myself, and honoring the love we share, tell her she is a good dog, and gently stroke her cheek. She surrenders allowing herself to focus on my attention, relaxing her body a bit more. With my focus on Beauty and the space containing she and I, I slowly reach my right hand back for the door handle. Just out of reach. The fears within push outward wanting to become terror. A breath to calm the fears. My left hand in front of Beauty's chest I shift my knees to the right. Beauty pushes against my left hand and arm, then thankfully surrenders a bit, settles back a bit. One breath, two breaths flowing deep, rich love to Beauty. I want nothing else yet I know I must allow an ever so small bit of attention to enable me to close the door. A turn of my head to locate the door handle. I see it and while feeling my hand against Beauty's chest I stretch in slow motion for the handle. As my fingers touch and then curve over the handle my body and energy turn back to Beauty and as my body shifts back to meet Beauty I pull the door closed. I hear the door close, every speck of me attention goes to sensing and watching Beauty's response. My attention balances between praising Beauty when she calms and letting her sense my willingness to release her if she panics. We hang there for a lifetime, a mere two seconds. To my relief, to my wonder, I sense *"I will trust you."* from Beauty as her weight shifts back onto the seat and her ears come partially forward. The energies I sense from Beauty repeat, *"This is exciting, this is scary, I choose to trust you."* In that moment I sense my future, Beauty's future shifting, opening, and from deep, deep within my belly I sense, *"Now Beauty is in our future."*

As Beauty accepts my scratching her cheek and saying, "**I am really happy.**" Ute's voice shifts from being secondary sounds I notice to words that communicate. Her voice has a familiar feel and sound as she says, "**This is so exciting.**" A pause, and another pause. "**I am going to getting in and drive now.**" A long second of my wondering "Am I ready? Is Beauty ready?" ends with the sound of the car door opening. While my mind shouts "Not yet!" my deeper self guides me to shift my focus to Beauty, to Beauty's needs. Ute says she will go forward around the building. I say backing up would be easiest.

More thoughts come, going unspoken, speech is a luxury secondary to Beauty's needs. A small part of me watches as Ute tries to back up, then tries to go forward. Engine noise says she is pressing the gas but the car goes nowhere. I hear my voice, "**Is your other foot on the brake?**" She says something as I feel the car suddenly move. I hear myself saying, "**That is why I use only one foot.**" while part of me quips, "Silly thing to say." and another, "Saying that had no value." Internal discussions cease as I notice Beauty's increase in body tension and movement. My world shrinks to Beauty and providing her a safe space to process her fears and excitement.

Somewhere in the first three minutes of our trip Ute tells me she will just go down Burnside to get us back to my home. I hear her and assume she means Burnside to 181st to Airport Way as we had agreed. As she drives past 181st I begin to panic as the many reasons why we should take 181st to Airport Way tromp through my mind. I struggle, the need to protect Beauty blends with a sense of betrayal. All my planning, all the trips home sharing my energies with Beauty cast aside. Within three blocks I recognize that my internal struggle only makes things more difficult for Beauty. My attention and energies are being pulled away from her as some of my energies become hateful. A breath as I decide to let go of what is happening with the drive and to return my focus fully to Beauty. The route along Burnside is noisy and sometimes chaotic. Again and again I let go of feeling betrayal as my focus returns to providing what Beauty needs.

Did the trip last 5 minutes or did it last 50 days? My logical mind says about 30 minutes. When I sense the amount of information about Beauty's state I sifted through I would say the trip was at least six months of study. I notice how each sound effects her, which ones cause tension, which ones are ignored. I notice how different scenery effects her. What does she ignore? What does she take in? I notice as her body movements indicate how unsettled she is, especially when she is disconnected from me, on the edge of panic. I notice how much her focus is inside the car or outside the car, doing a mini celebration when she lays next to me her head almost in my lap, much of the tension flowing from her body. Again and again I relax a bit when she sits or lays down. No state seems to last more than a block.

With each sound or movement or view that increases Beauty's tension my ego and mind begin telling me why "my route" would have been better. Sometimes the why is background noise. A couple dozen times after a fourth or fifth worried thought I feel myself breath "my attention is Beauty's", and let the thoughts fade away. Once when worried thoughts threaten to capture my attention I carefully notice and accept that I must keep shifting any thought of Ute's choice of a more difficult route to being grateful for her help, keeping the space clear of my judgments, supporting Beauty by staying connected with her and being grateful.

As we make the last turn onto my street some attention shifts to getting Beauty out of the car and into the house. Ute and I review the plan we made earlier, I go into the backyard with Beauty, she goes into the house and takes Fawn out for a walk. As Ute turns the car into the driveway I open every bit of awareness I can to Beauty. I am pleased that she seems more excited than scared. The car stops, Ute gets out, heads for the front door. I shift from looking at Beauty and scoot towards the backdoor and feel Beauty move so she is gently pushing me towards the door. At the door I pause, connect with Beauty's energies and sense she and I together in the backyard, sense *"Our home."* Warmth fills me as I sense from Beauty, *"Yes, our home."* Time and space shift. Suddenly I am both outside myself observing and the body taking actions. The door unlatches, swings open, and my energy shifts outward as my legs swing out of the car. Beauty is now pushing against me. She pushes harder, relaxes a bit, pushes harder, relaxes a bit. As I lean out of the door, Beauty pauses, as I stand and step out of the car Beauty steps to the floor, as I step to the side Beauty's front feet reach the ground. Amazingly by the time her back feet reach the ground much of the tension is gone from her body, by the time she has taken two steps her ears are up and forward, her tail is wagging slightly. Beauty's first steps are to follow Ute. A slight pull on her leash and **"Let's go this way"** is all it takes to head towards the back gate.

As I reach for the back gate latch I praise Beauty. She stops and pulls back a bit, tension spreads through her body. As the gate swings open her attention shifts to the opening and she relaxes slightly. She waits, unsure what I want, unsure she will trust me enough to pass through the gate. I know I must simply wait while she considers her choice. A long 5 seconds pass, a little tension leaving her with each tick. With the last tick my uncertainty becomes "it's time" and I notice myself opening my energy into the backyard, telling Beauty, **"Good girl."**, pulling gently on her leash and stepping through the gate. A moments hesitation and she steps to follow me. By the time her hips pass through the gate her tail is up and wagging. I experience a sense of awe and pleasure as she begins to trot into 'her' yard.

As we tour the backyard Beauty becomes more relaxed, a bit playful while guarded. Somehow I know it is time for praising Beauty, happy words, stroking her, calming myself, preparing for the last hurdle, entering the house.

We pass past the back porch three times as we tour, each time from within I sense a quiet "no". On the fourth pass Beauty pauses before the steps and looks back at me. It is time. She watches as I take the first step and then joins me for the two more onto the porch. Her body tenses in the small space, she is close to flight. I open myself further, drawing her into my awareness, holding her with me as I reach and open the screen door. A moment on the edge, a slight pull on the leash, and **"This is your new home."** as I reach for the backdoor doorknob. As I open the door inward I sense her energy moving with me into the house one moment before she steps forward, pauses, accepts my encouragement of a slight pull on her leash and steps into her new home. Now she is more curious than worried. We walk 15 feet into the room and stop. She turns to me with a quizzical look and relaxes as I reach down and undo her leash. With time still suspended I hear myself saying, **"Welcome home, Beauty**." From within comes a whisper of, *"Now Beauty is in our home. How much will you allow yourself to notice beauty?"*

Four Years Later

While I have been writing this book Beauty has been in the room with me. Sometimes sleeping on her dog bed. Sometimes laying close facing me. Sometimes coming to me letting me know it is time to take a break and go outside. Sometimes letting me know it is time for dinner by planting the sensations of chewing food in my mouth or making smacking sounds. Sometimes insisting it is time for a walk.

One of her behaviors surprises me. Occasionally I will get frustrated and vent my frustrations by speaking loudly or even shouting. When I do Beauty will stand up come within about 15 feet of me and without fear wag her tail with ears forward, mouth open, tongue out. I can almost hear her whisper of, "*It is okay. I want you to feel better. Are your ready to pet me?*" Often within moments I choose to allow calm and call her to me for pets and snuggles.

Over the last four years Beauty has also helped me to more easily, more often notice the beauty, the magic in my life. The ever present magic intertwined with beauty. The beauty always only an aware choice or two away.

Each day I am grateful for Beauty being part of my life. I will always be grateful for the beauty she continues to awaken within me.

About the Author

For many years I have been involved with dog and cat rescue ranging from fostering dogs to helping bring in strays. Bringing in Beauty was one such challenge, a challenge and opportunity to learn and grow. My thirteen years of study with a mystic opened my awareness in ways key to Beauty and I learning together. Beauty now lives with me in my dome shaped home in Portland, Oregon.